How to Succeed in a Highly Competitive Job Market

A Comprehensive Workbook for Executives

BRIAN CROUCHER

KOGAN
PAGE

For my wife, Sandra, and children, Annabel, James, Robert and William.

Thanks to Bee Brodie for preparing the original manuscript and also to Michelle Hogbin for proof-reading and expert advice.

First published in 1994

Kogan Page Limited
120 Pentonville Road
London N1 9JN
© Brian Croucher 1994

British Library Cataloguing in Publication Data

A CIP record for this book is available from the British Library.

ISBN 0–7494–1269–0

Typeset by Saxon Graphics Ltd, Derby
Printed and bound in Great Britain by Biddles Ltd, Guildford and King's Lynn

CONTENTS

FOREWORD

I have written this book to assist people currently out of work and also those in work, but seeking a new position for whatever reason.

I have concentrated on giving a detailed step-by-step analysis of what I actually did from the time that I was made redundant through to securing a new position some nine weeks later. Added to my own personal experiences are many practical tips and advice from a number of fellow professionals, all similarly engaged in the recruitment of personnel.

I suggest you read this book through, then treat it as a practical handbook. Write down your own specific answers to the various questions posed, and then put them into action. While I can't guarantee that you will succeed with every future job application, I feel sure that you will greatly improve your chances of a favourable outcome.

I do have an apology to make to the many women who will read this book. In order to avoid the he/she syndrome, I've assumed all interviewers, candidates etc are male. Needless to say, I could just as easily have made them all female.

Whatever your age, experience, circumstances or aspirations, I wish you all well in your job search, and I hope this book helps you on your way.

1. INTRODUCTION

I'd had a superb fortnight camping in France. The break had been especially welcome, as strict project deadlines had meant a lot of late-night finishes at work. The children had hardly seen me, being fast asleep before I returned home and not waking up until I had completed at least an hour's work the following morning.

All that seemed a long way away as I built my five hundredth sand castle on one of the wide sandy beaches, only to see my youngest son take great delight in kicking it over, spreading sand all over today's lunch of pâté, cheese, French bread and the inevitable bottle of 'vin de table'.

I had returned refreshed and 'raring to go' again. The project was on schedule, and the next four weeks were to be spent installing and commissioning a new IBM mainframe computer. I'd been planning this for the last two years, and here, finally, was the moment of truth.

When I walked into the office, however, I sensed all was not well. There was a message on my desk – I had to see the Financial Director at 9.30 am. When I walked into his office I noted that the Personnel Manager was seated at the far end of the table.

'Funny, he doesn't usually attend any of our meetings! ... Oh no, surely not! Not me!'

Every day one reads in the newspapers of factory closures or businesses cutting a number of jobs. My sympathies always go out to the individuals concerned, but I felt assured in the knowledge that it could never happen to me, because 'I'm essential to the smooth operation of the department, and in any case, this company is not seriously affected by recession'.

I was now greeted with the news that, following a reorganisation within my department, my job would become redundant from the end of the month. Imagine how I felt. I was 31 years old with a large mortgage, three very young children, and now no job.

Nine weeks later I started my new job in a new town, on a higher salary, with far better career prospects. The nine weeks had given me a chance to take a good look at myself and to plan ahead for the future, in terms of what I really wanted to do, where I wanted to live, and what I had to do to get there.

I look back now and think, I am thankful that redundancy happened to me when it did, otherwise I would not be where I am now.

2. WHEN THE BOMBSHELL HITS

Contents

- What goes through your mind when told about imminent redundancy
- The pain, hurt and grief felt
- Immediate priorities

Overview

Initially, on being informed that my position was to become redundant, the emotions I experienced were of total shock and disbelief. I could not believe this was really happening to me. I was absolutely stunned and did not know what to say. How can you do this to me? How am I going to tell my wife? Why me?

My feelings and thoughts on being made redundant.

The next 24 hours were probably the worst in my entire life. I experienced the following feelings:

1. Deep sense of rejection
   - How could I hold my head up in front of former colleagues?

2. Confusion
   - How was I going to pay the mortgage?
   - What would it do to the children?
   - How could I tell my friends and relatives?
   - What was I going to do?
   - I had a complete mental block, I just could not think straight.

9

3. Sickness
- a completely sleepless night;
- headache.

4. Failure
- I've lost my job, therefore I'm a failure.

5. Loss
- of self-confidence and self-esteem;
- of a secure job, car and benefits.

I was emotionally drained and, with my body aching all over, I was in no fit state to do anything or to face anybody. My mind was empty – I simply didn't know what I was going to do.

After a day, shock and disbelief gave way to feelings of anger and resentment. I thought of ways of getting even with the company and with the individuals directly concerned.

My thoughts were of: hurling a brick through the front window of the Finance Director, disclosing confidential information to the press concerning proposed factory closure plans and associated job losses, and destroying vital information on the company's main computer.

I am very glad I didn't carry out any such reprisal!

I quickly developed a close rapport with the Personnel Manager, who turned out to be of immense help to me in my search for alternative employment. He became my mentor, helped me to formulate an initial plan of action and put together the first draft of my curriculum vitae. He was able to think rationally and forced me to take control of myself. I slowly began to accept responsibility for what had happened and started to think about building a new career.

How to do it

Put aside your feelings.

My advice to others who find themselves in a similar position is to say and do very little. Once the decision has been made, there is usually no going back. Nothing you can say or do can make the situation any better, so just walk away from it. Get in your car and drive. Find a part of the countryside where you can get away from it all, where you won't be found. Climb to the top of a hill. Sit in a park. Find a deserted beach. Go for a long walk. Cool off.

Company takeovers, departmental reorganisations and factory closures are all too commonplace today. You are not the first to suffer, nor will you be the last. But unless you have actually been in this situation yourself, it is impossible to appreciate fully the feelings of despair, rejection, pain and anger which you will experience.

Remember, it's not *you* but *your job* which has become redundant. Regard yourself as temporarily 'in between appointments'.

Remember that even though these people are doing you out of a job, they are probably your best bet for securing your next position, because almost certainly any prospective employer will look to them for references. Furthermore, it is likely that they actually feel quite bad about it themselves, although they won't show it at the time. Would you like to inform someone that their job was about to become redundant?

You need your former employer's help.

There is, therefore, a fair chance that they will be able to assist you in your search for suitable alternative employment. This help may come in the form of career counselling or providing you with the names of people to contact. In short, keep your cool. Ask for help. Ask if they can offer any counselling or career advice, assistance with writing a curriculum vitae, and advice on how to go about applying for another job.

Before you do anything, ask yourself a simple question: '*Is what I am about to do or say going to improve my chances of getting another job?*' If the answer to that question is no, then don't do it, no matter how tempting it may seem at the time.

3. MAKE PLANS

Contents

- Getting a clear understanding of where you are now
- Developing a positive mental attitude
- Setting firm career goals, that is, establishing where you want to go
- Planning your route to get you there

Overview

You need to develop a positive mental attitude.

In any company there are primarily two sorts of people: the drifters and the achievers.

The main difference between them is that achievers have career goals: they have a clear vision of where they want to go and how they are going to get there.

I am amazed at the number of people, at all levels of an organisation, who just drift around in circles from one day to the next with little or no sense of direction and no real purpose in life. Typical catch phrases include:

- 'Oh dear, it's going to be one of those days again.'
- 'Que sera, sera'; whatever will be, will be.
- It doesn't matter how good you are in this place, it's just whether your face fits that counts.'
- 'Doing a good job round here is like wetting your pants; no one notices, but it leaves a nice warm feeling.'

If you have been affected by redundancy, you must get yourself into the right frame of mind. Start to think and act positively. Accept what has happened, and resolve to do something about it. Get your career back on the road, starting right now. This is the best opportunity you have had for years!

Developing a positive mental attitude is the first big step to make. Grit your teeth and say, over and over again:

'This is my big chance – I'm going to use it!'

Before embarking on any job campaign, however, you need a plan, just as you would if you were going to build a house or go on a long car journey.

You need to plan what to do.

It's time to take a good look at yourself. Get a clear picture of where you stand right now. Visualise in your mind where you want to get to, make written plans to get you there, then commit yourself whole-heartedly to them. Here's how.

How to do it

Write down answers to the following questions, being as specific as you can:

Sit down and think carefully about yourself, your circumstances and your aims.

1. What am I good at? For example:
   - communicating with people;
   - solving problems;
   - managing people;
   - getting things done;
   - selling;
   - coming up with new ideas;
   - making decisions.

2. What experience and skills do I have (both in work and outside)? For example:
   - industry experience;
   - track record;
   - major achievements;
   - qualifications;
   - training;
   - specialist knowledge.

3. What do I really want to do? For example:
   - type of work;
   - any particular company;
   - set up own business;
   - location;

13

- long-term ambitions;
- income target levels;
- status considerations.

4. What is the price I am prepared to pay? For example:
   - minimum starting salary;
   - benefits;
   - relocation to another area;
   - work away from home Monday to Friday;
   - attend evening classes;
   - go into full-time education.

5. How am I going to go about getting it? For example:
   - personal friends who can help;
   - companies to approach;
   - recruitment agencies to contact;
   - career advisers.

6. Where do I stand right now? For example:
   - cash in the bank;
   - income.

7. What are my main outgoings? For example:
   - mortgage;
   - local taxes;
   - gas bills;
   - hire purchase, credit cards, bank loans.

8. Who do I need to contact, should I need to defer payments? For example:
   - bank manager;
   - building society manager;
   - credit card company.

Well done! You have now got some firm plans written down. There's still a long way to go in the tunnel, but now there's a glimmer of light at the end!

4. WRITE A CV THAT IMPRESSES

Contents

- How a CV is used in the selection process
- How to write a CV that can't fail to impress

Overview

Q. What is a curriculum vitae?

A. It is a personal sales brochure; it's *you* who are on sale!

Q. What is its prime purpose?

A. To get you an interview (not a job; that is the purpose of the interview).

What is a CV for, and what does it do?

Your CV and accompanying letter or application form are the only information a company will receive about you initially, and therefore form the basis for the initial screening process. A nationally advertised vacancy will typically attract between 100 and 200 serious applications, so a high quality CV is essential.

I have personally processed hundreds of CVs at all levels, from trainee to senior manager and, believe me, there is nothing more *boring* than reading through dozens and dozens of CVs, mostly very similar, in order to carry out initial screening.

The majority of CVs are characterised by one or more of the following attributes:

Some common failings of a CV.

- printed on a low quality dot-matrix printer;
- photocopy of a photocopy;

15

- contain little information directly related to the position advertised;
- obviously written in a hurry, with little or no thought given to presentation;
- poorly laid out;
- waffly;
- too long;
- too short.

Many a good candidate has been overlooked, simply because of a poor CV. To illustrate this, let me use an actual example of how a sales executive was recruited into my former company.

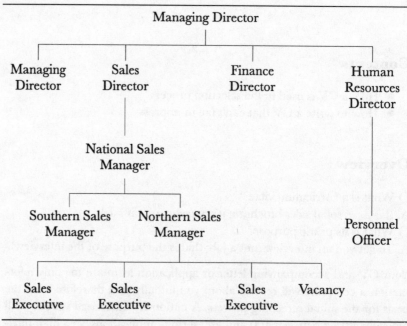

Figure 4.1 *Simplified organisation structure*

How a typical company recruits its staff.

The actual procedure used to recruit a sales executive was as follows:

1. The Northern Sales Manager obtains authorisation from the Sales Director, via the National Sales Manager, to recruit.
2. The Northern Sales Manager asks the Personnel Officer to advertise in the national press, and provides a draft job description.
3. One hundred and fifty applications are received. The Personnel Officer spends one hour processing them (note: less than 30 seconds each!) and

selects 25 candidates whom he believes best fit the requirements.

4. These 25 are then screened by the Northern Sales Manager for 45 minutes (note: less than two minutes each) and a short-list of eight is produced. The remaining 142 applicants are sent a 'we'll keep your name on file' letter, and their applications are subsequently binned.
5. The Northern Sales Manager asks the Personnel Officer to set up interviews with the eight short-listed candidates.
6. The first interviews are undertaken jointly by the Northern Sales Manager and the Personnel Officer, whereupon six candidates are rejected.
7. The National Sales Manager interviews the remaining two candidates and an offer is made to the successful applicant, who accepts.

The following points are worth noting:

1. The initial screening was carried out by the Personnel Officer who had received minimal information regarding the type of person required. His judgement was based on the applicants' age, experience and the quality of the CV.
2. Each application was read for less than 30 seconds. As a result, some very good candidates were almost certainly rejected.
3. The Northern Sales Manager had received no formal training in recruitment and selection.
4. Both the Personnel Officer and the Northern Sales Manager found the initial screening process very boring.
5. The people short-listed had the following attributes:

   - relevant previous experience and track record;
   - well-presented CVs, with the key facts clearly presented;
   - 'personalised' covering letters, expressing desire for job.

Other important points about your CV.

A well-thought-out, well-presented CV will greatly improve your chances of overcoming the initial screening process and of getting that all-important first interview. Do your homework. Gather all the facts and compile a slick, eye-catching CV. It could make all the difference between rejection and being short-listed.

There are contrasting opinions concerning the 'right' length for a CV. My opinion is that it should be two or three pages long. If it is any longer than this, it is essential that the key points can be extracted in under 30 seconds. Clarity, presentation and appeal are therefore as important as content.

It's also essential to keep your CV up to date at all times, no matter how secure or content you may be in your current position – you never know when you may need it. Are you 100 per cent sure your department will not be restructured in the next three months, or that an unexpected opportunity will not present itself? *Keep your options open – keep your CV up to date.*

While it's not possible to cover every different type of position, the following example serves to illustrate some of the key features to be included in your CV.

Remember, if you are considering applying for a number of different types of job, have several versions of your CV prepared, each geared towards a particular line of work. I did, and I'm sure it contributed to the high success rate I achieved with my job applications.

Follow the outline on the following pages and you will have a CV that can't fail to impress.

SUSAN DAVIES

202 West Street, Paddington, London W12 4QF
Telephone: 071-404 9324 (home)
            071-387 5852 ext 26 (work)
Date of Birth: 15 January 1964
Marital Status: Single
Nationality: British

CAREER SUMMARY

Strong commercial awareness with seven years' experience in Personnel Management including: Recruitment * Employee Relations * Industrial Relations * Policy Development * Training and Development.

EDUCATION AND QUALIFICATIONS

1984–1985 The London School of Economics & Political Science.
   – Diploma in Personnel Management
1981–1984 University of Durham.
   – BSc (Hons) Social Sciences (upper second)
1974–1981 Dudley Grammar School.
   – 3 'A' levels and 8 'O' levels

EMPLOYMENT

Jan 1991 to present – Human Resource Manager, The Pharmaceutical Company Limited, Nottingham

- Formulated a comprehensive and effective recruitment and training strategy for a manufacturing centre.
- Successfully implemented performance-related pay.
- Effective member of Personnel Policy Department Group.
- Trained managers to deliver team briefs.
- Published article on staff benefits.

December 1988 to January 1991 – Deputy Personnel Manager, The Travel Group, Hartlepool

- Controlled sickness absence through guidelines, statistics and training.
- Introduced highly effective recruitment and selection training.

- Produced personnel guidelines for managers.
- Personally responsible for successful management of Human Resource issues arising from company acquisition.

November 1985 to December 1988 – Personnel Officer, Townsend Holidays Ltd, Portsmouth

- Developed policies for discipline, grievance, data protection and health and safety.
- Managed redundancy programme for 200 staff.
- Prepared successful defence cases for two industrial tribunals.

ADDITIONAL INFORMATION

Hobbies: Running, travel.

Noteworthy achievements: Completed the London Marathon in 4 hours 25 minutes. My target is sub 4 hours by August 1994.

Driving: Car owner. Full UK driving licence.

Location: Prepared to relocate, if necessary.

5. BUILD A NETWORK

Contents

- The importance of building a personal network
- How to create your own network
- How headhunters work

Overview

'It's not *what* you know, it's *who* you know that counts.'

Why a personal network is so important.

This adage has been quoted time and time again by many individuals who are often despondent about their own career opportunities. It is not my favourite expression, but there is certainly an element of truth in it. My favourite expression is:

'It's not what you know, it's what you do with what you know that counts.'

Nevertheless, it is worth remembering that over half of all vacancies are never advertised (and this figure increases, the higher the position). If you can't beat them, join them! Not only does it take a minimum of effort, but also the reward can be massive.

I have got my own personal network, comprising over 200 names of people whom I have either met on a professional basis or who have been recommended to me by other colleagues. In addition, I am now being approached by professional headhunting agencies. Up until now it seemed that everyone else I knew had been the target of many a headhunter, but not me. I decided to do something about it – to let the word get around, to start selling myself and getting known in the right circles.

Build your own network, starting from now. Here's how.

How to do it

Find out about the job market.

1. Read job advertisement sections in:

- Local newspapers;
- National newspapers;
- Trade press.

Cut out relevant advertisements and keep them in a special file. Within a few months you will get a very clear picture of recruitment cycles, and which companies are the regular advertisers. A further benefit of this will be that it may provide ideas for career paths you had not initially considered. Get a feel for the types of job regularly advertised and note where demand is greatest. Get yourself on the mailing list of trade magazines; most are free of charge.

Tap into your colleagues' knowledge.

2. Ask your work colleagues:

- How did they get the job (if they are either coming into your company or leaving it)?
- Where was the position advertised?
- Did they register with any agencies, if so which?
- If a colleague is about to leave, ask if the company he is about to join has other vacancies.

Get the names and addresses of companies in your line of business.

3. Find out the names, addresses and key contacts within your company's main competitors.

They may jump at the chance of recruiting people with detailed knowledge about their major rivals. Similarly, consider your company's main suppliers and customers. They may be very interested in recruiting someone with detailed knowledge of the business.

Get your name known.

4. Join a professional body.

No matter what line of business you are in there will always be associated professional institutions with members from many different organisations. Ask around, find out for yourself the best organisations to join. Write articles for the magazines. Get your name known.

5. *Attend conferences and training courses.*

Go out of your way to meet new people and find out their line of business. This is a great way of building your list of personal contacts. If you get the opportunity to speak, then take it.

The best way I have found of keeping a record of personal contacts is to exchange business cards. Take business cards with you at all times. If you haven't got any, get some printed – they are relatively inexpensive and definitely worth having. When you come to file other people's cards, write on the back a very brief description of where and when you met and how you think they may be able to help you in the future.

Business cards are very useful.

How to be headhunted

Headhunting, or the 'recruitment of senior-level executives by intermediaries acting on behalf of client companies', is becoming an increasingly popular way of recruiting executives into senior management positions. Some people will argue that you should wait for headhunters to contact you. There are, however, a number of techniques you can adopt to short-circuit this process and to get yourself noticed, namely:

What is headhunting?

1. Send your CV to the headhunting agencies in your business.
2. Get yourself introduced by an influential friend.
3. Get your name known within the right circles.

Get yourself known to headhunters.

- Become appointed to the committee of a relevant professional or trade association.
- Write short articles for publication in industry journals.
- Get yourself a strong reputation.

The trouble with sending in speculative CVs is that leading headhunting agencies receive hundreds each week, and there is therefore a danger that your CV will be binned. So it needs to be very carefully compiled to meet the needs of the headhunters. Adopt the following guidelines:

Send a CV to headhunters.

- It must be short, factual, impressive and interesting.
- It should list events in reverse chronological order (ie most recent first) in a format easy to enter into a computer.
- It should be very specific about your particular industry sector.
- It should be either an original or a high quality photocopy taken from an original.

- It should be accompanied by a management summary letter, which summarises the key information in the CV, tailoring specific selling points in relation to the job being applied for.
- It should include salary details.

Summary

Building your own network of contacts is an old-established practice and a proven way of 'getting on'. It is a fact that a large number of vacancies are never advertised, and that many are filled on personal recommendation. Some companies even pay bonuses to employees who recommend people to join their organisation.

Get your name known by the right people, and start now. Wherever you go, and whoever you meet, keep thinking, 'How could this person help me move on?'

Action plan

A plan of action for building a personal network.

1. Make a personal commitment to be a member of at least one professional organisation. No matter what your trade, there will be one for you.
2. Write down the names, addresses and phone numbers of ten recruitment agencies who specialise in your particular field. If you want to take it one stage further, an introductory phone call can do no harm.
3. Attend seminars, training courses and presentations. Make a point of making at least one personal contact at each event – remember to take your business cards.
4. Get yourself on the circulation list of at least two relevant trade magazines. The address will be shown in the magazine (normally inside the front cover).

Study the newspapers on the days they advertise your type of job.

5. National newspapers feature specific job markets on different days. Find out which are the best newspapers to buy, and on which days. For general appointments, I recommend the following newspapers:

Financial Times: Thursday, mainly financial appointments
Daily Telegraph: Thursday, various appointments
The Times: Thursday, various appointments
The Sunday Times: Sunday, various appointments

The Guardian

Monday: media, marketing, secretarial

Wednesday: health, social services, finance, personnel

Thursday: computing, science and technology, general

Friday: European, housing, conservation, planning, leisure

The Independent

Monday/Sunday: computing

Tuesday/Sunday: financial/accounting

Wednesday/Sunday: media, sales and marketing

Thursday/Sunday: administrative, education, general

Friday/Sunday: legal

6. SEEK PROFESSIONAL ADVICE

Contents

- Talking over your situation with career counsellors and/or recruitment agencies
- Explaining how these people operate

Overview

There are many companies whose sole function is to place people into new positions. Sometimes the vacancies are advertised, sometimes not.

There are basically two different sorts of career/recruitment agencies:

1. Those who charge you (or your former company) for their services, that is, the out-placement or career guidance agencies.
2. Those who charge your new employer (typically 15–25 per cent of your starting annual salary), that is, the recruitment agencies.

When my former position became redundant, I found that it helped enormously to talk with both career counsellors and recruitment agencies. All of them had dealt with many people in similar circumstances to mine and were genuinely sympathetic and helpful.

How to do it

There are two main benefits of using recruitment agencies:

How to use recruit-
ment agencies.

1. They know the market place, the types of openings for people with your experience and skills, and the salary levels to expect.
2. They have contacts within many companies; therefore they often hear of vacancies before they are advertised.

Be very careful and selective about which agencies you use, and make sure that you retain control over which companies they approach on your behalf. Avoid the agencies which merely flood the market with your CV, especially if you are registering with more than one agency. Most agencies prepare their own résumé from your CV – make sure you personally see a copy before they send it out.

I suggest you use the services of between four and six different recruitment agencies. Whenever possible, make an appointment to see each one in person, rather than just talking over the phone – that way you can find out far more about how they operate. It also enables them to have a clear picture of you when they contact companies on your behalf – a picture paints a thousand words. Get to know one person well in each agency, who will become your personal contact.

Finally, don't overlook your present company. I always encourage my subordinates to speak freely about their career aspirations, and wherever possible I give them as much advice as I can. Remember, most professional managers would rather have an employee promoted or transferred internally than see him resign and join another company, if he was not happy in his current position.

Try for promotion
with your present
employer.

Go to your immediate supervisor or personnel manager and pose the question: 'I've been working in this position now for (three) years. I have gained a lot of valuable experience and my work has been of a high standard. I feel I am now a worthy candidate for promotion. What have you got to offer me?'

You have nothing to lose, whether you are fighting against the possibility of redundancy or seeking promotion. If you can come up with a strong enough case and you are persistent, then the chances are that you will be successful.

Remember, success goes to the activist!

Summary

Seeking professional advice was the best move I made after my position became redundant. Not only did I feel a lot better, but the career advisers I spoke to offered a lot of very constructive advice, and suggested career opportunities that I had not previously considered.

Furthermore, their advice was entirely free. Do the same – find the name of six recruitment agencies who specialise in your own particular area and talk it over. Most are available during the evening or at weekends if necessary. You have got nothing to lose, yet everything to gain.

7. HOW TO RESPOND TO ADVERTISED VACANCIES

Contents

- The need for a carefully prepared application
- How to write your own appealing introductory letter

Overview

Most job advertisements comprise two basic parts: the outline of the job; and a description of the skills and experience of the ideal candidate.

Although the ideal candidate probably doesn't exist, the wording within the advertisement will include several key words which will enable you to get a very clear idea of the sort of person required. By skilfully identifying the key requirements, and incorporating these into your introductory letter, you will have gained a significant edge over other applicants.

At one of the interviews I attended, I made a point of asking the interviewer why my application had been short-listed (I was one of only six people out of 170 applicants to be invited for first interview). The interviewer replied, 'It was your introductory letter – you wrote with a lot of enthusiasm and you obviously want the job'.

The first thing to do when applying for an advertised vacancy is to read the advertisement very carefully to determine exactly what is required of you. It seems simple enough, but you should see the number of applica-

What is in a job advertisement?

The importance of your introductory letter.

29

tions which are rejected because they did not conform to the format as stated in the advertisement.

How to reply to different types of advertisements.

Standard wordings within job advertisements usually fall into one of the following categories:

1. 'Contact Ann Morris on 021–345 6789 for further information, or alternatively write to her at ...'

This technique is becoming more popular with recruitment agencies. Here, a phone call will be worth its weight in gold because:

Phone calls.

- You will speak directly with the person who will be handling your initial application.
- You can project your enthusiasm for the position – this will hopefully stick in her mind when processing your application.
- You will have the opportunity to find out more about the job, the specific skills sought, the type of person the company is looking for etc. This is invaluable information to include in your management summary.
- It will give your written application a better chance of being noticed.

The phone call requires careful preparation. Prepare a draft copy of your management summary and have your CV to hand. Think of a couple of relevant questions to ask, such as location, work environment, size of department, company turnover etc. If you are speaking to an agency, usually they will not tell you the name of the company until they receive your written application, so don't ask over the phone. Remember that there may be hundreds of calls similar to yours being handled. Also, never discuss money at this stage.

Letter of application.

2. 'Write with full career details to ...'

Here, you should write a two-page letter of introduction, highlighting your most relevant skills. I also suggest that you include a copy of your CV. After all, you are armed with a high quality document, so make the most of it, but avoid making cross-references to it in your letter.

Application form.

3. 'Please contact G Smith for an application form.'

Do exactly that, preferably by phone. Do not try any other route – a complete waste of time. You should try to establish the name of the person to whom the application form should be sent so that you can personalise the accompanying letter.

Remember, your application is likely to be processed initially by:

Matters that must
be borne in mind
when replying.

- A recruitment agency;
- The personnel department; or
- A non-decision-maker in the relevant department (usually a subordinate).

This person is likely to be screening the applications on the following basis:

- Do they have the right background, that is, age, education/training, skills, previous experience?
- How presentable is their application?

The best way to convince this person that you are at least worthy of an interview is to format your application in the following way:

- Include a high quality CV, wherever possible, aimed specifically at that particular type of work, together with an introductory letter which includes a management summary.
- Complete the job application form.

Applying for jobs is a full-time occupation in its own right. If you have gone about it in a half-hearted manner (for example, mailing out CVs), then you are probably doing yourself more harm than good. Remember the old adage:

'If a job's worth doing, it's worth doing well.'

If you are really serious about a job move, you need to construct an informative and well-presented application, no matter which particular method you use.

To give yourself the best possible chance of getting at least to first interview stage, you need to write a dynamic introductory letter; here's how.

How to do it

Introductory letter with CV (or completed job application form)

Cover letters.

In the majority of cases, a job advertisement will specify that you forward a copy of your CV. You will need to send a suitable introductory letter with it, which is sometimes as important as the CV itself. Treat this letter with the attention it deserves and remember to include your management summary. Use an A4 sheet of white paper with matching envelope.

Examples of an
introductory letter.

An example of this follows:

Your address	8 London Road BIRMINGHAM B3 4EJ
Addressee	Mr E Davies Personnel Manager UK Autos Ltd LOUGHBOROUGH Leics LE12 8QT
Date	6th February 1994
Greeting. Use correct form of address	Dear Mr Davies
Reference	**YOUR REF: ST 5/12 – MARKETING MANAGER, SUNDAY TIMES, 5th FEB 1994**
Reason for writing	I was most interested to see your advertisement in the *Sunday Times* of 5th February for the position of Marketing Manager.
The message	I have over six years' very relevant experience within the automotive car industry and have developed strong marketing skills, especially in the last eighteen months. During this time, I successfully led a marketing team which has launched two successful marketing campaigns, increasing market share by 5 per cent. While my CV provides a general outline of my personnel background, career history and key achievements to date, I have summarised my skills and experiences which are particularly relevant to the position advertised. I hope this is useful to you.
Conclusion	I feel sure that I have the experience and skill to make a profitable contribution in the role advertised, and I would welcome the opportunity to discuss my application further.
Ending to match form of address	Yours sincerely (Signature)
Spell out your name here	**K JONES**
List any enclosures	Enc

MANAGEMENT SUMMARY: MR K JONES

POSITION: MARKETING MANAGER, UK AUTOS LIMITED

YOUR REQUIREMENT	MY EXPERIENCE/SKILLS
Graduate	I have a BA (Hons) Class 2.1 from Southampton University.
Four years' industry experience	I have been in the industry for over six years.
Ability to manage high investment marketing campaigns	Last year I was responsible for a £2m TV marketing campaign, which achieved an increase in market share of 5 per cent.
Good interpersonal skills	I enjoy all such aspects of the job. I am a regular presenter to the Executive Committee and have developed good working relationships with colleagues at all levels.
Creative thinking	One of my key strengths is identifying gaps in the markets and developing creative marketing campaigns to meet these needs. Of particular relevance was my idea to target and promote lease hire to the general public.

Introductory letter without a CV

Here you will need to summarise your CV on one side of A4, and include an identical management summary to the one in the previous letter. An example follows:

---

8 London Road
BIRMINGHAM
B3 4EJ

Mr E Davies
Personnel Manager
UK Autos Ltd
LOUGHBOROUGH
Leics LE12 8QT

6th February 1994

Dear Mr Davies

YOUR REF: ST 5/12 – MARKETING MANAGER, SUNDAY TIMES, 5th FEB 1994

Your advertisement in the *Sunday Times* of 5th February is of great interest to me, and I would like to apply for the position.

I am thirty-two, married and a graduate of Southampton University.

I am currently employed by Dorf UK, Small Car Division at Birmingham as a Marketing Executive responsible for a team of twelve. My key objective is to increase the market share of our small cars, in support of the company's production plants at Cardiff and Gloucester. I have held this position for three years and of noteworthy mention was my leading role of promoting lease hire of small cars to the general public. I take great pride in having achieved an increase of 5 per cent in our market share of small cars through the £2m marketing campaign I personally initiated.

Prior to this ... (etc)

I have summarised my skills and experience which are particularly relevant to the position advertised, and I hope this is useful to you.

I am seeking to broaden my span of responsibilities and I feel sure that I have the experience and skill to make a profitable contribution in the role advertised. I would welcome the opportunity to discuss my application with you.

Yours sincerely

K JONES

Enc.

Summary

To maximise your chances of getting an interview, follow the guidelines set out below:

Guidelines for getting an interview.

1. Read the job advertisement well, and be sure to respond in the way described.
2. Wherever possible make the first contact by phone, but do your homework first.
3. Always write a covering letter with either a CV or completed application form. Its content and layout are often equally as important as the CV/application form itself.
4. Include a management summary with every covering letter.
5. Get the covering letter typed if possible. If not, your best handwriting is fine (in fact, on some occasions employers insist on this, so that they can see a sample of your handwriting).
6. Give each application great care, no matter how boring or repetitive it may seem. Treat your application as a personal sales brochure – it has to be of the highest quality.

8. EXPLORING THE UNADVERTISED MARKET PLACE

Contents

- Outlining alternative methods of job hunting
- Illustrating the techniques to use

Overview

How do you go about finding a new job?

1. Read the jobs page in the newspaper. But so do thousands of other people.
2. Go to the job centre. But so do hundreds of other people.
3. Send speculative CVs to companies. But 95 per cent go straight into the bin.
4. Let a few people know you are looking for a job, and let them contact you. But you could wait for ever.

Quite simply, you have got two choices: you either proceed like everyone else and hope to strike lucky; or you do something about it yourself.

SUCCESS GOES TO THE ACTIVIST

There are four main ways of actively seeking jobs.

I can't emphasise it enough. You have got to be pro-active in an effective job search campaign. Your destiny lies in your own hands. If you want something, go out there and get it. It's not difficult, but you do need determination and courage to succeed.

Do it the wrong way and you'll waste valuable time and money. Do it the right way and you will be choosing between job offers. The techniques I'll cover are the following:

- Using recruitment consultancies.
- Writing speculative letters (with a difference).
- The telephone interview.
- Using personal contacts.

Remember, your goal in each of these cases is to get an interview. No more, no less. Don't pin all your hopes on one particular technique – use all four methods.

How to do it

Using recruitment agencies

Good recruitment agencies provide a valuable means of exploring vacancies not widely publicised. Bad recruitment agencies will do you more harm than good. The trick, therefore, is to choose the agencies you use with great care.

1. List 12 agencies which specialise in recruiting people with your particular skills.
2. Contact each agency by phone. Ask them how they operate.
    - How do they use your CV?
    - Do they have contacts within companies; if so, which ones?
    - What geographical area do they cover?
    - What sector of the market do they concentrate on?

Ways to find the right agency for you.

Look for those agencies which give you control over your CV. It is very important that you have the final say as to which companies they send your CV to. A good agency will always contact a prospective employer to establish whether or not there are any suitable vacancies. They will then contact you to ascertain whether or not you are interested in this company. Only then should they forward your CV. Avoid the indiscriminate CV mailers.

3. Ask around.
    - Which agencies regularly place people in your company?
    - Which agencies would your company use if they were recruiting?

4. Read the trade and local press to establish which agencies are regular advertisers.

When you have chosen a short-list.

From your original list of 12, select a short-list of six. Telephone them and arrange a meeting. It's best if you forward your CV and outline the areas which are of interest to you so that they can do some homework before your meeting. If it is inconvenient to go during the day, most agencies will see you during the evening or at weekends.

A picture paints a thousand words, hence a face-to-face meeting will give them a clear picture of you when they are liaising on your behalf with prospective employers. This is much more effective than merely sending your CV alone.

Write speculative letters

How to write a good speculative letter.

Two sorts of speculative letters are common:

- Speculative letters to recruitment consultants.
- Speculative letters to potential employers.

My advice is to avoid the first method – why waste time? – far better to telephone the consultancies direct. This is what they are there for and they are on *your* side, especially when they scent the smell of commission! Consequently, I will only cover letters to potential employers, which are an important weapon in your armoury.

No speculative letter should be written without a fair amount of time and effort being spent by you to make sure:

- It is addressed to the relevant person by name, for example, Mr B Smith, Personnel Manager (not just to 'The Personnel Manager').
- It has local colour (ie, it's specific to the particular company).

This letter should be considered as a personal sales brochure and its mission is to secure an interview. It therefore needs to be:
- short (maximum of one page);
- clear, and well laid out;
- to the point;
- professionally presented (on quality paper, and preferably typed or laser-printed, not photocopied);
- accompanied by your CV.

Before you send it, read it as if you were a potential employer. What impression does it make? Would you hire this person?

Two examples of such letters follow:

---

20 Brentwood Avenue
LLANELLI
Dyfed
DF21 SNW

Mr J P R Williams
Finance Director
Sportswear Industries
27 Hyde Park
LONDON
SE1 8NW

26 April 1994

Dear Mr Williams

I am writing to enquire whether you have any requirements which my experience and responsibilities to date may satisfy.

Currently I am employed by The First Manhattan Bank as Management Accountant within the Financial Econometrics Group. I have been with First Manhattan for nearly six years and I have a total of seventeen years' experience in the Finance sector, including three years as Management Accountant.

It is because of the lack of opportunities and career potential at First Manhattan that I am now considering alternative employment. For my part I am seeking a position with an organisation such as yours, which will provide a challenging environment where I could make a positive contribution.

Enclosed is a copy of my CV which summarises my career and gives some example of the type of work I have successfully performed, which I hope you will find relevant. Should you wish for any clarification I would be glad to provide further details. I would also be pleased to attend for interview to discuss any opportunities you may currently have or foresee in the near future.

I look forward to hearing from you.

Yours sincerely

Rhys Evans
Enc.

---

67 North Road
Evington
LEICESTER
LE4 2JD

Tel: 0533 501011

14 July 1994

J E Davis Esq
Head of Management Services
Brown Industries Limited
SPALDING
Lincs

Dear Mr Davis

I am writing to you to ask if you have any opportunities within your department which may be suitable for someone with my experience and qualifications.

Following a company takeover and subsequent restructuring of my department, my immediate career prospects with Smiths Limited are restricted. I am therefore seeking a Production Management position, preferably within the pharmaceutical sector, where I can build on over twelve years' experience and deliver my full potential.

Having researched your company, I have outlined in the following summary why I believe I can add value to your department. I have also enclosed a copy of my curriculum vitae, which I trust will be useful to you.

If you feel that my experience could be utilised within your department, I would be delighted to meet you to discuss any opportunities.

Yours sincerely

David Longbotham

Enc.

The telephone interview

Definitely very nerve-racking, but can pay a high dividend for someone with the courage to simply pick up the phone and call a company direct.

Here you are very much in control. You will, in all probability, have caught the recipient of your call unprepared and you will have a golden opportunity to talk your way into securing that all-important first interview.

Remember, your goal – getting an interview, *not* a job (that's the goal of the interview). Here is what you need to consider:

Telephoning employers can be tricky but very worth while.

1. Remember the AIDA principle, ie, you need to get the person's:
   - Attention;
   - Interest;
   - Desire (to know more);
   - Actions (afterwards).

Do some preparation beforehand.

2. You will not keep the person's interest for long; you therefore need to be to the point, yet thorough.

3. Do your homework first:
   - What are the company's main products?
   - What area most interests you?
   - What are the key skills sought?
   - What is the name of the person you need to speak to? (Note: the switchboard is a useful source of information.)

4. Your objective is merely to get an interview.

5. Try to find out as much as possible about the key skills required. You will be able to use this information in your written application.

6. Write down exactly what you are going to say. Read it out loud to yourself and try to predict the outcome or questions. Work out exactly how you are going to deal with the various scenarios.

7. Role-play with a friend as a rehearsal for the 'real thing'.

You should plan your call around the following three stages:

The structure of the telephone call.

Attract attention
   - your name;
   - what you do (very brief outline only);
   - what are you after;
   - get agreement to continue.

Produce interest and desire
- your main achievements;
- your main strengths;
- how you can add value to the company.

Agree actions
- Fix a date and time for an interview. If this fails, at least ask for contacts within other organisations who may have vacancies.

Some examples of what to say.

Examples of telephone interview techniques are as follows:
(Y = You; C = Company Representative)

Stage 1

Y: Good afternoon, Mr Davis. My name is Rose Smith and I am an experienced quality controller with extensive knowledge of the food industry, particularly baby foods, and I'm looking for a fresh challenge within the industry. Is this a good time to talk to you? I promise I'll be brief and to the point.

[If you get the 'OK', go to stage 2]

C: I'm tied up right now, can you call back later?

Y: Of course. Can you please give me a precise time when I know I can catch you at a good moment?

[Alternatively, he might say as follows]

C: We don't have any vacancies right now *or* Can you send me your CV?

Y: I understand, but can you tell me a little about the sort of key skills you would be looking for?

Stage 2

Y: I've recently successfully implemented a new quality control system at ABC Limited, which entailed controlling a budget of £1m and leading a team of twelve people. My experience in quality control within the food industry is very broadly based and has included positions within manufacturing, packaging and distribution.

Stage 3

Y: The purpose of my call is that I'm looking for a fresh challenge where I can really move my career onwards. I'm particularly interested in the continued development of quality assurance within the manufacturing environment. Is this an area in which you have much involvement? (Of course, you know it is from your research!)

[He replies that it is.]

Y: I am planning to be in your area on Monday. I'd be delighted if I could come in to see you for half an hour to discuss this further. Is 2 pm a convenient time?

Once you have fixed a date and time, it is a good idea to write down everything you have learned about the company during the conversation. Incorporate this information into your CV and management summary, and prepare your interview tactics and questions accordingly.

If the interview date is more than two weeks ahead, it is a good idea to write and confirm the interview date and time – less chance of a wasted journey.

I tried this tactic with about 20 potential employers. The lessons I learned were as follows:

Some useful points to bear in mind about telephoning.

1. The key people are usually tied up whenever you ring. You have to be very patient and persistent. Try 8.30 am.
2. If people promise to call you back, the chances are they won't.
3. You will be very nervous at first, but after three or four calls it will flow very naturally. Therefore save your best contacts until you are well versed.
4. Cold calling is largely unproductive. Do your homework first. A good source of information is the telephone switchboard. Be honest with them and say you are looking for a job in X department – ask who is the best person to contact, etc.
5. Have your CV to hand at all times.
6. Be confident in your own abilities, and come straight to the point.
7. Do not be put off by any early failures (if at first you don't succeed . . .).

Using personal contacts

The way to use personal contacts is as follows:

The best ways to make use of personal contacts.

1. To establish in which areas there are vacancies, and at what levels.
2. To identify who the main contacts are.
3. To get them to express your desire to join them.
4. To set up a meeting or interview.

43

5. To provide inside information about the company, the job and also the key skills sought.

A personal contact is a superb way of getting over the first hurdle and setting up the first interview. I have interviewed many people who have come via a personal recommendation, and usually they have a high success rate, provided there is a vacancy to be filled.

Remember, the wider your personal network the greater your chances of success. In many cases, if you hit at a good time, you may be the only candidate interviewed for the position (remember, over half of all vacancies are never advertised).

Summary

How successful you are in this field depends entirely upon how much effort you put in and how determined you are. By using the techniques outlined above, you have a clear opportunity to gain an edge over any other applicants. The key tips are:

1. Do your homework thoroughly.
2. Spread your net widely.
3. Don't put all your eggs in any one basket.
4. Be prepared to draw some blanks.
5. Have the guts to ring companies up direct.
6. If at first you don't succeed, try, try, try again.

Success goes to the person who is not only pro-active, but also determined.

GO FOR IT AND STICK TO IT!

9. INTERVIEW PREPARATION

Contents

- The necessity of doing your homework in preparation for each interview
- What you need to do

Overview

I have personally interviewed scores of people for positions at various levels from YTS trainee through to senior manager. In almost all cases I *wanted* the interviewee to succeed. I look for three critical success factors:

What an interviewer looks for.

- Can the interviewee do the job?
- Will he fit into the department?
- How much does he want the job?

Having outlined the format of the interview to the candidate, one of my favourite early questions, asked in a very casual manner, is: 'How much do you know about the company?'

Make sure you know the company's business.

The results are quite astounding:

- 50 per cent say they know 'not very much'.
- 40 per cent give a one-line answer ('you make curtain poles' etc).
- 8 per cent make a reasonable attempt, but clearly haven't done any thorough research.
- 2 per cent really impress.

To me, this is such a basic error on the part of potential employees. They are expecting us (the employers) to spend tens of thousands of pounds on them over many years, yet they haven't even taken the trouble to visit the local library to find out a little about the company's history.

WHY NOT?

A Saturday morning at the reference library could make the difference between a 'thumbs-up' and a 'thumbs-down' at interview.

DO YOUR HOMEWORK – AND DO IT THOROUGHLY.

Here's how.

How to do it

1. Sources of information are:

How to find out about the company's business.

- local reference library (tell the librarian exactly what you want to achieve and ask what the best books for that particular purpose are);
- the company itself (telephone the Publicity or Marketing Department and ask for some company literature – a copy of the latest annual report is a good start).

2. The information you need to know about the company is:

- company address;
- phone number;
- is it a wholly-owned subsidiary of another company?
- name of the Managing Director;
- name of the relevant director for your prospective new position;
- company turnover and profits;
- what the company does/makes;
- number of employees;
- where the main sites are;
- does it have any subsidiaries?
- who are its main customers?
- who are its main suppliers?
- who are its main competitors?
- what are the main factors affecting the market (for example, interest rates in the building industry)?
- is it expanding?

3. Also find out as much specific information about the relevant position as possible, such as:

- How does the department fit into the overall company?
- How many people are there in the department?
- How is it structured?
- What are the key skills needed?
- How could I contribute to the overall effectiveness of the department?
- How will I 'add value'?

4. Complete the questionnaire shown on the next page for each prospective employer and ask for a copy of the job description — one should exist for every vacancy.

Summary

It is not the person who is most qualified who succeeds at interview — it is the one who is most prepared.

Doing your homework can give you a clear advantage over the other candidates. Do it, and what's more, ensure you make it perfectly clear to the interviewer (in a subtle way) that you really have researched the company. You can do this by having a brief company dossier in front of you and by referring to it occasionally at interview.

Remember:

SUCCESS GOES TO THE ACTIVIST!

Prepare a dossier on each potential employer.

COMPANY INFORMATION

Company name/address..................
Phone number..................................
Wholly-owned ....
Managing Director............................
Relevant director..............................
Company turnover/profits...............
Company's business...........................
Number of employees.......................
Main site locations............................
Subsidiaries.......................................
Main customers.................................
Main suppliers...................................
Main competitors ....
Factors affecting market ....
Is it expanding? ....

SPECIFIC INFORMATION

How does department fit into overall company? .....
How many people in department?............................
How is department structured?................................

10. LAST MINUTE PREPARATION

Contents

- Planning your journey
- Overcoming nerves
- Last minute preparation

Overview

The plan

Your thoughts

'The interview is at 11 am. 100 miles on A roads and motorways will take about two hours. There shouldn't be any hold-ups at that time of day. Better give myself an extra 15 minutes – just in case!'

Your interview may not go as smoothly as you expect.

Reality

You have to stop for petrol. You get stuck behind a tractor. There are roadworks on the M1 – you sit in traffic for 30 minutes. The city centre is very busy. Parking is a nightmare – you have to leave your car a mile away and run in order to avoid being late. The company has four separate office blocks – where is the interview to be held? What's the name of the guy you are supposed to be seeing?

What sort of impression are you likely to make? Are you really in any position to do yourself justice?

49

There is much you can do to avoid the above scenario. Most of it is painfully obvious, but you would be surprised how few people use the following guidelines.

How to do it

Agree a suitable date and time

Make sure you have a convenient time and date for your interview.

The date and time should be convenient to both yourself and the employer. What is the best time for you in terms of:

- When are you normally at your best?
- How far have you got to travel?
- What condition are you likely to be in for the interview?

Most companies will be sympathetic to individual circumstances, so don't be afraid to telephone and suggest a more convenient date and time if the one offered to you presents problems. For senior positions, overnight accommodation may be offered (but only if *you* request it – there is no harm in asking).

Check your route thoroughly

Plan your journey as thoroughly as you can.

If you are travelling by car, make sure you have a map with you with detailed instructions on how to locate the actual building. Telephone well in advance and find out:

- what the local traffic is likely to be like at the particular time of day;
- exactly where the office is located;
- whether there are any local roadworks;
- where to park.

Arrive around one hour before the interview

There is plenty to do before the interview when you arrive.

Locate the office where the interview is to take place, then find yourself somewhere quiet where you can complete your preparation. This is key – do it thoroughly. Your final preparation should include:

1. Job details:

- Read and re-read all the relevant information about the position, including your own notes.

- Who will you report to?
- Who is interviewing you?

2. Perform a mock interview. Take the part of both the interviewer and the interviewee. Ask yourself the standard questions, and answer them convincingly aloud:

- Why do you want the job?
- What have you got to offer?
- Why should we choose you?
- What are your key achievements to date?
- What are your main strengths and weaknesses?

3. Overcome worry. There are many well documented methods of overcoming nerves, such as deep breathing, but one useful technique which I have successfully used to overcome unnecessary worry is as follows. Several days before the interview is scheduled to take place, write down all your concerns on a blank sheet of paper. To do this, draw three columns, headed 'Worst case', 'Consequence' and 'What I'm going to do'. Typical scenarios are as illustrated below:

Worst case	Consequence	What I'm going to do
I might get stuck in a traffic jam.	I might be late for the interview.	Check beforehand with the secretary. Ensure I have the phone number and change with me.
I might get very nervous.	I may forget the key points.	Write down the main facts, and have them with me to refer to.
I may not be the person sought.	I may not get the job.	I haven't got the job now, so I have nothing to lose by trying for it.

Visualise success

Give yourself a psychological boost.

Imagine yourself walking away from the office with a job offer in your hand. All the employees of the firm line up and give you a guard of honour. You are the answer to this company's problems. You succeed. You work here. This is where you come to work every day.

51

This technique is widely used by many of today's top sportsmen and sportswomen. Golfers, for example, visualise every shot before playing it, and see in their mind's eye the ball flying straight down the middle of the fairway onto the heart of the green.

Get the adrenalin pumping

Repeat twenty times with feeling the following lines:

- 'I am terrific'.
- 'I am the best candidate'.
- 'I get the job'.
- 'I succeed'.

If you can convince yourself, you have a far greater chance of convincing your would-be employers. *Anything you firmly believe becomes your reality.*

Summary

If you were going on holiday with your family and you had to catch a plane at a certain time, what would you do to make sure you didn't miss it?

I suspect your answer is along the following lines:

1. Pack the car the night before.
2. Check you have got your route planned.
3. Make sure you know where you are going to park.
4. Make sure you have got your tickets handy.
5. Plan to arrive at least an hour before you need to check in.

So what is different with your approach towards an interview? If you are really serious, the answer is '*nothing*'.

Remember to:

The important points in preparing for an interview.

1. Get there in plenty of time.
2. Go over your notes.
3. Psych yourself up.
4. Visualise success.
5. Relax.
6. Go for it!

11. A DYNAMIC FIRST IMPRESSION

Contents

- Your immaculate appearance
- A positive self-introduction
- Giving yourself a flying start

Overview

Fact 1: Most decisions are made in the first five minutes of an interview.
Fact 2: The rest of the interview is spent justifying that decision.

The first five minutes are the most important.

This is *not* how the textbook says you should interview people, but it is what happens in many cases in reality. You have to remember that over 50 per cent of all interviewers have had no formal training in interviewing techniques. Therefore you *have* to make a dynamic and lasting first impression – convince the interviewer that you are the person for the job, and then let him spend the rest of the interview justifying that decision.

Here's how.

How to do it

1. Report to the receptionist ten minutes before the scheduled time of the interview. Be particularly courteous – remember, receptionists and secretaries may be consulted later either in passing or as part of the actual

Twelve points to remember to get off to a good start.

interview process. If the receptionist has a particularly attractive brooch, for example, comment on it.

2. It is always a good idea to visit the toilet, to make sure you are impeccably presented (tie straight, hair combed etc). If nervous, take ten deep breaths.

3. Look around you. Observe the surroundings. Is there anything particularly interesting (photograph of the factory, quality of the reception area, age of the building etc)? Use this for your 'casual chat' lines.

4. If you are met in the reception area and accompanied to the interview room, use your 'casual chat' lines to keep some sort of conversation going, no matter how trivial. Remember, the first few minutes are critical. Avoid an awkward silence wherever possible.

5. Make sure you know the interviewer's name.

6. Shake hands positively and firmly, with a strong introduction line such as: 'Good morning, Mr Smith. I am David Jones and I'm pleased to meet you.'

7. Stand up until invited to sit down.

8. Keep your jacket on unless you are invited to take it off or the interviewer has taken his off – but even then ask first.

9. If your chair is in an uncomfortable position (for example, you are looking into the sun), ask immediately if you can move it – then do it.

10. Try to gauge as quickly as possible how good the interviewer is. A first-rate interviewer will naturally take control. A poor interviewer may be nervous and ill-prepared – you should therefore be ready to take the initiative if necessary.

11. It is perfectly acceptable to have a notepad and pencil to hand. Get these on the table immediately, but do not write copious notes – only key information.

12. Smile, relax, look the interviewer straight in the eye (but do not stare), and you are on your way!

Summary

First impressions often dictate the whole course of the interview. Make sure you are well prepared, well presented and give yourself a flying start.

A firm, confident handshake, together with affirmative introductory conversation and you are well on your way.

12. BODY LANGUAGE

Contents

- What body language is
- The tell-tale signs which indicate that someone is lying
- How body language can be used effectively at interview

Overview

Body language is a fascinating subject in its own right. It is especially important for people such as sales executives, who can interpret body gestures as possible buy signals. It is also important for you, the interviewee, to have a basic understanding of the art, so that:

- you don't commit any defensive blunders yourself during the interview;
- you know when the interviewer may be hiding something.

The most important thing to understand is that any one gesture can have a variety of different meanings. For example, sitting with crossed arms and legs, with chin down could be a signal of:

- cold;
- negativeness and defensiveness;
- a need to go to the toilet.

Therefore, gestures should never be interpreted in isolation, but rather in groups, or clusters, and should be used in conjunction with verbal communications.

Body gestures can be split into four main groups, for the purpose of interviews:

- hand to face movements;

Body language is a very useful clue to what the interviewer is thinking.

55

- crossed arms and legs;
- eye movements;
- head movements.

Hand to face

You have heard of the tale of the three monkeys who 'hear no evil, speak no evil and see no evil'. These classic gestures are the underlying basis for summarising human behaviour, in that every time we try to deceive, we try to cover it up with our hands. The only difference between the gestures of a human adult and a monkey is that human gestures tend to be more subtle. Their interpretation, however, is identical:

1. Hand placed over mouth: the person is telling a lie.
2. Hand touching nose: a version of the hand over mouth, ie the person is telling a lie.
3. Finger in mouth/pencil in mouth: common when a person is under pressure and seeking reassurance.
4. Eye rubbing: just as the monkey signifies in 'see no evil', usually coupled with the person looking in another direction. In short, he doesn't like what he sees.
5. Ear rubbing: 'hear no evil', that is, the person is trying to block out what he is hearing. He doesn't like it.
6. Head resting on hand: boredom. The person is trying to stop falling asleep by propping his head up.
7. Hand on cheek but not supporting the head (often with index finger pointing upwards): interest is being shown and the person is likely to be in thinking mode.
8. Chin stroking: a sign of decision making.

Conclusion

Most hand to face gestures are negative and many are used to cover up untruths. Play safe at interview – keep your hands well away from your head.

Crossed arms and legs

1. Crossed arms: the purpose of crossing arms was originally to shield the heart, and is a sign of:

   - defensiveness;

- negativity;
- nerves.

2. Crossed legs: while, in general, these indicate negative and defensive attitudes, they are more difficult to interpret and they can signify the following attitudes:

- nervous or defensive;
- reserved or holding back information.

3. However, they could also be due to:

- adopting a woman's pose;
- discomfort or cold;
- need to visit the toilet.

Conclusion

Crossed arms and legs form partial barriers between interviewee and interviewer. They normally represent defensive attitudes and can indicate that a person is holding back on a particular issue. Again, play safe – don't cross arms or legs.

Eyes

1. Eyes gazing at the other person's eyes/forehead: the serious, business-like gaze.
2. Eyes gazing from the level of eyes to neck: showing signs of social interest.
3. Eyes glancing sideways: with a raised eyebrow or smile this indicates interest. With lowered eyebrow or frown, this indicates suspicion or hostility.
4. Eyes wandering or closed: lack of interest.
5. Eyes looking at watch: a disaster! Means boredom or frustration.

Eyes can be particularly expressive.

Head

1. Upright: indicates acceptance of what the person is hearing, usually accompanied by occasional nods.
2. Tilted: interest is being shown.
3. Down: negative attitude, representing disapproval.
4. Both hands behind head: 'I'm smarter than you.'

The angle of your head shows the degree of confidence or alertness.

57

5. Shaking: a classic way to detect a covered-up objection, especially when it contradicts what is spoken. For example, 'Well, I've really enjoyed talking to you, and I'll contact you tomorrow.'
6. Nodding: signifies approval and a positive 'yes'.
7. Smiling: expresses confidence, enjoyment and can lighten a serious situation.

How to do it

Applying the theory of body language to the scenario of an interview can have a big effect on the outcome, whether or not the interviewer is able to recognise particular gestures. I suggest you follow the basic guidelines set out below:

Follow these guidelines to show positive body language.

1. Sit upright, attentive and alert. Don't slouch or prop your head up.
2. No matter how boring the interviewer may be, tell yourself, 'This is the most interesting conversation of my life.'
3. Look the interviewer straight in the eye, but don't stare.
4. Do not cross either your arms or legs.
5. Adopt an 'open' posture.
6. Keep your hands away from your face, except when in 'consideration mode' (that is, hand against cheek, with index finger pointing upwards).
7. Concentrate hard on the interview and the interviewer. Avoid letting your eyes wander and your concentration drift on to more pleasurable subjects.
8. Use your hands to demonstrate a point – but be careful not to overdo it.

Summary

Body language can be used in interview situations mainly to detect lies or defensive stands. A classic mistake to make when interpreting gestures, however, is to evaluate a particular gesture in isolation, as any one gesture can have a variety of different meanings, depending on the circumstances at the time.

A clever, well-trained interviewer can read the body gestures and match them against what is being said, whether reinforcing the point or contradicting it. Police interviewers, for example, are experts. That is why the interviewee's chair is placed right in the middle of the interview room, with lights shining directly into the person's face. This way, the slightest body motion can be detected to indicate whether a person is telling the truth, or not.

While you don't need to appreciate the finer points, it is important that you are aware of the various traps which you can fall into, regarding how your body gestures can give you away.

13. INTERVIEW SKILLS

Contents

- What are interviewers looking for?
- How to sell yourself
- How to make a lasting impression
- Dealing with an incompetent interviewer

Overview

The basic format of an interview.

By and large, most interviews I conduct follow a very similar format:

1. Introductions
2. We tell you about the position and the company
3. You tell us about yourself
4. We ask you questions
5. You ask us questions
6. Close.

In most cases we have a fairly good idea whether or not the candidate will be successful before the interviewee tells us anything about himself – the remaining 75 per cent of interview merely reinforces the first 25 per cent.

Some important general points about all interviews.

There are some key points to remember, which apply for interviews at all levels:

1. Over 50 per cent of all interviewers have not had formal training – some will be as nervous as you!
2. All interviewers *want* you to do well (whether on commission or not, no one *wants* to have to say 'no').
3. While the interview is in progress, the interviewer will be asking himself:

- Will this person fit in here?
- Has he got the right background and experience?
- Can he do the job?
- Does he really want it?
- How much preparation has he done?

4. A professional interviewer will be well-structured in his approach and will build up a complete picture of your skills to match those required for the job. Your objective is to be one step ahead and do this skills analysis beforehand as part of your interview preparation, that is, to assess what the key requirements are, and how these are likely to be evaluated.

5. Be positive and expect to succeed. If you expect to succeed, the chances are that you will. If you expect to fail, you surely will.

There are some classic signs to look for, and some obvious pitfalls which must be avoided. Here are some basic pointers.

How to do it

The dos

1. Be relaxed, natural and, above all, keen.
2. Gauge how skilled the interviewer is: is he in full control? Does he need help in keeping the conversation flowing?
3. Pay particular attention to what is being said. It's OK to make the odd note about a specific name etc, but avoid taking copious notes; just enough to let them know you are serious.
4. Don't waffle. If a question is not clear, ask for clarification before you answer.
5. Always try to relate your past experience with the current vacancy. Draw similarities and comparisons, and home in on specific achievements or strong points.
6. As part of your interview preparation, list the six key points you feel will give you an advantage over your competitors. Make sure these are all covered and cross them off in your mind when you go over them during the interview. Refer to them in your notes if you need to.
7. Make doubly sure you have done your homework on the company and the position on offer. If you cannot steer the conversation around to the information you have learned, bring up any specific points in your

A list of things to do in an interview.

61

questions at the end.

8. Try to make the conversation flow, as if you were talking over a drink in a pub. If you can develop rapport with the interviewer, so much the better, but don't overdo it.

9. Be well armed with questions to ask at the end (even if you know the answers!). Don't ask too many questions just for the sake of it, as this may turn the interviewer off.

10. Interviewers are always delighted with any references to the overall profitability of the company. Commercial awareness is a great asset to have. Think how you can add value to the company, not just to the department.

11. Be positive. Expect to succeed.

The don'ts

A list of things not to do in an interview.

1. Don't smoke under any circumstances.
2. Don't criticise your former company. If asked why you want to leave, give an honest straightforward answer, but don't dwell on it.
3. Don't ask about pay and benefits at this stage, unless they are particularly relevant to the job.
4. Don't lose interest, no matter how badly the interview appears to be going. If it's tough on you, it's likely to be tough on everyone else as well.
5. Don't look at your watch, or appear restless and in a hurry.
6. Don't expect to fail. If you do, you will. Developing a positive, winning mental attitude is more than half the battle.

The incompetent interviewer

How to spot an amateur interviewer.

Watch out for the 'amateur' or incompetent interviewer. They are easy to spot, usually by one or more of the following giveaways:

1. They have mislaid your application form.
2. The interview is in the interviewer's office.
3. Their desk is cluttered.
4. Interruptions by phone or by people walking in are frequent.
5. They ramble on for ages about the company, without you getting a word in edgeways.
6. They appear nervous.

7. The questions asked do not allow a flow of information, but point to 'yes/no' type answers.
8. They may paint a negative picture of the company.

Turn this around into an advantageous position for yourself. Consider the following methods to overcome each of the above points:

If you are being interviewed by an amateur, use this to your advantage.

1. Have several copies of your CV or application form with you.
2. Pay careful attention to the surroundings.
3. Compliment the interviewer on any features in the room (for example, a trophy or photograph).
4. Jot down exactly what you were discussing at the point of the interruption. Lead into the conversation upon resumption, referring to your notes, saying, 'We were discussing the restructure of the department, following the takeover in 1988'. The impression you will give is that you are organised, patient and have a good memory.
5. Show particular interest. Tell yourself, 'This is the most interesting conversation I have ever listened to', and pick up on points wherever possible. Be careful, however, not to interrupt – agreement and reinforcing sentiments are probably the safest entry lines.
6. Begin to take control. You may say, 'Mr Smith, I know your time is very valuable, so I have given careful thought regarding this interview and would like to propose the following format. First, I would like to tell you about my background, and why I am particularly interested in joining you. Then I would like to find out a little more about the exact role I would play in your team, and finally I would like to ask you about career development opportunities. Is this OK with you?'
7. Treat each yes/no question as if it was followed by 'Please give details of one specific example.' For example:

Q: Do you like to work in a team?
A: Yes, I certainly do. In my current position I am working closely with five colleagues on plans for the introduction of a new product in the spring. While much of the work is carried out independently of one another, I enjoy the camaraderie and the pursuit of common goals. We all put in that little bit extra, because no one wants to let the side down, and together we get a real sense of achievement when we reach milestones.

Summary

If you are serious about the job, you will have done your homework. If you have done your homework, you will be relaxed, confident and expecting to do well. If you are relaxed, confident and expecting to do well, you *will* do well.

The moral of the story is: always prepare thoroughly, well in advance, for each interview.

Careful interview preparation is the key to a successful interview.

14. STANDARD QUESTIONS TO EXPECT

Contents

- Examples of standard interview questions
- Suggested responses
- The importance of careful interview preparation

Overview

During every interview, there are favourite questions asked of candidates. Some are straightforward, such as, 'Why do you want the job?' Others may have more of a hidden meaning.

How to answer questions at the interview.

The secret of a successful interview is to keep the conversation flowing, to direct the conversation around your strengths and not to dwell upon any weaknesses. Try to work out what the interviewer is getting at, and be prepared to reinforce your answers with specific examples, where appropriate.

Below are some examples of standard questions you should expect, together with suggested styles of responses.

You should have answers prepared for each of these questions. Either write down your complete answer, or simply the main bullet points you would mention in an interview situation. The following are guidelines for preparing your own answers.

How to do it

Make sure you prepare your own answers to all these questions. Some suggestions are given.

1.* **Why do you want the job?**
   Opportunity to deliver my full potential and to progress within the company; to build upon my previous experience.

2.* **What interests you about the company?**
   I am particulary interested in the shoe industry, and I am naturally keen to join a major player in this field.

3. **What value can you add to this department?**
   My natural enthusiasm and proven skills, together with 15 years' highly relevant experience.

4.* **What has been your main achievement to date?**
   Describe a project you played a major part in and in particular how you overcame a specific problem.

5. **What are the benefits of working in a team and working independently?**
   Most jobs will require you to do both.

6.† **Why do you want to leave your present job?**
   Limited career development opportunities etc.

7. **How much do you know about our company?**
   Here's your moment of glory. They asked for it – now, sock it to them!

8. **How do you cope with pressure?**
   I don't panic. I react swiftly, yet calmly. I think the problem through, decide, then see the task through to conclusion.

9. **How will your boss react when you hand in your notice?**
   Naturally disappointed, as I've been a major contributor to the success of his team, especially over the last three months when I was involved in ...

10. **What are you looking for in your next job?**
    An opportunity to build on my previous experience, to broaden my horizons, and to develop my career ...

11. **What aspect of your current job do you enjoy most?**
    Problem-solving; it's demanding and challenging. I find I need to use a wide variety of skills in order to overcome the problems encountered, such as ...

12.†What aspect of your current job do you like least?

Routine administration (but you accept that it needs to be done).

13. Where do you see yourself in three years?

Be tactful; you could refer to your future boss's role.

14.*What are your main strengths?

Ability to get things done, decision making, leadership ...

15. What are your main weaknesses?

Impatience, frustration, when things are not moving quickly enough.

16. What are you doing about your weaknesses?

Always think of a weakness, as everybody has at least one, but turn it into a positive attribute. For example, you may see yourself as impatient at times if others cannot grasp new technology as quickly as you.

17. What projects have you worked on recently?

18.†What salary are you looking for?

Do not be specific. Give at most a vague response. For example, 'I am applying for positions in the range of £15,000 to £20,000'. (See Chapter 18 on effective salary negotiation.)

19. Why should I pick you, rather than any of the other candidates?

Because I feel I am particularly well suited in terms of ability to do the job, motivation and previous experience.

20.†Why did you not go on to further education?

21.†Why have you changed companies so often?

Give positive reasons.

22.†Why were you out of work between ...?

Be honest. If you were made redundant, say so.

23. How do you spend your leisure time?

I don't get a lot of time, but I am a particularly keen golfer, and I've played at ... courses etc.

24. What motivates you?

Success, recognition, achievement of objectives.

25. How would your boss describe you?

Teamworker, self-motivated, reliable, honest.

Key to the symbols:

* An ideal opportunity for you to really sell yourself. Have a comprehensive answer prepared, and be ready to speak at some length. This is your chance to impress the interviewer, and you should jump at it.

† An attacking question. Give an accurate answer of one or two sentences, but try to move on as quickly as possible.

Summary

A successful interview is one where the interviewee has spoken for about 70 per cent of the time and listened for 30 per cent, and where dialogue has flowed freely. The worst sort are those which are merely question and answer sessions.

Remember, the interviewer is looking for:

1. Ability to do the job.
2. Enthusiasm and confidence.
3. Proven track record and relevant experience.

The interviewer *wants* you to succeed, but to succeed you have to do your homework, both in terms of preparing answers to predictable questions, and also seeking out general information about the company.

The secret is to get one step ahead of the interviewer and to predict what questions will be asked. By giving careful thought to your answers, and even practising interviews with a close friend, you can develop your own interview style that leaves a lasting impression.

15. STANDARD QUESTIONS TO ASK

Contents

- The need for careful preparation of questions to ask
- How to deliver them and make a lasting impression
- The interviewer's likely reaction

Overview

At every interview, the interviewee will have the chance to ask questions. If the opportunity doesn't arise during the course of the interview, there is bound to be time at the end.

Why you need to prepare questions to ask at the interview.

This is your golden opportunity to ask sensible, intelligent questions which will give the interviewer the feeling that, 'This person is serious. He has done his homework, he's obviously keen'.

Again, careful preparation is the name of the game. Do your research. Find out as much as you can about the company. For example, new products, market developments, what the competition is doing etc. It does no harm to have these questions written down in front of you. Not only will you remember them, it will also let the interviewer know you really have prepared for this interview. Do not be afraid to pose questions, even if you already know the answer!

How to do it

Here is a selection of questions to adapt and ask at your next interview:

Examples of questions to ask at interview. Prepare some of your own as well.

1. Does the company have a policy of promotion from within, or does it prefer to recruit externally for senior positions (ie, what are the chances of promotion)?
2. What emphasis does the company put on personal training programmes for individual employees (ie, what training do you offer)?
3. What percentage of turnover is attributable to the export market (ie, how much are you currently exporting)? Is this on the increase?
4. How much is the company currently investing in information technology?
5. What would my priorities be if I was appointed?
6. Why has this job arisen? What happened to the predecessor?
7. I note from your 1992/1993 company results that your turnover increased by 15 per cent. How does this compare with your competitors – are you gaining market share?
8. How high is staff turnover in the department?
9. Where do you see the main career paths leading to, once I have firmly proved myself here? (Note: you may get this question thrown back at you – so beware!)
10. What is the size of department I will be working in?
11. How is individual performance assessed?
12. What is your policy on quality (BS 5750 etc)?
13. What is the company's mission statement (if it has one)?
14. I note from your current catalogue that you have recently launched a new product; how successful was the launch?
15. I note that your share price has fallen from a high of £2.60 to today's figure of £1.85. Are there significant reasons for this?
16. How will the introduction of new technology affect my role?
17. I note from your last annual report that you have been researching solar heating. What is the outcome of this study?
18. How does the job interact with different departments?
19. What is the general morale like within the company at the moment?
20. How does the company measure customer service? What efforts are you making to improve it? How can this department help in this respect?

Summary

There is no bigger let-down at the end of an interview than when the interviewer asks, 'I'm sure you would like to ask us some questions now –

do you have any specific points?' 'No!' Whereupon the interviewer promptly gets up from the chair and makes for the nearest exit.

The interviewer expects you to have done some homework, to be keen, and to ask relevant questions. Don't let him down – be well armed with a selection of questions, and listen carefully to the answers. It would not impress the interviewer for you to ask a question which has already been answered.

16. CLOSING THE INTERVIEW

Contents

- How to wind up an interview effectively
- The importance of a strong close
- Make a dynamic leaving impression

Overview

The importance of a strong close.

So many interviews which I have personally conducted have petered away almost to stalemate with the candidate unable to think of any further questions and obviously eager to make a quick get-away.

Needless to say, only a small percentage of these candidates proceeded to the next stage. Once again, it is all down to interview preparation. You need to have a strong close and thereby leave a favourable impression of yourself with the interviewer.

An old woodwork teacher once told me a tip about planing a piece of wood: 'If you look after the ends, the middle will take care of itself.' This is true to some extent with interview techniques – you need to make a dynamic first impression and an impressive, forceful finish. So when asked, 'Have you any further questions?', use this as your cue and hit them with your well-prepared closing gambit.

How to do it

At the end of the interview look the interviewer(s) in the eye and mention the following:

How to end an interview effectively.

1. Thank them for their time and interest in you. All interviewers are busy people and many find interviewing a bind. Thanking them for considering your application is a good way to reward them.
2. Summarise your main strengths in relation to the position offered.
3. Portray a sense of excitement about the prospect of joining the company.
4. Anticipate success, and expect to proceed to the next stage.
5. Do not portray any signs of hesitation or indecisiveness. If you do have any further nagging doubts, these can always be cleared up afterwards.
6. Be highly enthusiastic and determined throughout. You can always change your mind later, and remember that you are making no commitment until you accept any offer made.

Consider the following example:

'Before I go, I would like to thank you for your time. I found our discussions very constructive and I find the prospect of working for you very exciting. I have no doubt about my ability to do the job and I am particularly pleased that I will be able to build on my previous experience. When will we speak again?'

The six points above combined into one sentence.

Be careful, though. Unless you sound totally convincing, this closing speech could come over as being completely rehearsed and therefore not sincere. I strongly suggest that you rehearse several versions, and in doing so convince yourself of your sincerity. Tailor the actual wording to the content of the interview, so that it comes over as authentic and genuine.

The main thing is to say something, even if it is simply:

'Thank you for your time – it has been a most constructive interview and I am really excited about this opportunity. I sincerely hope my application will be successful.'

Summary

Consider the format of a typical James Bond film:

Think of this analogy when considering the interview.

- riveting initial five minutes to grab your undivided attention;
- eighty minutes of the main plot;
- dramatic final scenes involving car chases, explosions and an unexpected twist.

Q: What is it that you remember about the film?
A: The beginning and the end.

Q: How did you rate the main film?
A: Only as good as the opening and closing scenes.

This does not mean that you should not pay particular interest to the main body of the interview – in many ways this is where the real 'you' will come over and it is this part which you need to prepare fully for.

The final part, however, is where you can score heavily over other candidates by a simple statement expressing your thanks, interest and keenness. Don't underestimate the impact this can have.

17. AFTER THE INTERVIEW

Contents

- What you should do immediately after the interview
- Your follow-up procedure

Overview

'Phew! Thank goodness the interview is over. Now where is the nearest pub – I deserve a drink after all that.' *Wrong*! It's at this particular moment, when what was said in the interview is still fresh in your mind, that you need to start your follow-up procedure.

Although I have interviewed scores of candidates, I have yet to receive a follow-up letter from any of them! In my opinion, the ten minutes it takes to write one could mean the difference between getting the job and not. I use this technique myself to portray the following points:

- It shows you are keen and interested.
- It shows you paid attention to what was said.
- It shows you are a thorough professional.
- It helps to crystallise in your mind your own particular strengths and weaknesses, and it gives you time to address any issues before your next meeting.

After you have left the interview, sit down and write a follow-up letter.

How to do it

What to put in the follow-up letter.

1. Answer the following points straight after the interview. I normally do this in my car, or even on a park bench, but always within ten minutes of the interview:

   - the name(s) and job title(s) of the interview panel;
   - the job title of the position applied for (if not originally specified);
   - what the work involves;
   - the critical success factors (ie, the most important aspects of the job);
   - where in the interview did you do particularly well (ie, your strengths)?
   - where did you struggle (ie, your weaknesses)?
   - why should they choose you?
   - what was the next step (ie, who is to contact whom, and when)?

Other points to note.

2. Get the letter typed. Alternatively, write in your best handwriting, using a fountain pen.
3. Address your letter to the main interviewer, and send only the one copy – any more is overkill.
4. Send the letter as soon as possible, and always use first class post. Speed is essential here, as decisions can be made at extremely short notice.
5. Make sure it is specific: ie, that it doesn't give the impression of 'just another standard follow-up letter'.
6. If you were put forward by an agency, phone the agency, expressing how keen you are and how well you thought the interview went. These comments *will* be relayed back to the company. If there were any weak points, point these out to the agency and tell them what you intend to do about them. The agency is likely to be on commission and therefore is on your side.
7. If you have not been contacted within a week, telephone the company (or the agency) and follow this up – it is not uncommon for interview papers to be 'filed away'. At worst, yours will be put at the top of the pile. You can take this opportunity to re-emphasise how keen you are to get the job. Ask them bluntly, 'What do I need to do to convince you I'm the right person for the job?'

A good follow-up letter may resemble the following example:

Dear Mr Smith

Thank you for your time yesterday. I found our meeting most constructive.

The position of Marketing Manager which you outlined is particularly appealing to me. It offers a great challenge over the next two years, especially as there are obvious opportunities for the proven performer.

I feel that I am particularly well qualified, given my in-depth knowledge of the shoe industry and my proven man-management skills. I am confident I can rise to the challenge and contribute to the success of the department from day one.

I believe our immediate priorities are to:

1. Consolidate our market share by a review of the pricing and discount structures offered to our main customers;
2. Launch a customer care campaign to bring about a speedy resolution of major customer issues.

I would be delighted to discuss this opportunity with you further at your earliest convenience.

Yours sincerely

Summary

If you want the job, you have got to stand out from the crowd and get an edge over the other candidates. A follow-up letter costs next to nothing to produce, and could tip the balance between yourself and other strong candidates. Take the trouble to write. Do it carefully, but above all do it quickly – to arrive no later than 48 hours after the interview.

18. EFFECTIVE SALARY NEGOTIATION

Contents

- When to discuss salary
- How to negotiate the best deal

Overview

Beware of questions about salary.

'How much are you looking for?' This is the killer question to be asked in an interview. If you reply:

- too high – you could eliminate yourself from consideration;
- too low – you could do yourself out of a lot of money, or, even worse, eliminate yourself from consideration.

The golden rule in salary negotiation is:

NEVER DISCUSS SALARY UNTIL YOU HAVE BEEN OFFERED THE JOB.

The reason for this is as follows.

Before an offer is made, the interviewer can be considered to be the buyer and the candidate is the salesman. The buyer obviously wants to buy at the lowest price, and the salesman wants to sell, but not necessarily at any price.

After an offer is made the *interviewer* becomes the salesman (he is trying to attract you by 'selling' the position and the company to you) while the candidate becomes the buyer. The candidate therefore has a much firmer control of the proceedings and is able to negotiate from a position of strength.

Unless you happen to hit the exact level when asked what salary you require, you can do yourself far more damage than good should you give a direct answer to this direct question.

The secret is to stall the interviewer, give a vague or passing response, and wait until the job has been offered.

How to do it

Consider the following responses to the question, 'How much are you looking for?' Look the interviewer straight in the eye and reply:

How to deal with questions about salary.

1. 'In all honesty, I would prefer to discuss salary once we have agreed that I am the person for the job. I know you pay well for good people, so I would rather not let it be an issue at this stage. Is that OK?'
2. 'Oh, somewhere in the twenties. The most important aspects to me are job satisfaction and career opportunities. Is there a defined salary range or is this open for negotiation?'

Try to answer the question with another question, to take you away from a defensive situation back to level terms.

If you are pushed again for a direct answer, you have very little choice but to reply accordingly. This is where doing your homework is essential. You should have found out what the salary range is for the position advertised, and you should pitch your response at the upper end of the range. For example, if the advertised range was 'circa £20k', 'to £20k' or '£15k to £20k', I would reply, 'My current package totals around £17k, and I am looking for an advance upon this figure to attract me out of ABC Limited.'

Remember, you can always negotiate downwards, but it is far harder to negotiate upwards. Think of it as like selling a house – if the buyer is interested, he will not go away if the price is too high in the first instance.

What to do when you are made an offer

Over 90 per cent of people, when made an offer, will either accept it or turn it down in its original form. Far better to do neither and phone up the company and speak directly to the person who made you the offer of say, £20,000, and say something like, 'Hello, Mr Smith. This is John

Once you are offered the job, then you can talk about salary.

Jones. Thank you for your offer for the position of Factory Supervisor. I am in the process of weighing up a number of options and I would like to discuss the salary you have offered. Is this figure cast in stone, or is there some room for negotiation?'

Note that:

1. You may or may not have another offer – the interviewer will never know.
2. You have not declined the offer merely by questioning the salary.
3. You have nothing to lose, and the worst that can happen is that the employer is not able to offer you any more than the original £20,000. The chances are that he will be able to increase his offer, if he wants you badly enough.

Summary

The golden rules of salary negotiation.

Follow the golden rules of salary negotiation and you will win the best possible deals. The rules are:

1. Never discuss salary until after you have been offered the job.
2. Let the employer make the first move when discussing salary.
3. Answer a salary-related question with a question of your own.
4. If pressed, give a salary range, rather than a specific figure.
5. Don't necessarily accept the first offer. The chances are that the employer is deliberately offering you a salary level which gives him some room for negotiation upwards. A well-prepared phone call to discuss the offer can pay huge dividends.
6. Stick up for yourself. Don't sell yourself too cheaply just because you really want the job. If the interviewer is interested in you, he will make sure the money is available.

19. OTHER SELECTION METHODS

Contents

- Informal evenings
- Recruitment fairs
- Group selection days

Overview

An increasingly popular way of recruiting people is to adopt the format of open days, recruitment fairs, and to invite several candidates to attend a group selection day.

There are a number of other ways of recruiting people.

I have co-ordinated many such events, usually because of the need to recruit a number of people in a short time. Handling all the applicants in one go seemed a preferable approach, as opposed to conducting many separate interviews over the course of many weeks.

These events have many benefits over the normal process of selection by interview, including the following:

1. It allows the employer to see the 'real' you.
2. It is quicker.
3. It allows the employer to compare candidates against one another, and thereby select only the best.
4. It gives you a practical opportunity to demonstrate how you work in a team.

Although these events can be good fun, you have to remember that you are still being judged and evaluated. However, you need to adopt a slightly different approach from a normal interview situation in order to succeed. Here are some 'inside' tips.

How to do it

Rules to remember for selection days.

1. Get yourself noticed. At the end of the day the selectors will have to assess all the people they met during the day. Individuals become just a sea of faces, and many good candidates may get overlooked simply because they didn't stand out from the crowd. Wear an eye-catching tie, a particularly bright brooch or another clearly distinguishing article of clothing.
2. Develop rapport with the selectors. Talk about your hobbies, where you come from or something you are involved in at the moment. Ideally, you need to find out what the pet subjects of the selectors are, and talk along these lines if possible.
3. Carry several spare copies of your CV with you and also some business cards. Have some passport-sized photographs to hand. Clip these to your CV as an aide memoire.
4. Ask the selectors how they intend to narrow down the field to a short-list. If appropriate, give them one of your photographs – it will greatly assist them and will also get you noticed.
5. Just as in an interview situation, do your homework carefully before-hand. As a last resort, you may be able to pick up some literature about the company on the day. Read any such information thoroughly and prepare a series of questions for each company you intend to see. Never go in blind or unprepared – you won't stand out.
6. In team exercises, the final solution is normally not as important as the way you work within the team. Make sure you are the one who takes the notes, who volunteers to act as the spokesperson and offers advice freely. You should not go overboard – this could backfire if you come over as aggressive.
7. Enjoy yourself. Such events are meant to be as relaxed and as normal as possible, so smile and have a good time.

Summary

The important thing about recruitment fairs and other such events is that you still need to do your homework in exactly the same way as if you were attending a formal interview.

When you meet the company representative try to develop rapport. Get talking about anything, ideally on his/her favourite topic. Get yourself noticed by:

- Your appearance
- Your personality
- The amount of preparation you have carried out.

These events are intended to give you the opportunity to really shine and to bring out the 'real' you.

Go prepared, be positive, be assertive and stand out from the crowd.

20. 101 WAYS TO LOSE, SEEK AND WIN A JOB

Coping with redundancy

Chapter 2

1. Accept the news in a positive manner (easy to say!). Tell yourself that there is a reason for this happening, even though it may not be apparent at the time.

2. Find out the details about your redundancy package and also how the company will help you to find alternative employment. Arrange an interview with your company's Personnel Officer as a matter of urgency.

3. Tell your family and friends. It may hurt your pride, but news will quickly spread anyway. Don't look for sympathy (you will get plenty), but rather ask them for ideas and names of people to contact and for personal introductions.

4. Get away from it all for 48 hours to get over the initial shock. Release all feelings of pain, bitterness and sadness. You'll cry a lot – the more the better!

5. Dismiss any thoughts of getting your own back on the company or any specific individuals. This will do you no good at all.

Chapter 3

6. Draw up a personal finance plan and identify:
   - your regular outgoings;
   - your total savings;

- any income (including benefits from the DSS).

Work out exactly how long you can survive before you:
- need to dip into personal savings;
- need to borrow money.

7. Contact the manager of your bank/building society/hire purchase company. Enquire about the possibility of deferring payments.

8. Assume responsibility for what has happened. Take full control of every event. Get out of the 'Que sera, sera' attitude (whatever will be, will be), and resolve to get yourself out of this situation as soon as possible.   **Chapter 2**

9. Believe in yourself – you *will* get over this.

10. Remember that it was *your job* and not *you* which became redundant. You are not redundant, but simply temporarily in-between appointments.

Make plans

11. Use this opportunity to sit down and take a very hard look at yourself. Even if this process takes a week to complete, it is time well spent. Be totally convinced that you have answered the following questions.   **Chapter 3**

12. What am I good at? List ten strengths.

13. What experience and skills do I have? List ten attributes regarding your qualifications, experience and major achievements.

14. What do I really want to do? Am I really happy in my current line of work, or have I got a burning desire to do something completely different?

15. What is the price I am prepared to pay?
- Salary?
- Move to another area?
- Work away from home Monday to Friday?
- Obtain further qualifications?

16. Should I consider setting up my own business, either on a full or part-time basis?
- What have I got to offer?
- What about buying a franchise?

- What courses are available?
- What about working as an independent distributor? (This is what I am now doing on a part-time basis!)

17. Commit yourself to a full-time job search campaign. Establish a routine work pattern. For example:
    - Visit the reference library on Monday and Friday mornings.
    - Set up specific times each day for telephone calls; for example, every weekday from 2 pm to 4 pm.
    - Set up appointments with recruitment agencies on Tuesday and Thursday mornings.

18. Avoid the temptation to 'decorate the lounge' or 're-tile the bathroom'. You will, of course, need to mix your job search activities with pleasure, but plan your leisure activities as if you were in normal full-time employment.

19. Don't panic. Look for the best in every situation. Think of the analogy of a car driver whose car had been damaged by someone who drove into the back of it. Looking on the bright side, the immediate response was, 'Oh well, at least I'll get a brand new bumper and rear panels out of this.'

20. Write all your plans down on paper. Talk them through with your immediate family and agree them. Once agreed, commit to them and resolve to see them through to successful completion. Having a firm plan is a major achievement and a big step forward. You need to know what your objectives are, and how you intend to achieve them.

Curriculum vitae

Chapter 4

21. Consider a CV as your personal sales brochure. It needs to be accurate, well-presented and it should be easy to pick out the key points on it at a glance.

22. There is no 'right' length for a CV, but remember that some potential employers may only spend 30 seconds looking at it. I suggest, therefore, that two sides of A4 is the optimum length.

23. Avoid lengthy paragraphs. Instead, use bullet points and a consistent layout, ideally presenting your experience in reverse chronological order (ie, most recent events first).

24. Don't go into too much detail in your CV. Avoid mentioning specific job titles, salary levels or your precise requirements.

25. Remember that the purpose of a CV is to get you an interview, not a job.

26. Your CV must be typed and printed on a high quality laser printer. Avoid photocopies if at all possible – the extra cost of having laser quality prints is a small price to pay, and it can make all the difference in the selection process.

27. Contact a professional CV preparation company. These can be found in the *Yellow Pages* under 'Graphic Artists', or alternatively in the classified ads section of leading Sunday newspapers (for example, the *Sunday Times*). Contact at least three such agencies and compare costs and services provided. The minimum requirement is for DTP (desktop publishing) facilities and laser quality printing.

28. Keep your CV up to date. You never know when you may need it. Review it at least every three months.

29. Within your CV, use action verbs (for example, 'achieved, overcame, succeeded, led, designed, transformed' and identify yourself as a problem-solver and an achiever.

30. Always try to link your role with the goals of the company as a whole. How did you contribute to the success of the company? Were you involved with any cost-cutting scheme?

Build contacts

31. If you have been affected by redundancy, be entirely open with your family, friends, neighbours, professional associates, work colleagues and anyone else who may be able to assist. If they can't help you directly, they may have their own contacts who can. There is nothing to gain by trying to keep the news to yourself, and certainly no shame to be felt. Obviously, you need to be extremely careful who you tell about seeking a new job if you are in full-time employment.

32. Do not overlook your current employers as people to discuss your career plans with. Early warning of unrest may result in salary increases and/or promotion if the company feels you are worth keep-

Chapter 5

ing. It takes courage to do this, but any professional manager should at least give you a sympathetic hearing.

33. Look in the recruitment sections of the main trade magazines and national and local newspapers. Identify the top dozen recruitment agencies in your own field. Contact them, initially by phone, and make an appointment to see them.

Chapter 6

34. Determine how each of the recruitment agencies works. Use only those who can 'add value' to your application by introducing you personally to their major clients. Avoid the CV mailshotters – they can do you more harm than good.

Chapter 5

35. Make a habit of swapping business cards (if you haven't got any of your own, then get some!). When you obtain someone else's business card, write down on the back of it brief details of where you met this person and how he may be able to assist you with any career move, either now or in the future.

36. Keep your own 'scrap book' of interesting or possibly useful job advertisements, even if you are not actively involved in looking for a new job at the time. Try to establish patterns followed by the regular advertisers.

37. Join a professional body. Get your name known, and volunteer for office.

38. Attend conferences and training courses. Go out of your way to meet as many people as possible and remember to take a supply of your business cards to exchange.

39. Take time to find out the names, addresses and key contacts within your main competitors. They may jump at the chance of recruiting you.

40. Look beyond your own specialist area. I responded to several different advertisements in the *Sunday Times* regarding possible new business ventures. However, make sure that you get independent financial advice before making any form of commitment.

Respond to advertised vacancies

Chapter 5

41. Find out in which magazines or newspapers and on which particular days the relevant jobs are advertised. Be sure to get your own copy delivered on a regular basis.

42. Read the job advert well, and respond exactly as requested. For example, if it states, 'Contact Mr Smith for an application form', then do precisely that and contact Mr Smith, preferably by phone.

43. Wherever possible, phone up the advertiser (either the company itself or an agency) and find out exactly what the job entails, and what sort of person is sought. Tailor your application to meet these requirements.

44. Write an introductory letter and tailored management summary with each application. Ideally, these should be typed, but if not then your best handwriting will do. Also, include a copy of your CV and business card, unless specifically told otherwise.

45. Respond within 48 hours of seeing the advertisement.

46. Take great care with each job application. Treat each one as a personal sales brochure.

47. Never pin your hopes on any one application. Advertised vacancies will almost certainly attract a large response, so keep several applications on the go at any one time.

48. If you haven't heard within seven days, telephone the company and find out what the short-listing procedure is. The very worst this can do is to get your name known.

49. Expect success with each application. Anticipate an interview arising from each one.

50. Don't be put off if you don't meet the exact requirements specified in the job advertisement – the ideal candidate rarely exists. You should, however, meet at least 50 per cent of the requirements specified.

Chapter 7

Explore the unadvertised market place

51. Responding to advertised vacancies is easy. It is also easy for hundreds of other applicants to do likewise. Exploring the unadvertised market place, however, is very much down to you. The more active you are, the more successful you will be.

Chapter 8

52. Contact your network of recruitment agencies. Build upon the relationships already developed, and revisit them if necessary.

53. Get in touch with your network of personal contacts. Ask them for names of other people to contact. Ideally, get them to arrange personal introductions, or at the very least to advise them to expect your phone call.

54. Write speculative letters to potential employers. Set yourself a target of, say, three letters per day.

55. Follow up speculative letters with phone calls. If it is clear that you have drawn a blank, then try at least to get referrals into other companies.

56. Accept that you may need to make many phone calls from home. Sure, it's not cheap, but it is a small price to pay in relation to the possible gain.

57. People who say they will call you back invariably won't. You need to be extremely patient and if necessary call them back a second or third time. Persistence is the name of the game, until they grant you an interview.

58. Stick at it. Don't be put off by a few 'failures'. Treat each 'failure' as being one step closer to finding the right opportunity for you.

59. Have a go at telephone interviews. It is nerve-racking at first, but you will get better and better with each such call. Time spent researching the company beforehand is time well spent.

60. Remember, your goal at this stage is merely to get an interview, not to get a job.

Prepare thoroughly for each interview

Chapter 9

61. Get a copy of the job description for each position you apply for. Read it through very carefully and, as in the management summary which you have prepared, identify what skills or experience you have to offer against each of the main criteria.

62. Make sure you complete your homework on the company. The best sources of information are your local reference library and the com-

pany itself – ring them up and ask for any sales literature or for a copy of their latest annual report. The switchboard receptionist will inform you who you need to speak to.

63. Remember that it is not necessarily the person who is the most qualified who succeeds at interview – it is always the one who is most prepared. Do your homework well – show them just how keen and well-prepared you are.

64. Make sure you know exactly where the interview is to be held. Ask for a local road map, and also for instructions on where to park.

Chapter 10

65. Give yourself plenty of time, and ideally plan to arrive about an hour before the interview is due to start. Arrange to stay overnight locally if you have a long journey and an early appointment.

66. Use the hour before the interview to go over your notes and 'psych' yourself up for the interview. Get into a positive frame of mind – get the adrenalin flowing.

67. Conduct the whole interview process in your mind before the interview itself takes place – right from the initial handshake through to leaving the building. Expect to do well. Visualise success.

68. Contain any nerves you may have. You haven't got the job before the interview, so you've got absolutely nothing to lose.

69. Visit the loo – make sure your appearance is immaculate. Look at yourself in the mirror and build yourself up by saying 'I look terrific', 'I perform brilliantly in the interview', and 'I succeed'.

Interview techniques

70. Offer a firm handshake, and make a dynamic first impression: 'Hello Mr Smith, I'm David Jones, and I'm pleased to meet you.'

Chapter 11

71. Develop rapport as quickly as you can with the interviewer. Casual conversation on the way to the interview room is a good start (talk about the weather, your journey, the building you are in etc).

72. Stand up until you are invited to sit down. Keep your jacket on and don't smoke under any circumstances.

73. Have a small notepad and pen handy. If you wish, place them on the

91

table in front of you, and don't be afraid to refer to your notes when it comes to your opportunity to ask questions.

Chapter 12

74. Sit upright. Look the interviewer straight in the eye, but don't stare. Don't cross your arms or legs (defensive barriers), and beware of any hand to face motions (these could be interpreted as a lie).

Chapter 13

75. Concentrate hard on what is being said. Tell yourself that this is the most interesting conversation you have ever had.

76. Don't interrupt the interviewer, but, where appropriate, summarise what is being said and ask any relevant questions at opportune moments.

77. Try to keep the conversation going. Avoid a question and answer session, and back up your answers with specific examples wherever possible.

78. If asked a particularly awkward question, give yourself time to think by stalling the interviewer. You can achieve this by asking for clarification of particular points. It is far better to do this than to launch into a monologue of unrelated material – there is nothing more annoying to an interviewer than having to listen to waffle. Pausing before answering is considered to be classy.

79. Remain confident and optimistic, no matter how badly you may think you are doing. Remember that if it is hard for you, it will also be hard for the other candidates.

Chapter 14

80. Make sure you have prepared answers to the standard questions you expect to be asked. Your answers should come over as spontaneous replies, but you should have established the framework for your responses well in advance.

Closing the interview

Chapter 18

81. Avoid discussing salary levels until after you have been offered the job. Before this time, you are in a no-win situation, and an incorrect answer (either too high or too low) can completely undermine your application. If pressed, then quote a salary range at the top end of that being offered.

82. Make sure you have a list of questions to ask at the end of the interview. Refer to your notes if you wish.

Chapter 15

83. As a final closing line, summarise the main points of the interview and thank the interviewer for his time. Anticipating success, ask when you will be speaking again.

Chapter 16

84. Remember that the selection process is still continuing after the interview has finished. If you are being escorted to the main entrance, it is very important to sound keen, confident and optimistic. Ask the interviewer how many people they are interviewing and what the general response has been like. Above all, if you do have any doubts or concerns about your ability to do the job or to fit into the organisation, keep these concerns to yourself at this stage.

85. As soon as you leave the building, find somewhere quiet where you can write down the main points of the meeting. For example:

Chapter 17

- What were your strengths?
- Where did you do badly?
- How could you contribute?
- What is the next step (who is going to contact whom)?

86. Write a short summary letter, addressed to the senior member of the interview panel. Keep this letter very brief, and aim for it to be received within 48 hours of the interview.

87. If an agency was involved, phone them to let them know how the interview went. Although they will be on your side (they will undoubtedly be earning commission if you get the job), continue to be very positive and confident that you will do well in the position. This information will certainly be relayed back to the interview panel.

88. If you have not been contacted within a week, phone the company or agency and find out what is happening.

89. At recruitment fairs or group selection days, your main aim is to make an impact, that is, to stand out from the crowd. Treat each such event as if it were a formal interview, so do your homework beforehand. Also, remember to carry business cards, copies of your CV and passport-sized photographs of yourself.

Chapter 19

90. Remember that interviewers want you to do well – they want to find the right person for the job. The most important criteria are:
    - Your ability to do the job
    - How well you will fit in
    - Keenness.

The new job

Chapter 18

91. The right time to discuss salary is after you have been offered the job. Now you can negotiate from a position of strength.

92. How you negotiate depends upon individual circumstances. My advice is not to turn down a job offer if the only problem is salary. Phone up the company and tell them the salary level you had in mind. If they are unable to improve on the offer immediately, I recommend that you tell the company that you will be keeping the offer on hold for a short while in order to allow you to weigh it up with others which you anticipate you will be getting (whether or not this is true).

93. Avoid falling into the trap of accepting the first job which is offered to you if you are temporarily unemployed. If you've been offered one job, the chances are that others will follow. If you are uncertain, ask for more time to consider.

94. Never accept an offer until it is unconditional (that is, it doesn't depend on references or a medical), and make certain you have all the relevant details in writing. A verbal offer is not enough.

95. Before accepting an offer, talk the situation over with your current employers. They may be prepared at least to match the salary offered – you have nothing to lose by talking it over.

96. Maintain good contact with your former employers – you may need to use a former work colleague as a referee for any future career moves.

97. If your application has been unsuccessful, phone the company up and find out what the main reasons were. Incorporate any such feedback into future applications.

98. If you have been unsuccessful, ask if they know of any other compa-

nies who may have vacancies at the present time. If possible, establish the name of the relevant person to contact.

99. If you do find that you have not had much success with job applications, take the trouble to find out why, and use each unsuccessful application as part of a learning exercise. If necessary, have someone take a fundamental review of your applications – it may well be that there is a common reason which you have not detected yourself.

100. Expect the unexpected. You will not succeed at some interviews where you felt you did particularly well, and you will be pleasantly surprised at others which you felt went badly. Don't let disappointments get you down – you didn't want that particular job anyway!

101. If at first you don't succeed, try, try again. It is a tough world out there, but you can be sure of one thing – if you try hard enough, you *will* be rewarded in the end.

EPILOGUE

The information contained in this book details exactly what I did from the time my former position became redundant through to when I started a new job nine weeks later.

In hindsight, redundancy was probably the best thing that could have happened to me at that particular time. I had been unhappy at work for many months and my family had not really settled into the area where we lived. I had been intending to relocate back to the South West of England for some time, but I had not been planning on the particular events which took place.

Since this time, however, life as a whole has improved considerably. My wife and I enjoy our new Christian-based lifestyle, and we have since been blessed by the safe arrival of our fourth child.

While seeking a new job, I also looked at starting my own business. If you have never run your own business before, it is certainly worth considering. Getting started is not as difficult as you might imagine, but you do have to be prepared for both the ups and the downs.

Whatever your career aspirations, I wish you every success, and I hope that this book helps you on your way.

RECOMMENDED READING

Body Language, Allan Pease, Sheldon Press
Great Answers to Tough Interview Questions: How to Get the Job You Want, Martin Yate, Kogan Page
The Headhunting Business, Stephanie Jones, Macmillan. Lists the leading executive search firms in London.
The Right Way to Apply for a Job, Arthur Wilcox, Paperfronts
The Right Way to Write Your Own CV, John Clarke, Paperfronts

Further reading from Kogan Page

Career Counselling for Executives, Godfrey Golzen
Changing Your Job After 35, *The Daily Telegraph Guide* (7th edition), Godfrey Golzen and Philip Plumbley
Going Freelance (4th edition), Godfrey Golzen
How to Master Selection Tests, Mike Bryon and Sanjay Modha
The Job Assault Course, MC Lindsay Stewart (a book for the military)
Job Sharing: A Practical Guide, Pam Walton
The Mid-Career Action Guide: A Practical Guide to Mid-Career Change (2nd edition), Derek Kemp and Fred Kemp
Offbeat Careers: 60 Ways to Avoid Becoming an Accountant, (2nd edition), Vivien Donald
Portable Careers: How to Survive Your Partner's Relocation, Linda R Greenbury
Putting Redundancy Behind You, Sheila Cane and Peter Lowman
Working Abroad: The Daily Telegraph Guide to Working and Living Overseas (15th edition), Godfrey Golzen
Your Employment Rights, Michael Malone

A SELECTION OF CAREER ADVISERS

Head office addresses:

Career Analysts
Career House
90 Gloucester Place
London WIH 4BL
071–935 5452

CLP Concept
Mariner House
Prince Street
Bristol BS1 4HU
0272 308805

Connaught Mainland
32 Savile Row
London W1X 1AG
071–734 3879

InterExec
Landseer House
19 Charing Cross Road
London WC2H 0ES
071–930 5041

New Careers
6 John Street
London WC1N 2ES
071–242 9921

Pathfinder Partnership
Omega House
6 Buckingham Place
Bellfield Road
High Wycombe
Bucks HP13 5HW
0494 452791

CW00371478

BUENOS AIRES

Directed and Designed by Hans Höfer
Edited and Produced by Kathleen Wheaton

APA PUBLICATIONS

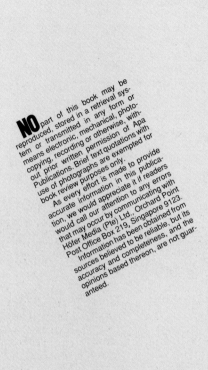
BUENOS AIRES

First Edition (Reprint)
© **1990 APA PUBLICATIONS (HK) LTD**
All Rights Reserved
Printed in Singapore by Höfer Press Pte. Ltd

ABOUT THIS BOOK

When APA Publications of Singapore launched its series of *CityGuides*, Buenos Aires was a natural early selection for the kind of deep, searching examination characteristic of all the *Insight Guides*.

Apa Founder **Hans Höfer** turned his attention to South America after directing Insight teams outward from Southeast Asia where his first book, published in 1970, won high honors. That edition, *Insight Guide: Bali*, set the standard followed in every succeeding volume in the vast library of travel literature published by Apa. Each of these books includes fine photography, great writing and clear, frank journalism. They reflect the training that Höfer, a native of West Germany, received in the Bauhaus tradition for book design, typography and photography. The Apa standards are maintained by assigning a single project editor to each book to coordinate the work of the best available local writers and photographers.

The *CityGuides* were conceived as a natural extension of the *Insight Guides* series. Most of the great cities of the globe are like small countries, each one with its particular history, habits, and ways of looking at the world. The true spirit of a city tends to be somewhat hidden: on its back streets, and in what might be called its collective personality. The focus of the *CityGuides* is on the physical setting and the cast of characters who have made the city unique.

The task of turning these ideas into printed pages fell to **Kathleen Wheaton**. A native Californian, project editor Wheaton studied Spanish at Sanford University and spent two years after college in Spain, where she wrote for a local paper and taught English. Wheaton was project editor for *Insight Guide: Spain*, an assignment that sparked her interest in the Spanish influence on the New World.

One of the most prolific contributors to the book was **Patricia Pittman**. Born in Washington, D.C., Pittman received a political science degree from Yale University in 1980. In 1982 she went to Argentina with a Ford Foundation-funded human rights project and has worked from her home in suburban Buenos Aires as a free-lancer and consultant to Americas Watch and the Ford Foundation.

Most of the history section was written by Australian journalist **Anthony Perrottet**. Perrottet studied history at Sydney University before setting out on an 18-month trek across South America. Enchanted by stories from relatives who had worked as wool classers in Patagonia, Perrottet traveled from Colombia to Tierra del Fuego, writing news and travel features for the *Australian Sunday Times*, the *Sydney Morning Herald*, the *Wellington Evening Post*, the *South China Morning Post* and the *London Daily News*.

Former Buenos Aires Herald editor **Dan Newland** has a first-hand perspective on the city's turbulent past, having lived in Argentina since 1973. Newland has contributed to the *London Daily Express*, the *London Daily Telegraph*, *Newsweek* and *Business Week*.

Uruguayan journalist **María Esther Gilio** is well-known throughout the Spanish-speaking world for her incisive interviews, many of which are anthologized in such books as *Protagonistas Sobrevivientes* and *Emergentes*. In the early 1970s, her book on Uruguayan urban guerillas, *La Guerilla Tupamara*, won Latin America's most prestigious literary prize, the Casa de las Americas Award. Her writing appears in the Argentine daily, *Clarín*, and countless other publications throughout Latin America.

National Public Radio correspondent **David Welna** went to Argentina in 1981, shortly before the Malvinas/Falklands War. Born in Waseca, Minnesota, he received a degree in Latin American studies from Carleton College and has traveled extensively in Latin America, spending a year in Brazil on a Watson Fellowship. At that time, Welna became intrigued by Argentina and subsequently reported on the war from Buenos Aires.

Michigan-born journalist **Don Boroughs** has had a particular interest in Argentina since he

Wheaton   *Pittman*   *Perrottet*   *Newland*   *Gilio*

played the role of Che Guevara in the musical *Evita*. After receiving a degree in photography from Rochester Institute of Technology and a degree in magazine journalism from Syracuse University, he traveled through 19 of Argentina's 24 provinces. Boroughs made his home in the barrio of Palermo, where he wrote for the U.N. publication *Mazingira* and *The Progressive*. Boroughs contributed several articles and more than 40 photographs to this book.

Joseph Hooper spent a month in chic Barrio Norte, visiting the cafés, museums, and the cemetery while preparing a chapter on that neighborhood. Born in Baltimore and educated at Sanford University, Hooper was Arts and Entertainment Editor for the *Palo Alto Weekly*. He has traveled extensively in South America and has written travel pieces and other articles for *San Francisco Magazine*, *Esquire*, *Vanity Fair*, and *UltraSport*. Hooper lives in Manhattan, where he writes features for the weekly magazine, *Seven Days*.

Free-lancer **Louise Byrne** spent two and a half years traveling through Australia and Asia, and has contributed to such travel publications as *Berlitz Travel Guides* and *Half the Earth*, a feminist travel guide.

Five Buenos Aires-based writers brought their particular expertise for special features to this book. *Buenos Aires Herald* sports-writer Eric Weil was born in England and has been a journalist in Argentina since 1951.

Reuters correspondent **Rex Gowar** was born in Argentina to British parents and studied literature at Essex University in England. He returned to Argentina in 1978, where he has written on sports for a number of publications.

Judith Evans is a correspondent for the *Wall Street Journal*, and contributes pieces to *The Independent* and the *New York Times*. She also lectures on the tango and architecture.

Helga Thomson applied considerable knowledge to the chapter on Argentine painting and printmaking. Of German-Argentine descent, Thomson has studied printmaking in Buenos Aires, Paris and Washington D.C. She has won several awards for her work, some of which is included in public and private collections in the U.S., Argentina and Europe.

No guidebook to Buenos Aires would be complete without the epicurean touch of food writer **Dereck Foster**. Argentine-born Foster is food and wine editor for the *Buenos Aires Herald* and owner-editor of the gastronomic magazine *Aromas y Sabores*.

Former *Buenos Aires Herald* news desk editor **Virginia Newland** brought her life-long familiarity with the city to the Travel Tips. She is a native of the Floresta barrio of Buenos Aires.

The original photography for *Insight Guide: Buenos Aires* is the result of the tireless work of two outstanding Argentine photographers. **Fiora Bemporad** is best known for her penetrating portraits of famous Argentines from Borges to Alfonsín. A porteña with Italian roots, Bemporad's photography has won numerous prizes and has been extensively exhibited in Argentina and Italy.

Buenos Aires-based photographer **Eduardo Gil's** inimitable vision can be seen on the cover and throughout the book. Gil worked as a commercial airline pilot and studied meteorology and sociology before dedicating himself fulltime to photography. His work has appeared in *Clarín* and *Newsweek*, among other publications.

Other contributing photographers include **Miguel Doura**, **Jorge Schulte** and **Alex Ocampo**.

Grateful thanks to cartographer **Isabel Suárez de Rosa**, who applied her fine attention to detail and endless patience with "Tramites" to the mapmaking process.

Special thanks must also go to *Ediciones de la Flor* editor **Daniel Divinsky** for his kind advice and encouragement, and to **Bernardino Rivadavia**, whose unique perspective on the city gave the editor many new insights. **Jose María Peña** of the Museum of Buenos Aires and historian **Felix Luna** also freely contributed some of their vast knowledge of the city's history.

—Apa Publications

Welna

Boroughs

Hooper

Byrne

Weil

HISTORY AND HERITAGE

PLACES AND FEATURES

TRAVEL TIPS

THE PARIS OF SOUTH AMERICA

The air of Buenos Aires—this is the air that captivated the Spaniards, and every day I'm more convinced that they baptized her, "The City of Good Airs," because they were seduced by her perfume and her illusion.

—Ramon Gomez de la Serna

By the time you enter Buenos Aires on Avenida Nueve de Julio, you will have heard that you are riding along the widest street in the world, headed straight towards the world's widest river, the Rio de la Plata. A huge obelisk looms in the middle of the avenue, and on either side are heavy-limbed subtropical trees and Parisian-style office buildings, some with balconies where employees are looking out at the traffic. The damp air smells of diesel, grilled meat and caramelized sugar.

By this time you will also have heard, often, that Buenos Aires resembles a European capital. At first glance, the comparisons are evident: there are tidy plazas with Rodin statues in them, sidewalk cafés, *pret-a-porter* windows where beautiful women gaze simultaneously at the clothes and their own reflections. You are in the heart of South America, but you can drink tap water and eat raw salads, and buy almost any new magazine or exquisite cosmetic. Very likely, you will have arrived from a great distance, and through a haze of weariness and perhaps the miracle of a different season you left behind, you have a Victorian traveler's anticipation of pleasure and grace.

Buenos Aires is an old-fashioned city; her charms and quirks refer mostly to the 19th century. Here, you will want to stroll along boulevards, dawdle over several courses at lunch, poke into bookstores, have tea and cakes at five, go to the opera, spend Sunday at the races or walk in the graveyard.

Preceding pages: Belgian cobblestones; doorway; old schooner; Colon Opera House; guards; waiters and stuffed cows; helicopter's eye view. Left, reflection of clock tower. Right, mask vendor posing with his wares.

Buenos Aires or *la gran aldea* (the big village), is a city with a population of four million where the telephone and the post office are such doubtful mechanisms that business is conducted and bills are paid in person; where an unknown shopkeeper will say, as you fumble for the right number of *centavos*, "Bring it tomorrow;" where part of the ritual of shopping involves having your purchase painstakingly wrapped in

colored paper, even if it's only toothpaste.

Everyone stands on ceremony. Say *"perdon"* to a fiercely-dressed punk and he will politely step aside. Ask a passer-by for directions and he will not only answer you at length but probably give you his name card.

European dreaming: Throughout her convulsive and sometimes bloody history, Buenos Aires has kept her eyes fixed lovingly on Europe. The sweeping Avenida de Mayo is a tribute to Madrid's Gran Via; the Colón Opera House faithfully emulates La Scala; swanky Barrio Norte is a shrine to the Right Bank. At the turn of the century, rich Argentines went to Europe to school and to shop. It wasn't unheard-of for these families to take a cow along with them—so the children would not have to drink strange milk—and they brought back clothing, furniture, and art.

The opulent municipality meanwhile imported statues for public intersections, cobblestones (there are very few stones in the pampas), and occasionally whole buildings, such as the hallucinatory waterworks (Obras Sanitarias, 1950 Cordoba) which was shipped over tile by tile from England and France.

This reverence for the Old World reveals itself in small ways as well as in grand (the people of the port), and they love the city for reasons which could strike visitors as peculiar. The *porteño* who gives you a tour of his favorite neighborhood is apt to point out an English-style train station, with its scalloped roof and wrought-iron railing, a Spanish cupola, an Italian balustrade covered with moss. "Now, stand here and look up this street, through the sycamores. Don't you feel as though you're in the South of France?"

Obligingly, you look, stand, and imagine as instructed. Different cities and moods fade in and out cinematiically. Gradually, a common thread begins to emerge: every-

gestures. There are scores of humble cantinas named after villages of Galicia or Calabria, where old men in berets play card games they learned a long time ago. "I'm not really Argentine, I'm Spanish (or Italian, or Polish or Irish)," someone might say. "I still have my passport. I only came here 30 years ago, to work."

"Are you going back, then?"

"Ah, no, why would I do that?"

People in Buenos Aires might keep citizenships or bank accounts in other places, but unless there is an urgent political or economic reason, they don't often move back home. They call themselves *porteños* thing looks as though a local builder had been handed a drawing and told, "Please, recreate this." Buenos Aires doesn't look like Europe; it looks like pictures of Europe—like a Spain or Italy a homesick immigrant might see in a dream.

Homesickness and history: Why are *porteños* so homesick? It's a question they like to consider. In the late 19th century, when most of the immigrants came, Buenos Aires appeared to hold out the same kinds of golden promises as New York, as well as a graceful, Latin way of life. In the 20th century, dictatorships and economic woes caused many of those promises to fail; add to that, some say, the nostalgic Southern European temperament, and you get a city in a permanent state of longing. In the 1930s one Spanish immigrant wrote, "Most disconcerting of all...is that one cannot swear to one's beloved to look at the same star during the nights of separation. Even the moon is useless, because the moon she sees has not arrived here yet."

During the Second World War, Spanish journalist Ramón Gómez described Buenos Aires as a balcony on the world: "Sitting on divans in tranquil houses...we can see when the news is false, when history is mistaken, when the great man dies." *Porteños* might

which became suddenly magically wealthy—than to Barcelona or Milan. For all their formality, *porteños* share with their North American cousins a certain expansiveness, a willingness to confess their salaries and emotional lives to a stranger on a bus. Looking at some of the oversized villas sprinkled here and there in Barrio Norte, you're reminded not so much of an Italian noble as of the self-made mogul in *Citizen Kane*. As in San Francisco, in Buenos Aires the golden age was so recent that history has an intimate feeling. Museums seem more like dusty attics, and are full of family treasures—spurs, pistols, letters—whose signifi-

boast that the great dangers of the nuclear age don't touch them, but they are intensely eager for news from abroad. Morning newscasters often hold up instant facsimiles of the *New York Times* and *Le Monde* to the television cameras.

This air of remoteness, however sophisticated, gives Buenos Aires an identity that is more American than European. Buenos Aires is also closer in spirit to San Francisco—another muddy Spanish port town

cance is obscure to outsiders. In the Fernandez Blanco Museum, which houses colonial silver, you can overhear a well-dressed woman murmur, "Look, isn't that just like the *mate* we have at home?"

In the National Historical Museum, a gaily-painted colonial hacienda on the edge of Lezama Park, visitors wander through rooms full of portraits of handsome military men. As you exit, you will have learned that most of the streets of Buenos Aires were named after soldiers, but the historical narrative remains mysterious.

This is less the fault of museum directors than it is the result of the *porteño* attitude

Left, polo game at Palermo field. Above, retired gentlemen relax on a park bench.

towards the past, which tends to be a personal, inviolate set of beliefs. Borges describes this near-religious approach in his poem, *The Mythological Founding of Buenos Aires:* "To me it is a fairy tale that Buenos Aires was founded. It seems as eternal as water and air."

In Buenos Aires, history and politics are synonyms. A conversation about a president in office a century ago will be no less emotionally charged than a discussion of Peronism or the recent military government. Not that you shouldn't ask questions; simply be prepared for a passionate reply. In general, *porteños* want very much to tell

Sunday caller, and with difficulty restrain their children from laughing and swinging on the quaint wrought-iron gates. The presence of populist Evita does not sit well with many aristocrats whose ancestors lie nearby, but there is usually an admirer or two standing beside the brass plaque bearing her name, and a bouquet of carnations. If the porter at the cemetery entrance happens not to approve of Peronist politics, he will merely say to enquirers, like a haughty butler, that she is not here, and he doesn't know where she is.

In the park outside, teenaged boys take clusters of purebred dogs for walks, and little

their side, like feuding family members trying to engage the sympathies of a houseguest.

Sightseeing: The figure who still arouses the most fervent controversy is Eva Perón. In Argentina, she is worshipped as a saint and reviled as a prostitute. Abroad, she is probably the Argentine who is best known to the world; tourist board officials wryly concede that her grave in Recoleta Cemetery is the monument visitors to the city most often ask to see.

On Sundays, the cemetery is a promenade for well-born mourners, who go in and out of the baroque pantheons with flowers, like any

girls in impractical gauzy dresses climb on the roots of a giant rubber tree. The setting is slightly macabre, attractive and sensual.

All around the cemetery are the city's most elegant shops and cafés. As an antidote to an afternoon of boutiques and cream pastries you could spend the evening in a raucous Italian cantina in the *barrio* of La Boca, where diners get up between family-style courses and dance around the tables.

An alternative activity, quite popular with *porteños*, is attending an experimental theater production in the bohemian quarter of San Telmo, where at some point during the play the performers are certain to defy their decorous upbringings by undressing.

No matter where you go, the sense of being part of a scenario is always present. The city thrives on spectacles, whether it's an impromptu tango show on a sunny back street, a gala opera opening at the Colón, or a political march with drums and songs and flapping banners. Whatever the occasion, the spectators are also actors in the drama; at the polo matches they are glamorous, slender and nervous as the horses on the field; at soccer games and political rallies they are young and furious with loyalty; at the racetrack they are elderly and dandified, full of wild hope and melancholy.

After you have been in the city for a while—after you have eaten leisurely suppers, sat in jazz clubs and walked in parks, bought Italian shoes or an antique box, seen *La Bohéme* and an old Bergman film, you might find you crave horizons.

You set out for an *estancia* in the countryside or the beach at Mar del Plata, or Punta del Este, or even the sweeping plains of Patagonia. When you come back, either by river ferry or across the pampas, there is nothing to obstruct your line of vision, and you can see Buenos Aires from a fairly long way off.

Probably no other city is so welcoming

For *porteños,* half the enjoyment of any outing is the opportunity to join a crowd, to observe and to be observed. Even a meal in a restaurant is a chance for people to feast their eyes on one another. In the words of contemporary novelist Luisa Valenzuela, "when you walk in, everyone turns around to look, not at who you are but what you are wearing." For a curious visitor, this love of show is greatly statisfying: so much of Buenos Aires willingly meets the eye.

Opposite left, political rally is fortified by hamburgers, and right, a pretty *porteña*. Above, classical musicians at a concert-demonstration.

late at night. The restaurants are jammed at one in the morning, there are street musicians playing to crowds along Calle Florida, and whole families are eating ice cream beside illuminated fountains. At such times, it seems impossible that *porteños* almost universally claim to be melancholic. With its sweet climate, stage-set prettiness and dedication to refined pleasures, Buenos Aires might be a kind of urban paradise, and *porteños* the lucky characters of fairy tales. But there are those long, lonely vistas outside. The borders of the city are the edges of their stage, and all around are endless water and endless pampas.

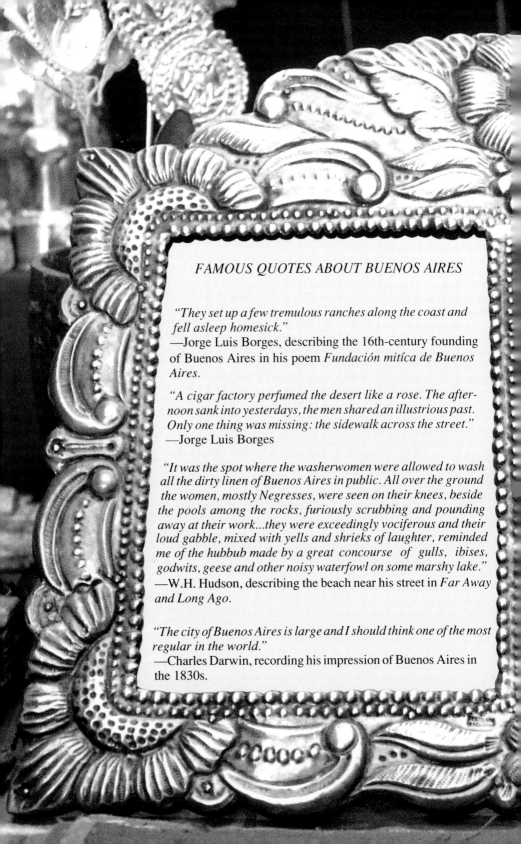

FAMOUS QUOTES ABOUT BUENOS AIRES

"They set up a few tremulous ranches along the coast and fell asleep homesick."
—Jorge Luis Borges, describing the 16th-century founding of Buenos Aires in his poem *Fundación mitíca de Buenos Aires.*

"A cigar factory perfumed the desert like a rose. The afternoon sank into yesterdays, the men shared an illustrious past. Only one thing was missing: the sidewalk across the street."
—Jorge Luis Borges

"It was the spot where the washerwomen were allowed to wash all the dirty linen of Buenos Aires in public. All over the ground the women, mostly Negresses, were seen on their knees, beside the pools among the rocks, furiously scrubbing and pounding away at their work...they were exceedingly vociferous and their loud gabble, mixed with yells and shrieks of laughter, reminded me of the hubbub made by a great concourse of gulls, ibises, godwits, geese and other noisy waterfowl on some marshy lake."
—W.H. Hudson, describing the beach near his street in *Far Away and Long Ago.*

"The city of Buenos Aires is large and I should think one of the most regular in the world."
—Charles Darwin, recording his impression of Buenos Aires in the 1830s.

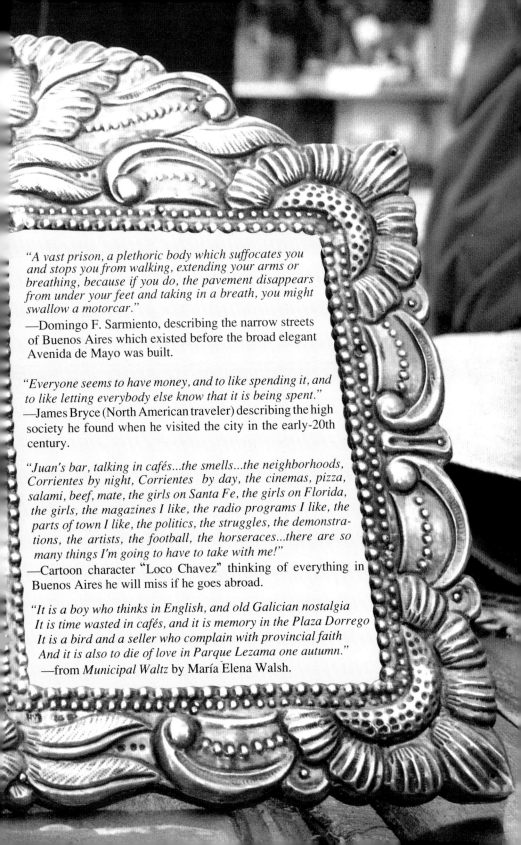

"*A vast prison, a plethoric body which suffocates you and stops you from walking, extending your arms or breathing, because if you do, the pavement disappears from under your feet and taking in a breath, you might swallow a motorcar.*"
—Domingo F. Sarmiento, describing the narrow streets of Buenos Aires which existed before the broad elegant Avenida de Mayo was built.

"*Everyone seems to have money, and to like spending it, and to like letting everybody else know that it is being spent.*"
—James Bryce (North American traveler) describing the high society he found when he visited the city in the early-20th century.

"*Juan's bar, talking in cafés...the smells...the neighborhoods, Corrientes by night, Corrientes by day, the cinemas, pizza, salami, beef, mate, the girls on Santa Fe, the girls on Florida, the girls, the magazines I like, the radio programs I like, the parts of town I like, the politics, the struggles, the demonstrations, the artists, the football, the horseraces...there are so many things I'm going to have to take with me!*"
—Cartoon character "Loco Chavez" thinking of everything in Buenos Aires he will miss if he goes abroad.

"*It is a boy who thinks in English, and old Galician nostalgia*
It is time wasted in cafés, and it is memory in the Plaza Dorrego
It is a bird and a seller who complain with provincial faith
And it is also to die of love in Parque Lezama one autumn."
—from *Municipal Waltz* by María Elena Walsh.

EARLY HISTORY: PRECOLUMBIAN
TO THE VICEROYS

Few of the world's great cities have had so inauspicious a start as Buenos Aires.

A series of accidents, mistakes and defeats followed one another as the Spanish explored and tried to settle the Rio de la Plata region. Wild dreams of gold and silver in the early years contrasted sadly with the reality of Buenos Aires as a lonely outpost stagnating at the fringe of the Empire.

The ill-fated explorers: To Juan Diaz de Solis, the first European to lay eyes on the Rio de la Plata, the muddy estuary was a certain passage to the riches of the East and the fabled kingdoms of Orphir and Tarsis. A Portuguese explorer working for the Spanish crown, the enthusiastic de Solis made a landing on the east bank in 1516 but unfortunately only took six men with him. He quickly encountered a band of Querandí Indians, one of the many wild nomadic tribes that had roamed the region's plains for centuries. De Solis and his hapless crewmen were set upon, killed, and—if the chronicler is to be believed—devoured while the rest of the crew watched helplessly from the boats.

Ten years later, the more cautious but no less imaginative explorer Sebastian Cabot made his way upstream. It was Cabot who optimistically gave the name "river of silver" to the muddy waters after he reached modern-day Paraguay and secured some metal trinkets from the Guaraní Indians.

Convinced that he was on the track of "the Kingdom of the White Caesars," Cabot hurried back to Spain. But to secure the discovery, he left guards in a roughly pallisaded fort called Sancti Spiritus. The region's first permanent settlement was promptly attacked by Indians, its buildings burned and its inhabitants slaughtered.

A false start at Buenos Aires: Cabot's few trinkets easily convinced the Spanish king that vast wealth must be hoarded somewhere near the Rio de la Plata. He commissioned the aristocrat don Pedro de Mendoza to find it, sending him off with what would be the largest expedition to ever leave for the New World: 1,600 soldiers, three times more than Cortez needed to conquer Mexico, set sail in fourteen ships.

In 1536 de Mendoza arrived in South America to make the first attempt at settling Buenos Aires. In a solemn ceremony at what is today the *barrio* of La Boca, he gave it the grandiose title *Puerto Nuestro Señora Santa Maria de Buen Aire*—a reference not to pure antipodeal airs but a patron saint currently fashionable with European navigators.

But while conquistadors and missionaries were busily pillaging great and opulent Indian empires in Peru, Mexico and Central America, de Mendoza's expedition found not a piece of gold. The Indians of the pampas were elusive and hostile. Forcing them to find food for the settlement quickly provoked war. Within eighteen months, starvation, disease and Indian raids had already killed two thirds of the population.

A Bavarian foot soldier, Ulrich Schmidl, who gave the first written account of Buenose Aires, observed:

"The situation was so terrible...that it wasn't enough to just eat rats or mice, reptiles or insects. We had to eat our shoes and leather and everything else."

Schmidl records that three Spaniards stole a horse and later admitted under torture that they had eaten it. The robbers were hung in the main square. The next morning, it was found that other *porteños* had hacked the flesh from the robbers' thighs and taken them home to devour.

Not long after, Indians attacked the settlement with flaming arrows, forcing de Mendoza to take refuge on board the moored ships. Admitting that his mission had been a spectacular failure, de Mendoza moved the entire outpost to Asunción, where there were plentiful vegetables, wild game and more cooperative Guaraní women.

Unfortunately, de Mendoza contracted

Cartoonist Oski satirizes conflicts between Spanish explorers and Indians at the city's founding.

syphillis and died on his way back to Spain, Meanwhile his second-in-command had marched off into the Paraguayan Chaco in search of treasure, but ill-fate probably befell him too, for he was never to be heard from again.

Juan de Garay's second attempt: It was not until 40 years later that settlers tried again with Buenos Aires. This time the conquistador Juan de Garay moved down from Asunción with 66 men and an unknown number of women. Known more for his pragmatism than his intellect, de Garay succeeded where de Mendoza had failed: at what is today the Plaza de Mayo, he chose

Bolivar and Hipolito Yrigoyen was traded for a horse and a guitar.

Life was certainly not easy at the new settlement and many gave up and returned to Asunción. The missionaries constantly complained that there was no way to stop animals wandering into their makeshift chapel, while the rest of the settlers were more concerned by the occasional Indian raid. De Garay lost his reputation for pragmatism when he took a summer siesta by the river bank and was surprised by Indians and killed.

The backwater of the empire: For its first 100 years, Buenos Aires was little more than

the first *cabildo* or town council, and planted a "tree of justice". Then, de Garay proceeded to draw up a classic Spanish grid plan for Buenos Aires on a piece of cow hide.

With food supplies coming from Asunción, the settlers left the Indians alone and went ahead with the business of building a town. Everyone received a plot of land each, and were given rights to capture the horses which de Mendoza had left behind to grow wild and breed on the pampas. The only single woman, a widow named Ana Diaz, received the entire area now at the intersection of Florida and Avenida Corrientes, while the block now on the corner of

a collection of shacks lost in a lonely swamp. It remained on the outskirts of the Spanish Empire in the New World, which had as its center Lima and the mines of Upper Peru. For the Spaniards, the region had little to offer: all the quests for silver came to nothing and the native Querandí could not be press-ganged into agricultural pursuits; they continued roaming and hunting in the pampas and to harass intruding Europeans.

Buenos Aires was far less important than other inland towns such as Cordoba and Tucuman. It was the last link in a chain of settlements which stretched to Peru, supplying the mines with food, mules and clothes.

The great problem that bedeviled Buenos Aires for the first 200 years of its existence was the prohibition of free trade into or out of its port. The Spanish Crown insisted that it did not have the seapower to protect merchants crossing the Atlantic from enemies and pirates.

This meant that most goods to Buenos Aires from Europe first went via the Caribbean to Panama, overland to the Pacific, by boat to Lima, then transported by ox-cart the thousands of miles to the Rio de la Plata.

Porteños complained that woollen clothes cost ten times more in Buenos Aires than in Spain thanks to this trading arrangement. A horse-shoe cost more than a horse. There were acute shortages of every manufactured good, from soap and cooking oil to nails and weaponry.

The response to this illogical situation was to turn to smuggling with the Portuguese in order to survive. Even so, Buenos Aires in the 17th century enjoyed only a tenuous existence. At its 100th anniversary in 1680, the town had only 5,000 inhabitants and had just built its first brick house.

One early traveler to Buenos Aires reported that it was a fairly wretched place, with most adobe huts and a population of "poor devils without a shirt to their backs and their toes sticking through their shoes." Anybody who could afford European clothes only wore them on special occasions to avoid wearing them out.

Colonial society was dominated by those born in Spain and the white *criollos*, or Spaniards born in the New World. In the country towns these people were rigidly separated from *mestizos* or people of mixed blood who were the artisans and laborers. Buenos Aires was somewhat more egalitarian, since Garay had started the settlement with nearly all *mestizos* and very few Spanish women made the arduous journey to the Rio de la Plata. Spanish artisans found themselves mixing easily with *mestizo* workers.

The Church continued to play an important role in providing education and organizing the religious fiestas that would bring *porteños* together. The Spanish daily routine and pastimes were imported: mass, siestas, evening promenades, cock-fights, billiards and bull-fights. The educated *criollos* would gather in one another's houses to discuss the latest European philosophies or poetry.

Meanwhile Indian tribes often cut the trade routes to Peru and left Buenos Aires isolated from the Empire. A more organized culture of Araucanian Indians was pressing up from Southern Chile, mastering the wild horses of the pampas and regularly knocking down the Spanish forts.

A smuggling capital: As the 18th century approached, Buenos Aires began to develop its illegal trading until it became one of the great commercial centers of South America—completely without the Spanish Crown's approval.

Porteños developed a skill at avoiding rules and regulations that would continue to the present day. Spain tried dozens of schemes to control the secret trading—at one stage even banning the use of money—but were powerless against the *porteños'* wily schemes.

The annual "permission ship" granted by the crown to bring goods was restocked by smugglers in its mooring for weeks. Foreign boats would declare themselves "in distress" with false leaks and pull into Buenos Aires for "refitting" while dropping merchandise by night. Poorly paid town officials would "confiscate" illegal goods only to resell them to their original owners at mock auctions. The founding of Colonia del Sacramento by the Portuguese in 1680 provided a permanent smuggling outlet.

Buenos Aires also became a slave market: a compound to sell black slaves was set up at the present site of Retiro train station. *Porteños* blamed the slaves' unhygienic conditions for various epidemics running through the town, but they accepted the slaves in the name of profit. Freed blacks, given the lowest social status in the town, made up at least a quarter of the population by the 19th century.

But the real fortunes were to be made in cattle hides—Rio de la Plata leather equipped soldiers in endless European wars.

Gruesome portrayal of cannibalistic ending to the first attempt to found Buenos Aires.

Cattle-hunts or *vaquerìas* occurred less and less as *estancias* (cattle ranches) were set up. Huge tracts of land were set aside for a few Spanish families, whose names would recur again and again as the power-brokers of Argentina.

Mule-breeding was less glamorous but only slightly less profitable. By the 1750s Buenos Aires boasted an elite who walked the streets in the finest French silks and even had two-story brick houses.

'La Gente Perdida': From the earliest days of Buenos Aires, individuals had fled to the country and mixed with the Indians. Fleeing criminals, escaped slaves and deserting guishable from those of the Indians.

The wandering, vagrant population had always irritated the *porteño* officials, who tried to licence the gauchos, tie them to the new estancias, and forbid them from using knives—all without success.

One English traveler in the period wrote in despair: "Vain is the endeavor to explain to him the luxuries and blessings of a more civilized life!"

Saga of the Jesuit missions: The Jesuit presence in what is now the north of Argentina and south of Paraguay has become well known with the Academy-Award winning movie *The Mission* starring Robert De

militia-men lived at the fringes of society and were known as *la gente perdida:* the lost people. They developed their own harsh, nomadic lifestyle on the pampas, following and killing cattle herds for fresh meat and hides (which they traded for *yerba mate* or alcohol.) The men developed their own style: special knives or *facones*, distinctive bagged trousers, Spanish hats and woven Indian shawls. Now called gauchos, they were known for gambling, horsemanship and knife fighting.

The women, called *chinas*, played a subsidiary role in this macho lifestyle, raising children in small huts which were indistin-

Niro and Jeremy Irons.

In 1609 the Buenos Aires cabildo supported the Jesuits in setting up Indian missions to protect Spanish holdings. Free from taxes, the missions brought Guaraní Indians together in societies which organized every moment of daily life. By 1700, more than 50,000 Guaraní Indians were growing crops, rearing sheep and making musical instruments in conditions far better than those of other plantations.

The missions suffered early losses from raids by slave traders. However, the Jesuits learned from their mistakes and organized a standing army of Indians which became the largest, most efficient military machine in the Rio de la Plata region. And its position remained unchallenged for 100 years.

When in 1750 the Spanish gave the missions to Portugal, the Indians rebelled and defended themselves. Only in 1768 when the Jesuits were expelled from the Spanish Empire was the system's weakness revealed: the paternalistic structure collapsed without the priests, leaving the Guaraní totally unprepared to deal with any change. Most fled into the jungle and the missions quickly became overgrown ruins.

Spain appeases the porteños: The Spanish Crown eventually had to admit that

smuggling in Buenos Aires was out of control and that corruption and inefficiency were rampant.

In 1776, Spain made Buenos Aires the capital of a new vice-royalty of the Rio de la Plata which stretched from modern-day Bolivia to Paraguay and Uruguay. Trade was opened up and some administrative reforms made.

Left, Pauke print depicts prominent role of Jesuits in colonial B.A. and above, 1806 artilleryman.

The man sent to be the first viceroy was the Spanish general Pedro de Cevallos, a religous fanatic hated by his own men for his ruthlessness. Considered the last of the conquistadors, he managed to capture Colonia del Sacramento from the Portuguese at a time when Spain was being soundly defeated everywhere else in the world.

De Cevallos puffed the pride of *porteños* by telling them that Buenos Aires was Spain's "most important bastion in America, whose development we must encourage by every means possible, for here we will win or lose South America."

With the growth of trade bringing unseen prosperity, Buenos Aires began to improve its image. The streets were paved and lit, a hospital and orphanage were built, theaters were opened and Spanish professionals began to migrate to the new capital. By the end of the 18th century, Buenos Aires had eight churches and a main cathedral.

But visitors were still not overly impressed by the improvements. Another English traveler at the time remarked dryly:

"The city of Buenos Aires, observed from the outer anchorage, has an imposing appearance. The public buildings and cupolas of the various churches give it a certain air of grandeur which vanishes as soon as we draw near."

Buenos Aires remained notorious for its terrible sanitation. Most of the population depended for their drinking water on vendors who filled their leather vats with the same river water used for bathing and sewage. Disease was rife and visitors reported that the streets were full of lepers, and rats the size of rabbits.

But all of Spain's reforms finally backfired. The boost in *porteño* self-confidence provided by the new wealth only served to encourage the idea of ending all ties with Spain, while the new administrators sent by the crown were only seen as meddlers by the local *criollos*.

When in 1796 war with Britain finally cut Atlantic trade routes, leaving piles of goods to rot in the warehouses of Buenos Aires, *porteños* decided that connections with Spain were undesirable.

The Crown's authority would never be fully restored in Buenos Aires again.

INDEPENDENCE AND CIVIL WAR

The street names of Buenos Aires constitute a roll-call of heroes from its struggle for independence and the civil wars that followed. Although *porteños* seized power to improve their commercial prosperity, the provincial towns refused to cooperate. It was not until 70 years later that Argentina would settle down as a political unit with Buenos Aires in control.

The British take over: The *porteños'* eventual separation from Spain was partly due to longstanding resentment against the Crown and partly due to outside influences beyond Spanish control: the examples of the French and American revolutions, Enlightenment ideas of popular participation in governmment and, above all, the misguided plans of an Englishman by the name of Sir Home Popham.

Popham was commanding a British naval force on its way back from South Africa in June 1806, when he decided, completely without orders, to capture Buenos Aires. Like all good Britons of the time, he felt that if foreigners would not trade with the British willingly, they should be forced to do so. Popham landed his Scottish highlanders, backed by gunboats, to take the city. The Spanish viceroy promptly scurried for cover in Cordoba, for which he would never be forgiven by the *porteños*.

Proclaiming the Rio de la Plata region to be a 'New Arcadia' for British merchants, Popham sent home boats full of war booty. The takings, which were emblazoned with the word TREASURE in gold, were paraded through the streets of London in horse-drawn wagons.

Its appetite whetted, the British government sent massive reinforcements to Buenos Aires. But before they could arrive, the *proteños* had already tired of the British, rebelled and easily captured the whole occupying force. The British colors were hung in

Left, Gaucho Soldier in Rosas' army. Right, Monvoisin painting shows *porteña* mourning Civil War dead.

the Church of Santo Domingo, where they can still be found today. Captured officers spent their time fishing and horse-riding in *estancias* of the provinces, while *porteños* hastily organised a popular militia using captured weapons and anything else they could find.

The new British commander, General George Whitelocke, found himself in Montevideo with no less than 70 boats full of merchant goods which were supposed to be sold to *porteños*. A weak and indecisive leader, Whitelocke decided that his predecessors had been defeated by a Spanish conspiracy rather than a popular uprising.

Whitelocke ordered his troops to land and retake Buenos Aires, but the *porteños* were ready. The British were caught in the narrow streets of the city as patriots showered them from the rooftops with "musketry, hand grenades, stink pots, brickbats and all sorts of combustibles."

Four hundred British soldiers were killed in the chaotic confrontation, as many wounded, and over 2,000 captured. The enemy fell back to Montevideo and White-locke was recalled to London for court-martial. Days of celebration followed the victory in Buenos Aires: a new confidence had been achieved by the *porteños* for soundly defeating a powerful foreign invader without the slightest help from Spain.

The viceroy returned from his hiding-place in the provinces but his prestige had been shattered. A Portuguese spy in the city at the time noted that "Buenos Aires is, in fact, a Republic already."

The independence movement: The ejected British also left behind the memory of their cheap manufactured goods and had

Aires became crowded with merchants, soldiers, *estancieros* and bureaucrats debating the best course for the future.

The climax came on May 25, when the viceroy and the *cabildo* watched the assembling militiamen in the Plaza de Mayo and admitted that they no longer controlled Buenos Aires. They surrendered their power to a *junta criolla* which declared that it would rule in the name of the Spanish Crown. It was only on July 9, 1816 that full independence was announced for the whole Rio de la Plata region in the provincial town of Tucuman, which is why Argentines celebrate two national independence days.

given the *criollo* merchants their first taste of unrestricted trade. These merchants led the push for local autonomy, organizing the militia under their own control so that the independence movement would never become a truly popular revolt.

Napoleon's invasion of Spain provided *porteños* with the opportunity they had been awaiting. In May 1810, news arrived in Buenos Aires that the interim government of Seville had fallen and that there was now no direct link with the Spanish Crown. For four tense days, the leading *porteño* citizenry pressured the viceroy to hand over his authority, while the muddy streets of Buenos

Before that date, however, Buenos Aires saw a bewildering number of experiments at the new experience of self-government ranging from new juntas to triumvirates, congresses and directorates.

Despite this, Buenos Aires remained the only South American capital that the Spanish never managed to recover and *porteños* carried their struggle to other countries. The campaign was led by the only historical figure to have kept the universal respect of Argentines: General Jose de San Martin. This polite and reserved veteran of the Spanish war against Napoleon, returned to his home country after hearing of the events of

May 25. Realizing that the newly-declared Republic could never be safe while its neighbors were Spanish-dominated, San Martin spent years preparing for a massive expedition to Chile.

The crossing of the Andes was timed with clockwork precision, not only liberating Santiago but later freeing Lima, the Spanish capital in South America. San Martin became depressed by the constant bickering and growing chaos back in Buenos Aires and tried to convince the other great liberator of the continent, Simon Bolivar, that a new monarchy was the only solution. After Bolivar refused to agree, San Martin gave up on

who had fled to South America after the Waterloo fiasco.

The civil wars begin: No sooner had the *porteños* declared the viceroyalty of the Rio de la Plata to be independent than the whole of Upper Peru, Uruguay and Paraguay announced that they wanted to be separate from Buenos Aires. Soon, the various provincial towns that now make up Argentina, were declaring their own autonomy.

The inhabitants of the interior were understandably not as thrilled by the idea of Buenos Aires' leadership as the *porteños* themselves. The *criollo* merchants saw vast profits in opening up the whole country to free

South America and went to France, where he died, lonely and disillusioned.

During these years, *porteños* accepted aid from wherever they could get it. The Irishman William Brown had deserted the British Navy and arrived in Buenos Aires to eventually lead a naval squadron which broke a blockade. Jean-Jacques D'Auxion, who commanded *porteño* troops, was said to have been one of Napoleon's own generals

Left, *mataderos* or slaughter houses flanked the city and were the source of its wealth. Right, 1831 Pellegrini painting of the Cabildo.

trade, indifferent to the fact that this would destroy the provincial economies.

Porteños were also hurrying to trade with their old enemies, the British. They knew that woolen ponchos, modeled on Tucuman's products, could be bought from Manchester factories at a fraction of the Tucuman price, while Sheffield knives would easily outsell those from Jujuy.

The division between Buenos Aires and the interior is often described as a struggle between Unitarist and Federalists: the Unitarists wanted to keep a strong central government in Buenos Aires and the Federalists wanted to preserve local autonomy. But the wheeling and dealing in the many complex civil wars that followed, often made the distinction meaningless.

From the confusion after Independence, emerged the figure of the *caudillo*, the local strongman, usually a landowner from a traditional family who took control of each of the provinces. They fought with Buenos Aires and among themselves, developing a habit of chopping off their defeated enemies' heads and hanging them in the main plaza of their towns.

Buenos Aires tried to win over the *caudillos* by offering a new constitution, but instead, they marched on the city with their gaucho armies and captured it, forcing *porteños*, at least for the time being, to accept federalism.

Buenos Aires under Rivadavia: A brief respite from the civil wars during the 1820s allowed *porteños* to take stock of their newfound freedom. Under their Anglophile governor Bernardino Rivadavia, it appeared that very little had changed.

Travelers were still astounded by the number of accidents caused by racing horse-and-buggies in the city streets. They noted the number of children hanging around smoking tobacco in the plazas and were shocked by wild black dances at night in San Telmo. One English writer observed that Buenos Aires now had five cafés—one of which he thought superior to anything in London but not up to Parisian standards—while the port area was crowded with bars and brothels.

Young single foreigners arrived from the poorer parts of Europe to find work, with many Irish and Basques accepting the lonely and rough life of sheepherding in the country. Another English traveler noted that an Irishman digging ditches on an *estancia* could earn enough in three weeks to buy 1,500 sheep, while his homeland offered nothing but starvation.

In the same year as Independence, landowners became richer with the introduction of the *saladero*: a crude factory which processed every last part of cattle and horses amid an overwhelming stench of blood and gore. Hides, salted meat, hair and melted hooves left in the many schooners that passed by Buenos Aires.

Rivadavia tried to make some more profound changes but only provoked further civil war. He first upset the large landowners by proposing to create a democracy of small landowners such as in the United States. He then enraged the Church with his anti-clerical measures, creating a university free from religious control and setting up a public library which boasted the works of the most radical French thinkers.

The people of the interior rose up against Buenos Aires yet again under the banner "Religion or Death." More turmoil followed, with years of war, assassination, alliances and back-stabbings until the most infamous of all *caudillos* appeared on the scene: Juan Manuel de Rosas.

The restorer of the laws: Rosas still arouses passionate debate among *porteños*. He is denounced by some as a cruel and bloody tyrant while praised by others as a nationalist hero.

The "Caligula of the River Plate" came from a wealthy ranching family of Buenos Aires province. He handled himself with equal ease among the urbane *porteños* and the gauchos of the pampas, where he had slept under the stars in his youth and learned to tell the weather by chewing blades of grass. Rosas had already led militia troops against Buenos Aires in the name of Federalism, but the chaos of the civil wars was so destructive that *porteños* decided to call on this *caudillo* to protect them.

From the moment of assuming governorship in 1829 until his expulsion 23 years later, Rosas ruled Buenos Aires as if it were his own private *estancia*. He silenced his critics through censorship, intimidation and exile—sending to Montevideo the intellectuals who later became known as "the Generation of '37."

As the *caudillo* of Buenos Aires province, Rosas soon became *de facto* ruler of Argentina by defeating various provincial leaders. When he left the governorship for a short break to kill Indians instead, *porteños* invited Rosas back with virtually unlimited dictatorial powers.

Pictures of Rosas were hung over church altars: "Rosas the Restorer of the Laws" next to "Christ the Redeemer." Many schools were closed, radical books banned and the

Buenos Aires *Carnaval* supressed. Bureaucrats who did not do their master's bidding could expect a nocturnal visit from the secret police called the *mazorca*, who assassinated their victims by slitting their throats.

Rosas' residence in what is now Palermo Park was known as *el Versailles criollo* for its sumptuous mansion, sculptures, park and zoo. His city residence in Monserrat was famous for its giant telescope.

The dictator paid constant lip-service to Federalism, going so far as to force all *porteños* to wear a ribbon of the Federalist color—red. Even fashionable ladies of the aristocracy obeyed this directive, while which allowed Buenos Aires province to prosper while dooming many of the provincial industries to destruction.

Under Rosas' rule, porteños increasingly had to tolerate more wars against *caudillos*, as well as various blockades of the Rio de la Plata by the British and the French, to break the protective tariff. The dictator started a 12-year siege of Montevideo which *porteños* jokingly called "the Troy of the River Plate," but when the British took the Falkland Islands in 1833, Rosas only managed a stern note of protest to London.

The cost of maintaining Rosas' army and wars was soon intefering in the happy pur-

Rosas' wife appeared in scarlet satins and his gauchos in scarlet ponchos. All legal documents began: "Long live the Federation and Death to the Unitarist Savages."

Yet it was Rosas more than anyone else who guaranteed the end of Federalism and the supremacy of Buenos Aires. He crushed uprisings by other *caudillos*, ensured *porteño* control of revenues from trade, and introduced a system of protective tariffs

Nineteenth-century Bacle print spoofs the exaggerated *peinetones* or combs which were fashionable in the early-19th century.

suit of profit by *porteño* merchants, which turned his own supporters against him. When one of Rosas' former military commanders, Justo José de Urquiza, turned against him and marched on Buenos Aires, many *porteños* rebelled.

Rosas was defeated and his supporters massacred. Buenos Aires was sacked by looters, forcing foreign boats to put marines ashore to protect their merchandise.

The ageing dictator himself fled on a British ship to Southampton, where he spent the next 25 years wasting his considerable fortune trying to recreate the conditions of his old *estancia* on a plot of English soil.

Life after Rosas: Forty years of independence and chaos had still not profoundly changed life in Buenos Aires or provincial society. But the Rosas years had shown how the city could be a political capital of the Rio de la Plata. In the decades that followed, economic growth and the unification of Argentina went hand in hand.

The provinces had once again defeated Buenos Aires, but they could not control it. Exhausted by wars, everybody at last agreed to a new constitution. In 1862, Bartolome Mitre became the first President of *La Republica Argentina*. The theory of Federalism was maintained, with the national gov-

est minds coming from Europe. Meanwhile the "Generation of '37" returned from exile in Montevideo to fill the city's cafés and supply Argentina with statesmen, writers and historians who would paint the Rosas years in lurid colors.

The most influential of these was Domingo Sarmiento. He had followed the final campaign against Rosas with a printing press on an ox-cart to send out propaganda condemning him as a tyrant. Sarmiento divided the world into "civilization"— which was represented by all things European—and barbarous: *caudillos*, gauchos and Indians.

ernment ruling from Buenos Aires as the guests of the provincial rulers.

An economic boom followed, based on sheep farming and agriculture. Argentina accepted its neocolonial role of selling raw materials to industrial countries and buying back manufactured goods. Steamships with regular schedules helped trade and brought Buenos Aires closer to Europe, while the expansion of railroads backed by British investors tied the provinces even more securely to their only port.

Porteños now culled from the interior anyone with even the slightest talent, imagination or ambition. They secured the bright-

The old *caudillo* with his motley cavalry bands no longer fitted in with Argentina's new style of politics. The country's leaders would increasingly dress in collar and tie, eager to appear highly cultured and urbane.

The gauchos who still roamed the pampas and made up *caudillo* armies were seen as a threat to Sarmiento's great dream for the country. Rosas had already tried to control them, but now, codes were introduced to regulate their movements, dress, drinking habits and diet. Thousands of gauchos were pressed into military service as punishment for not possessing a passport they could not even read.

President Mitre led wars to exterminate the gauchos, advised by Sarmiento that they were "biped animals of the most perverse stripe" whose carcasses were only good to fertilize the earth.

Soon, the *gaucho* was virtually extinct as a social grouping, leaving only an idealized literary memory.

In the great literary work of the 1870s, *The Gaucho Martin Fierro*, Jose Hernandez would lament:

"And listen to the story told by a gaucho who's hunted by the law, who's been a hardworking father and a loving husband - yet in spite of all that, taken to be a criminal."

Buenos Aires at federation: It was not until 1886 that the final step towards nationhood was made when Buenos Aires was separated from its province and declared the capital of Argentina.

Poised before the great expansion of the 1880s, the city was still known as *la gran aldea*—the big village. Most of its buildings were still colonial style, built around courtyards, sparsely furnished and unheated. Streets were mostly unpaved and the port's facilities still inadequate.

Although Buenos Aires had banks, factories, tramways, a gasworks and a telegraph station, many of the *porteños'* habits had not

CORONEL JULIO A ROCA 1874

Meanwhile, the Araucanian Indians continued to threaten *estancias*. One raid as late as 1876 broke through the defensive forts to reach within 155 miles (250 km) of Buenos Aires. After this, General Julio Roca embarked upon the "conquest of the wilderness" with the simple expedient of killing any Indian who stood in his path and herding the rest into reservations. For his efforts, *porteños* made him President.

Opposite page, the *pulperia* or combination saloon and general store. Above left, first President Bernardino Rivadavia; right, President Roca.

changed since pre-Independence days. They still took long siestas after huge lunches of roasted meat with little alcohol, drank *mate*, went to mass, and kept strong family ties.

But compared to the provinces, the city was a cosmopolitan center. The monotonous pace of the conservative interior was only livened by the occasional cockfight or game of billiards. In Buenos Aires, the migrants were arriving and with them came new ideas, and a new wave of restaurants, cafés, hotels, brothels and even foreign-language newspapers.

Yet the changes had just begun. Buenos Aires was on the verge of its Golden 'Age.'

WEALTH AND IMMIGRATION

The close of the 19th century saw Buenos Aires change from a dusty, colonial town to the "Paris of South America," a center of commerce and culture claiming to be unmatched in the hemisphere. Development of the pampas brought unimagined wealth and waves of immigrants from Europe. However, it was not long before the end of the Argentine dream was in sight.

The "great leap forward": An agricultural revolution on the vast pampas beyond Buenos Aires proved to be more important in shaping the future of Argentina than all the civil wars and conflicts of the 1800s. Booms occurred first with wheat-growing, followed by sheep-raising and finally with cattle. Expansion into the fertile plains went on unchecked for the next 40 years, making the pampas the richest area in Latin America and the Argentine *estanciero* (rancher) a near-mythical figure of wealth, to stand alongside the Brazilian rubber lord and Texan oil baron.

The most dramatic change was made in the production of beef. In the mid-19th century, only a fraction of the meat on slaughtered cattle was used; most of it rotted in the open air and was picked at by wandering gauchos. Meanwhile in Europe, beef was selling at outrageous prices and considered a luxury on the finest dinner tables. With slow shipping and no refrigeration, the problem was to getting the beef across the Atlantic before it went bad.

It was in 1876 that an experimental shipment of frozen beef first arrived in Buenos Aires from France. The elated *estancieros* threw a grand banquet for the Frenchmen. Their enthusiasm was only slightly dulled by the discovery that technical imperfections had left the meat unchewable after the three-month voyage. But within years Argentine beef was crossing the Atlantic in large quantities to be sliced on European tables.

Preceding pages: gaucho woos his pretty *novia*. Left, Turkish immigrant with hookah. Right, dockside warehouse.

Bigger and faster steam ships began transporting live cattle until Argentine stock was found to be ridden with foot and mouth disease. A new Chicago-based technique was soon developed to chill rather than freeze meat, increasing both the beef's quality and the *estancieros'* massive profits.

Cultivation of the pampas skyrocketed to keep up with the new demands. Railways were laid across the country by British com-

panies, to move produce as quickly as possible towards Buenos Aires and other coastal ports. Argentina was soon outstripping its rivals, Canada and Australia, in agricultural advances, and some observers predicted that it would overtake the United States.

The immigrants arrive: Laborers were needed to keep the boom going, and these were made available through immigration. Before 1880, only a trickle of foreign workers stayed in Argentina. Overnight they became a flood, the greatest influx of immigrants in relation to population patterns in world history.

The majority of immigrants were peasants

from northern Italy, with the next largest group coming from Spain. Nearly all paid their own way across the Atlantic with a thirdclass passage, spending weeks crammed below decks in a constant battle against seasickness and food poisoning.

Most arrived penniless, secure only in the knowledge that two weeks' work in Argentina would cover the cost of the fare.

The newcomers' first taste of Buenos Aires was usually five days' free lodging at the dreaded Immigrants' Hotel, a horse barn which was eventually upgraded in the style of a concrete prison. Anyone who was able picked up a cheap hotel room, contacted

Immigrants were instead offered two-year tenancy leases in the pampas, moving on when they expired. The landowners provided the seed and tools, the immigrants the brawn. Their existence as tenants was harsh and lonely; the nearest town was often 30 miles (50 km) away. Staying for such a short time, farmers rarely bothered to construct anything more permanent than a hut of straw and thatch with sheepskin for a door.

Their only social contact would be the local store, usually at the distant railway station, which was a development of the gauchos' *pulpería*: some idle conversation could be had over cheap red wine, meat and

relatives or drifted around the waterfront. By the turn of the century, the system was refined so that laborers were off their boats and into Retiro station on the same day, where a train would whisk them to the pampas.

But unlike in North America, the immigrants were not able to buy their own small plots of land. The Argentine *estancieros* refused to break up their huge tracts of territory, easily ignoring laws passed to control concentration of property. Even the plains opened up by Roca's Conquest of the Desert were snapped up by the richest *porteños*, avoiding the 100,000-acre hectare limit on purchases by using false names.

dry biscuits. The farmer lived without roads in the countryside, let alone churches, doctors or schools.

Not surprisingly, the vast majority of immigrants ended up staying in Buenos Aires and other coastal ports, only making seasonal forays into the pampas at harvest time. They worked in the meat-packing plants, railways and service industries needed to channel the produce to the outside world. Those who did well formed a new middle class in the city: they became the shopkeepers, bank clerks, teachers, minor officials and small factory owners of the 20th century.

It was the *estanciero* who amassed vast fortunes from the boom, living in the capital with holiday houses in Tigre and Mar del Plata. The phrase "rich as an Argentine" fell into common usage in France as the *porteño* playboy began to cut a notorious figure in the salons of Paris (women had to wait some decades before escaping needlework and cooking classes).

These *estancieros* became leaders of a tight-knit group of some 200 families, comprising leading bankers, politicians and businessmen. Educated in Europe, cosmopolitan and aloof, they set about shaping the city of Buenos Aires to their ideals.

made sure that the benefits of the pampas revolution stayed in the capital, changing the face of the city.

Buenos Aires shed its Hispanic colonial atmosphere to become an expression of *porteño* admiration for all things French. The Plaza de Mayo, which had been full of garbage and marketstalls, was cleared and a lawn was planted. The Casa Rosada was completed. Garay's 16th-century street plan was finally cast aside and streets widened into grand avenues, to be lined with Parisian cafés, jacarandas and footpaths made of Swedish marble.

Palermo Park was remodeled along the

The transformation of Buenos Aires: *Porteños* greeted the centennial of independence in 1910 with boundless optimism, convinced that the future was assured by beef, wheat and sheep. "We are living the most glorious day," announced one writer ecstatically, "better than the trumpeted century of Pericles, better even than the Renaissance." Buenos Aires was now the largest city in Latin America and second only to New York in the hemisphere. *Porteños*

Above, European immigrants gather in the bleak dining hall of the Immigrant Hotel.

lines of Paris' Bois de Boulogne, while the Avenida 9 de Julio was planned after the Champs Elysée. The British architects of Retiro and Constitution railway stations resisted the fashion and copied them from London and Liverpool instead.

Horse-drawn carts gave way to electric trams in the chaotic streets. Travelers who had once complained about *porteño* horsemanship now found automobile drivers in the city no more considerate and decidedly more dangerous. A subway line was opened only 10 years after New York's. Meanwhile, engineers scoured the world for a grade of asphalt which would not melt in the summer sun and provide comfortable coach rides for well-to-do young ladies.

The modern-day contours of Buenos Aires were defined: Florida became a shopping area, Corrientes a focus for cabaret and dance, north of the Plaza de Mayo, the banking center and the waterfront, the red-light district. Beyond these were the *barrios*, where most people lived and worked. Each *barrio* had its own shops, priests and bar.

As Buenos Aires became more sophistacted the gulf widened with the 'interior': most pampa towns remained colonial backwaters where nobody of talent or importance would consider staying. One English traveler of the time, aghast at the dusty main squares and dirt roads, wrote: "If a man ever wishes to know what it is to have an inclination to commit suicide, let him pass a week in a camptown in the Argentine."

The rise of the radicals: Despite the changes occurring over the turn of the century, political power remained in the hands of the few old *estanciero* and business families referred to simply as "the oligarchy." A nominal democratic system was arranged so that the oligarchs could choose presidents and congressmen from their own ranks, while corruption in the courts and bureaucracy bent the system to their needs.

A protest movement against the oligarchs' grip grew in the 1880s with the Unión Cívica, pulling together students, university professors and scattered groups from the *criollo* middle class. After a failed attempt at revolution in 1890, this was transformed into the Unión Cívica Radical, forerunner of today's political party of the same name. The Radicals' infuence extended under the leadership of Hipolito Yrigoyen, a figure still revered by party members: a shy and introverted man, Yrigoyen was a poor speaker and dictatorial in his methods, but a brilliant organizer. He undertook the tedious shuffling and manouvering for support that made the Radicals a powerful force.

Yrigoyen's demand was simple: free elections. Once it was obvious that the only thing "radical" about the middle-class protest movement was its name, the oligarchs decided on a strategic retreat to protect their interests. A democratic poll was held in 1916 with universal male suffrage (women had to wait until the regime of Perón for the vote). Yrigoyen won the presidential race by only one ballot in the electoral college. He was drawn through the streets of Buenos Aires by throngs of young supporters, hailing what they hoped would be a new age of reform.

But the Radicals proved from the very beginning they had little interest in changing the old order. Although the university system was updated, most other reforms were either blocked in Congress or failed through party division.

Argentina stood still. Anarchist cells were formed in Buenos Aires, leading strikes which the Radicals were eager to crush. *La Semana Trágica* or 'Tragic Week' of 1919 followed a general strike, with rightwing vigilante groups storming the slums of the capital in search of 'Bolsheviks'. Three years later, Yrigoyen allowed the Army to break a shepherd's strike in Patagonia and carry out mass executions.

Between the wars: Buenos Aires in the 1920s became the cultural mecca of Latin America. The Teatro Colón put the city on par with Berlin and Milan for opera and ballet. A dozen newspapers thrived. Art galleries opened along Florida. Writers flocked to the city from across the Hispanic world, lured by the reputation of literary magazines such as *Martin Fierro* and the works of poet Leopoldo Lugones, novelist Manuel Gálvez and the young Jorge Luis Borges.

As a freer age was ushered in, women walking alone on the streets were no longer denounced as whores or insane. Bohemians gathered in the café Tortoni to imitate the latest rage from Paris, from nude follies to "cocaine mania."

Even tango emerged from the dark bars of La Boca once it became fashionable in France, reaching new heights with the work of singer, Carlos Gardel. Yet, despite the heady enthusiasm and wild parties of small *porteño* cliques, the cracks were already showing in the great edifice of Argentine prosperity. The country was still contentedly supplying raw materials to Europe and developing little industry, making no allowance for changes in the world economy. A nearly senile Yrigoyen was reelected president in 1928, only to face the Wall Street

Crash the next year. He did nothing to soften the impact of the world depression and let corruption run out of control. The Radicals appeared completely unable to deal with the situation.

Meanwhile the Argentine army had spent the 1920s practising the goosesteps taught by German instructors and admiring Rosada and took over the government.

Two years later Uriburu passed control to a series of conservative presidents, who led Argentina through *La Década Infame* "the Infamous Decade." Firmly back in power, the oligarchy continued to run the country as if it were still in the 1890s.

As the "Infamous Decade" of the 1930s

Mussolini's Italy from afar. Increasingly critical of democracy, they made on Sept. 6, 1930, what would be the first of many interventions,: General José Uriburu strolled unopposed with his troops into the Casa

Revolution of September 6, 1930 in which Radical President Hipolito Yrigoyen was overthrown.

progressed, the middle class became increasingly restive. But the great wellspring of discontent would be the workers, many of whom were the children of immigrants. Crammed into one-room family houses, working long hours for unprotected wages, they still had no political voice.

Into this void stepped Juan Domingo Perón.

PERÓN TO THE PRESENT

The two most significant events in Argentina's last four decades of history have been the rise to power of Juan Domingo Perón in the mid-1940s and the return to real representative democracy in 1983.

Perón was the most influential personality in Argentina's history to date, and one of the best loved and most hated leaders in contemporary political history.

Perón is remembered by his detractors as a cruel and ruthless dictator who modeled his regime on that of Italy's Benito Mussolini and Germany's Adolf Hitler, and who plundered the wealth and well-being of the nation. He is seen by his admirers, meanwhile, as the great benefactor of the unsung worker, the man who made all Argentines equal, created a national industry and ended the feudal exploitation of the laborer by the landed gentry.

Perhaps, as is usually the case with remarkable figures in history, a little of both views is true. But one thing is certain—no Argentine, even today, more than a decade after the leader's death, is indifferent to the name of Juan Domingo Perón.

Born in the little town of Lobos about 60 miles (100 km) southwest of Buenos Aires in 1895, Perón joined the Army when he was 16 years old. He attended officers' training and on receiving his commission, made rapid progress through the ranks. He stood over six feet tall and possessed the kind of daring and flintiness which made him the target of admiration and envy in the cadre and the ranks. He was a champion swordsman, an efficient boxer and a good skier. But he also did well in the classroom, especially in history and political science.

Perón was indeed influenced in his early political career by the Italian dictator Benito Mussolini. In the 1930s, he served as Argentina's military attaché in Rome, seeing with his own eyes the rapid inroads made in Europe by Mussolini's and Adolf Hitler's nationalism.

During World War II, as during World War I, Argentina remained nominally neutral although in practice, the country was split and at severe odds over the issues of the Second World War. Neutrality was basically a matter of economics. In both World Wars, Argentina was a universal supplier of food and leather.

In 1938, at the start of the conflict, the Conservative Coalition government of Roberto Ortiz came to office.

Ortiz's administration followed the relative stability of six years under the Progressive Conservative government of Agustín Justo. But the new government quickly proved itself unequal to the task of preserving that stability in the face of growing controversy over the issues of World War II.

Less than four years later, in 1942, Ortiz fell ill, resigned and died shortly thereafter. He was replaced in office by his Vice-President, Ramón Castillo, who was slated to serve out the rest of Ortiz's term until 1944. But he didn't last a year.

Perón's rise to power: In June of 1943, Generals Arturo Rawson, P.P. Ramírez and Edelmiro Farrell mustered troops at the Campo de Mayo Army base outside Buenos Aires and marched to the center of the city where they took over the Government House and ousted Castillo.

Perón was, from the beginning of the uprising, one of the chief aides to the new ruling junta.

Efficient, opportune and highly politicized, Perón accepted greater and greater responsibilities from the three generals, garrison types who knew next to nothing about politics and "people power" whose strength was that they had all the weapons.

Early on in the regime Perón was named labor secretary, and it was here that he began to gather his power base among the country's largely unprotected and ununionized workers. He began working on draft legislation to benefit workers, particularly lower-class laborers, expanding his sphere of influence into the social welfare secretariat as well. Finding Colonel Perón ever willing and able to accept greater responsibility, the generals, in 1944, also named him minister of war—in time for him to foresee the outcome of the Second World War and break the regime's neutrality and rather obvious friendship with the Axis and declare its sudden loyalty to the Allies. By 1945, Perón had also become vice president of the nation. Now without doubt the real power-figure in the military government, Perón pushed through measures to further endear him to the workers.

All through this period, a personality cult was growing around what workers saw as their own *caudillo*, and now that cult was rapidly extending to his beautiful young actress mistress, María Eva (better known as "Evita") Duarte.

It was logical that this should happen. Buenos Aires society was a class-conscious place where the rule of thumb was that you had to be from "a good family" and often one of "the" families in order to get anywhere. Perón and Evita were living proof that this wasn't necessarily true, and that you only had to be smarter, bolder and bigger than the rest to get to the top. He was a smalltown boy and she was a poor girl from the wrong side of the tracks. But they persevered and soon he was the real power behind the power and she was at his side. They could make the country do their bidding.

Their chance to prove this came in 1945. Perón's gathering of worker support was beginning to worry influential sectors of society that put pressure on the military regime to do something about it. The fear among the wealthy was that Perón might eventually lead the workers in a move toward a communist state. The last straw came when he began laying the groundwork for the formation of an umbrella union organization, aimed at "Peronizing" labor as a whole, called the General Confederation of Labor (CGT).

The regime stripped him of his official posts and packed him off to the Martín García military prison on an island in the middle of the River Plate near Buenos Aires. But the generals had not reckoned on the tremendous charisma and already consummate political strength of Eva Duarte. Evita quickly rallied the workers of Buenos Aires area, and solicited the help of sectors of the army loyal to Perón.

Perón had been in jail for less than a fortnight before being released. He made a triumphant return to Buenos Aires on October 17, 1945 (the date is still celebrated by Peronists as the anniversary of the founding of Peronism) and spoke from the balcony of Government House to some 300,000 people gathered in Plaza de Mayo below. The speech, in which he promised to become President and lead the nation to strength and social justice, was also broadcast nationwide on radio.

Several days later, Perón married Evita, to the delight of followers who were becoming ever more swept up in the fairytale glamor of the life of Juan Perón.

The discredited generals called elections for February of the following year. After a brief campaign—in which the liberal opposition claimed it had been repressed by the Federal Police and Peronist strongarm squads—Perón was voted into office with 56 percent of the popular vote.

"Justicialism": His domestic policy was dubbed Justicialism, because the idea behind it was to give social justice to long-oppressed workers. (The Peronists of today are known as Justicialists and their movement as the Justicialist Party). The opponents of Peronism, however, called the policy "distributionism," since, they claimed, it distributed the reserves and assets of the nation among the workers, thus gradually impoverishing the state.

Whatever it was, it reshaped society in Buenos Aires. Justicialism showered Perón's most fervent followers, laborers known in Peronist lingo as *los descamisados* (the shirtless ones) with social benefits, housing and jobs in the public sector. All workers benefitted from guarantees against dismissal and received blanket wage-rises and institutionalized fringe benefits.

On the business front, Perón controlled prices and foreign trade and carried out an ambitious nationalization program, bringing the formerly British-owned railways under state control and taking over other foreign interests in public utilities and other areas of industry.

With regard to foreign relations, Perón may very well have been the inventor of a political philosophy known in the world today as the "non-aligned" stance—and of which, despite decades of political upheaval and change, Argentina is still a major exponent. Perón, however, called it the Third Position: it belonged to neither communism nor capitalism.

The fairytale Evita: In a purely personal sense, Perón put Argentina on the map. In the post-war days, people, both in Argentina and other countries, weary of the seriousness was gaining and put her power to work to change the lives of workers in the only way she knew how: by granting their wishes one by one like a fairy godmother.

The waiting room of her office in what is today the palatial headquarters of the Buenos Aires city council was the size of a good-sized ballroom. (Under subsequent governments the room was actually used as a ballroom reception hall for large diplomatic gatherings.) She held audience for the public, person by person, in her plush, high-ceilinged study with its tall french doors. Her waiting room was generally peopled by throngs that wanted favors from Peronism or

and realism of war days, were looking for Cinderella-like success stories. Juan and Evita Perón became celebrities in the US and Europe. They were a kind of Latin American royalty, seen as the romantically intriguing rulers of a distant land.

Indeed, although he was an elected leader, Perón ruled with confidence in the backing of the majority and with the iron hand of a military leader. Evita, for her part, thrived on the kind of worldwide royal social status she

Thousands of supporters show their loyalty to the Peróns on Oct 17, 1945, the founding date of Peronism.

answers to their dreams of a job, a pension, or a home. And many humble workers walked away with the answer to their dreams clearly in sight.

It has been said that Evita was the real power behind Perón. This is, without a doubt, an oversimplification. But it is nonetheless obvious that Evita's charisma and her considerable control over Peronist labor were strong support for Perón's own powerful personlity and authority, and for his significant support within the Armed Forces. It was thanks to a monumentally crowd-pleasing campaign carried out by Evita in 1951 that Perón was re-elected by an even wider margin than the one he had managed in 1946.

It is little wonder, then, that it came as a real blow to Perón and Justicialism when Evita died the following year of uterine cancer, at the age of 33. The shock and sorrow of millions of workers dramtically shrouded Buenos Aires. A grief-stricken Perón had Evita's body specially embalmed so that it would remain intact indefinitely.

With Evita gone and new problems of state—worsening terms of trade, growing inflation, dwindling reserves—to occupy Perón, the General Confederation of Labor began to take wings of its own, even while remaining loyal to Perón. This once again began to spark fears, among rich landholders and other business interests which had already been stung by Perón's social and domestic economic policies, an eventual turn toward communism. These sectors had the ear of conservative sectors of the army linked to the regime Perón deposed in 1946.

The situation came to a head with a military rebellion that began in June 1955. A naval battery in the River Plate supported by airforce fighter planes blasted and strafed the main square of the city, setting Government House on fire and tearing up the facades of government buildings nearby. Under air and naval support, a detachment of marines sought to take over Government House, but failed in the attempt.

After that attack, in which scores of people, including many innocent bystanders, were killed or injured, Perón was on his way out of government, and out of the country. In mid-September of that same year, Perón was forced to flee the country aboard a Paraguayan gunboat provided by his friend General Alfredo Stroessner who had just come to power in that neighboring country.

Exile and chaos: Perón went off to exile, first in Paraguay and finally in Madrid. The powerful Argentine leader would spend the next 18 years watering the roses in his sumptuous Spanish villa, holding interviews and working on his political writings. He would marry again—in 1961 he married cabaret dancer María Estela Martínez (better known by her stage name, Isabelita") whom he met in Panama in 1956. But he was also planning his return to Argentina.

Back in Buenos Aires, official anti-Perónism became a psychosis. Writing or saying the name of Perón in public was forbidden. Playing or singing *La Marcha Perónista*, the Perónist anthem was banned.

But Perónism, despite being banned from two elections in the shaky years from 1955 to 1973, remained a dominant factor in Argentine politics—it was largely responsible for the fact that not a single military or civilian government in those 18 years managed to consolidate the popular power necessary to rule effectively.

Throughout this period of chaos and confusion in which generals played musical chairs with political power, the country's youth were becoming ever more alienated and frustrated. Argentina thus became the perfect breeding ground for guerrilla movements and political terrorism. In the face of growing civil strife and open opposition to military rule, the way was paved for new democratic elections.

And this time they were indeed democratic, since they did not forbid the running of any party, not even Perónism. More than 20 parties, from the extreme right to the extreme left, ran in the 1973 elections. But the main positions were Radicalism and Perónism.

The intervening years had split Perónism to such an extent that one could find philosophies in Perónist ranks from the staunchest of rightists to the most radicalized leftists: Practically the only thing these Peronists had in common was Perón.

While the party was not banned from the polls, Perón himself was. But it was made clear in the Justicialist campaign that Perón was on his way back to power in Argentina. It was leftwing Perónist Héctor Cámpora who was running for president, but the campaign slogan affirmed that a vote for Cámpora was a vote for Perón.

Cámpora won the election with 48.7 percent of the popular vote. Lanusse handed the presidency over to him on May 25—a national holiday marking the start of Argentina's 1810 revolution against Spanish rule. On June 20 (Flag Day), 1973, less than a month after Cámpora's inauguration, Perón returned to Argentina, 18 years after his hasty departure. But his triumphant return was marred by the deep split between left and rightwing Peronists who turned out to meet him at the Ezeiza International airport. Push led to shove in the crowd of leftists and rightists who awaited their leader and Perón's plane, in the end, had to be rerouted to another landing field as a gunbattle broke out between opposing factions in which over 100 people were killed or wounded.

The following month, Cámpora resigned after just 49 days in office. He was provisionally replaced by Lower House congressional chairman Raúl Lastiri, who called extraordinary elections for September to legitimize the return of Perón. In those polls

later, when Perón died of pneumonia in the rainy Buenos Aires winter month of July.

Mourning workers ground the nation to a halt, and hundreds of thousands of tearful Argentines queued in the cold and rain for blocks in order to file past the coffin in the rotunda of Congress where the President's body lay in state. A shaken, politically inept Isabelita assumed the presidency of a country as the violence broke out between the right and left factions.

As the violence increased, Mrs Perón's feeble grip on government began to slip to an ever greater degree. In the end, she had even lost the backing of Perón's own CGT labor

Perón captured 7.4 million of the 12 million votes cast and by October 15, 1973, Perón was starting his third presidency, with "Isabelita" as his vice president.

By now, the once seemingly indestructable Perón was 78 and on his last legs. His doctor had warned him that the pressures of the presidency and the humid bone-chilling winters of Buenos Aires could kill him. The doctor was proved correct less than a year

Perón's second wife and widow, Isabel, poses with advisors during her brief term as *La Presidenta.*

movement. In 1975, a strained and nervous Isabel Perón was sent out of the country for a rest and was temporarily replaced by Senate President Italo Luder, who signed a decree declaring a state of siege and ordering the Armed Forces to annihilate armed leftwing subversions.

But this was not enough to save the Perónist government. Battered by general strikes, nearly 800 percent annual inflation, a paralyzed economy and increasing civil strife, the government was totally discredited and removed from office in a bloodless military coup on March 24, 1976.

Dark days: Or at least the revolt itself was

bloodless. What followed was the darkest period in Argentine history.

Armed with the order of the deposed Peronist government to "annihilate subversion," the new military regime set about doing just that. Once real armed leftist subversion had been crushed, however, the regime began to use the repressive machinery it had set up, to eliminate any resistance to, and criticism of, military rule.

In the period from the mid to late 1970s, at least 8,900 people "disappeared;" a large proportion of them in and around Buenos Aires. Hundreds more languished at clandestine detention centers or in regular jails,

and his own economic team, the balance which had saved the regime from a storm of condemnation, went haywire.

Projects produced by Videla's team fell apart, inflation began to reheat and the value of Argentine currency began to crumble. Unwell and politically unprepared, Viola lost the confidence of his peers, and was replaced by General Leopoldo Galtieri.

But it was too late for Galtieri to rescue the National Reorganization Process. The bottom had fallen out of the economy, industry was stalled, projects for which enormous international loans had been granted were paralyzed and creditors began wondering

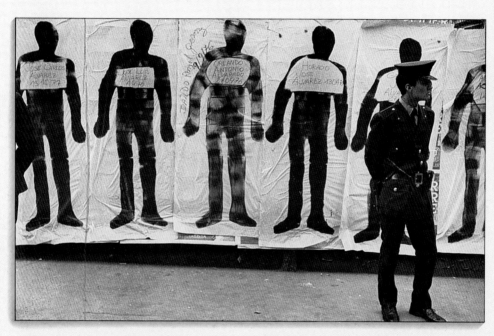

held under the state of siege decree.

But the National Reorganization Process, as the regime became known, tempered its fearsome policy of "national security" with an ambitious policy of economic recovery that promoted foreign investment and offered encouragement for private enterprise.

This careful balance between harsh authoritarian rule and liberal economics was kept under the political leadership of General Jorge Rafael Videla and Economy Minister José Martínez de Hoz in the first three years of the regime. But when Videla was replaced, as planned, after this first period by Army Commander Roberto Viola

about Argentina's ability to pay back the loans. Inflation was checked by severe austerity measures which in turn gave rise to unemployment.

Return of democracy: To stem the tide of protest against him, Galtieri sought an issue on which he could base a consensus on which to continue to rule. And he found one: the islands known to Argentines as the Malvinas and to the British as the Falklands, which lay just a few hundred miles off the southern coast of Argentina.

On April 2, 1982, the country awoke to the news that the nation's armed forces had reclaimed the islands in a military operation in which not a single Birtish subject had been killed or injured. By noon, Plaza de Mayo was brimming with tens of thousands of well-wishers, waving flags and carrying signs reading, "the Malvinas are Argentine." It would have been difficult to guess that just the week before, in this same square, anti-government rioters had been shouting insults at Galtieri and battling with the police.

But Galtieri's glory was short-lived. The subsequent war between Argentina and Britain lasted only ten weeks and ended in a hmiliating defeat for Argentina and the loss of thousands of lives, British and Argentine. The announcement of the surrender brought another night of anti-government street violence in which rioters fought police in an unsuccessful attempt to break down the doors of government house in the apparent hope of laying hands on Galtieri.

Utterly discredited, Galtieri was forced to resign and was replaced by General Reynaldo Bignone, backed by military junta which promised and delivered an immediate political opening, making way for the democratic elections in which Argentina's current President, Raúl Alfonsín, came to office.

Human rights trials: The strides taken by the Alfonsín administration toward the stabilization and democratization of Argentina since the President took office on December 10, 1983, have been impressive.

For a start, for the first time in Argentine history former military rulers were brought to trial. The trials of nine former junta members were based on evidence collected by the National Commission on Missing People (CONADEP) which Alfonsín formed on taking office. Five former military rulers were sentenced to terms ranging from 12 years to life for their parts in crimes against humanity from the mid to late 1970s.

Subsequently, there have been other trials of military and security personnel for violating human rights. Legal action has been taken to fight corruption. Three generals, including General Galtieri, were also tried for their part in the South Atlantic fiasco.

Left, silhouettes of the "disappeared" victims of the dirty war. Right, jubilant supporter of Raúl Alfonsín cheers his election in 1983.

Pressure from the military and conservative sectors of society have recently caused the government to rethink its stance on the human rights issue in the interest of maintaining democratic stability. A statute of limitations placed a time limit on the introduction of evidence against human rights violators from the military regime and it appears that responsibility for these crimes will ultimately lie with command level officers only.

But despite the limitations, this is a unique experience in legislation in Argentina and in the whole of South America. Long-time political observers tend to agree that this is

the first completely democratic government in Argentina's last half-century of history.

Peronism too is in a process of democratic change. This has been evident in the development of a renewal movement within the top opposition party which is based on the need to consolidate Justicialism on the premise of strong party politics and social and legal issues, rather than on the now intangible personality cult built around General Perón.

With both major parties deeply involved in this process of change, most observers feel that this is a propitious time for the building of a long-lasting democracy.

POLITICS IN THE STREETS

Buenos Aires. Easter Sunday, 1987. For hundreds of thousands of citizens, the traditional mid-day meal was canceled. A section of the military had organized an uprising and, in response, the *porteños* flooded the Plaza de Mayo to symbolically defend democracy.

President Raúl Alfonsín addressed the crowds. He instructed them to wait for him in the plaza while he went to the military barracks to negotiate a solution. There were drum rolls, whistles blowing, political banners and Argentine flags waving. The crowds jumping in unison chanted "*El que no salta es un militar*," (If you're not jumping, you work for the military). Another song ended "this afternoon, the people are in the streets." That afternoon the rebels surrendered, and few doubted that the mass rally was the key factor which had persuaded them to give up their plans to overthrow the Alfonsin government.

This was not the first, and surely will not be the last, street rally in Buenos Aires. A large part of politics in Buenos Aires happens on the streets. Marches, political graffiti or citizens gathering on Florida Street to discuss current issues, all form part of the tradition of Argentine politics.

The amount of physical space occupied, the location of the banner, the slogans chosen, constitute part of the language used by the protesters to communicate among themselves and to those not present. One sector may be shouting "Dear Raul, the people are with you," while another chants back the "*La gloriosa jotape*" (the Peronist youth song)". A third group tries to reconcile the two with another slogan "The people united, will never be defeated."

Since the Peronist government of 1945, most major historical events has had physical manifestations in the streets. An impor-tant date in the history of this phenomenon was October 17, 1945, when Evita called the workers to Plaza de Mayo to protest Perón's detention. Thousands of people marching over the bridges from the south constituted what historians now consider the birth of the working class as an integral part of Argentina's political system. Perón later institutionalized the practice with innumerable rallies, in which he spoke to the crowds from the balcony of the Casa Rosada, with the people chanting their response, accompanied by the beating of great kettle drums called *bombos*.

In a country where voting rights are not guaranteed and negotiations behind closed doors have been the norm, street protests, for many, were the principal form of expressing opinions. During military governments that followed the overthrow of Perón, rallies were often met with repression. Yet in other periods the marches have taken on a festive atmosphere.

Political graffiti: When rallies became too dangerous, graffiti took their place. This was especially true during the exile of Perón, when groups of young people with cars, painting material, and even lawyers on call in case of an arrest, crept out in the dead of night to scrawl messages on walls.

Since then, graffiti has become part of the fabric of political life. During the military government slogans such as "Down with the dictatorship," and "Where are the disappeared?" were countered by paramilitary phrases like "Death to the subversives." Today graffiti varies from "IMF out of Argentina" to "Family yes, Divorce no" and, of course, the standard "Vote for ..."

Wall painting is an accepted part of any political campaign, and no matter how many times a building's facade is whitewashed, the next dawn will reveal yet another layer of political graffiti. Although graffiti is illegal, police tend to look the other way. There are even artists who specialize in these paintings and who market their services for a reasonable fee.

Alarmed by a restless military, 300,000 *porteños* rallied in April 1987 to show their support for democracy.

THE PEOPLE OF BUENOS AIRES

Once you've met them, they will stand out in any crowd—their Italian-accented Spanish, their flair for style, their striking intensity. These are *los porteños*, the inhabitants of Buenos Aires, so-named for their proximity to the port on the Rio de la Plata. Any description of them is invariably colored with ambiguous adjectives: sophisticated, self-important, skeptical, stylish, verbose, clever, and (always) melancholic.

A hardware storekeeper in downtown Buenos Aires once tried conveying to me how idiosyncratic his fellow *porteños* really were. "The entire world's peoples," he explained, "can be divided into four areas: East, West, Japan, and Argentina." Surely he meant Buenos Aires in that last category, since it is the *porteños*, not the twenty-odd million Argentines who do not live in this city, who have earned such peculiar renown.

Just who is *el porteño*? A popular joke has it that he is a Spaniard who talks like an Italian, dresses like a Frenchman, and thinks he is British. Indeed, it often does seem that in this southernmost country of the world, Europe is more a state of mind for the *porteño* than a far-off place on the map. "Buenos Aires," writes Argentine expatriate Eduardo Crawley, "playacts at being a city that really belongs in the northern hemisphere, and, although it somehow drifted down to the South Atlantic, it is still attached to the parental body by an imaginary umbilical cord."

Such other-worldly attitudes are by no means a recent fad. In his 19th-century tome exalting the "civilization" of Buenos Aires versus the "barbarism" of the backlands, the educator and former Argentine President, Domingo Sarmiento, wrote that Europeans visiting Buenos Aires fancied themselves in the salons of Paris: "Nothing was wanting; not even the insolence of the Parisian elegant, which was well imitated by the same class of young men in Buenos Aires."

Style is everything: Putting on airs seems to suit *porteños*. In a city where theater thrives (they say you can go to the theater every night for a month and never see the same performance twice) and where the lurid tango is still danced punctiliously, if not universally, illusions become very much a part of reality. What meets the eye is crucial: *porteños* relish seeing and being seen. They choose carefully what they wear for this city's daily pomp and when they wear it. They carry themselves like dancers, some erectly, others with proud weariness. In vain Buenos Aires, one must always be prepared for the scrutiny of others's eyes and reflecting surfaces.

This obsession with appearances is perhaps part of the *porteño's* unrelenting quest for respectability. Intellectual achievement is highly esteemed and flouted. It is a rare well-educated *porteño* who does not remind others of his or her academic background with a title refecting his degrees. Lawers and PhD's (and countless others with more questionable credentials) are "Doctor," college graduates are *Licenciado*, and engineers and architects wear their professions like badges before their names.

Nothing establishes more immediately one's public respectability than the automobile. Possession of this status symbol earns the *porteño* respect for it consecrates him as a full-fledged member of the middle class, the station in society that epitomizes the notion of respectablilty.

If the *porteño* also owns some land, so much the better. In this elegant cow town flanked by slaughterhouses, nobody gets more respect than someone whose wealth is derived from the land. But getting dirt under the fingernails is not the landed gentry's method of farming. They hire others to perform that kind of work so they may devote themselves more fully to the pleasures of the great city.

Residents regard Buenos Aires with a

Preceding pages: the traditional August Cattle Show; the younger, less traditional Argentine generation sharing a joke. Right, tango singer attracts crowds in San Telmo.

kind of ingrained reverence, as if living there were a privilege akin to belonging to an exclusive social club. That privilege is not without its strictures. Up until the goverment returned to civilian rule in 1983, men who wore shorts on the streets were arrested for indecency. Eating in the parks is still frowned upon. You will not likely find a *porteño* visibly drunk in public. Nor will you see litter accumulate for long on the streets.

This sense of order fits snugly with the ritualistic ways of the *porteños*. Buenos Aires is a city that moves in rhythms. More so, perhaps, than other cities. *Porteños* are a homogeneous group with defined tastes, and

they defy sleep on sheer hedonistic willpower. You will find them thronging the streets at 3 a.m. on weekends, as if their biological clocks were all running several hours slow.

This fascination with the city's night and its indoor diversions parallels the *porteños'* fascination with his own dark sides and secrets. Perhaps no other city in the world has such a brooding, introspective populace. For all the glories of life in "the pearl of the River Plate," *porteños* are afflicted with a chronic sense of malaise. They spend a great deal of time on the analyst's couch; there are three times more psychiatrists and psycholo-

few stray from the established norms. They know what they like and they like what they know.

Look on the dark side of life: What *porteños* seem to like most is the night. The *porteño* is like a cat: he prefers to sleep when the sun shines and prowl when darkness wraps the city. The hour has then arrived for the seduction of the bright lights and box offices of Lavalle and Corrientes. *Una salida,* or an evening out, can begin with either food or entertainment, provided it starts late and ends at dawn. *Porteños* sometimes brace themselves for such carousing with a late afternoon nap, but more often

gists per capita in Buenos Aires than there are in New York State. Though loath to admit it, *porteños* take a certain relish in life's complications. It's that much more grist for the verbal mills that grind away over coffee or a bottle of wine. While it is debatable whether the human condition really is more poignant in Buenos Aires than elsewhere, *porteños'* capacity for talking about the sorry hand that life has dealt them is unrivalled.

You can see the *porteño* passion for talking most vividly in the street debates that form spontaneously on pedestrian malls like Florida and Lavalle. Red-faced, rapidly gesticulating interlocutors argue over who's responsible for the mess they're in, but the exchanges rarely come to blows. Talking, even when it sounds more like shouting, is considered dignified. Street fighting is regarded as behavior befitting only barbaric louts (unless, of course, a woman's honor is being defended).

Three topics dominate *porteño* conversation: money, games and sex. *"La guita,"* which means money in the local argot, never seems to stretch as far as do *porteños'* consumer appetites, particularly during inflation's frequent gusts into the triple-digit range. There's a sense that money eludes any

sex. The manifestations of this preoccupation are ubiquitous. Watch the ads on television for a graphic illustration of the selling power of sex. Or listen to passers-by. Attractive women frequently are the targets of declarations of love (some exquisitely poetic, others vulgar) from passing men. Historian James Scobie describes the gaucho ideal of virility as finding its *porteño* expression in the strutting, precise steps of the tango, a perfect showcase for the macho's "aggressive parade of masculinity."

Most *porteños* these days are sexually active before finishing high school, although less conspicuously so than in north-

personal control. Nearly everyone dreams of winning one of the many local and national lotteries. Many of these games of chance are connected to sports, and they fuel already abundant discussions about soccer clubs and *"los burros,"* as *porteños* affectionately call the horse races.

Sex and family: What stirs *porteños'* passions even more deeply than soccer and money is the topic that even when not on their tongues is still usually on their minds:

Left, the sidewalk cafés around Recoleta Cemetery attract the elite. Above, all dressed up for a Sunday in the park.

ern latitudes. Private accomodations are not always available for love affairs, so *porteños* frequently resort to the city's officially regulated trysting establishments. These *albergues transitorios*, or temporary hostels, are as dignified as a *porteño's* public demeanor; from the outside, they look like funeral parlors. Known informally as "*telos*," they do a brisk business during lunch hours and on weekends.

Despite liberal pre-marital sexual attitudes, the family remains a sacrosanct institution among *porteños*. Families tend to be small and cohesive, often with three generations under the same roof. Children are

THE JEWS OF BUENOS AIRES

By far, Latin America's largest concentration of Jews is in Buenos Aires. Most estimates put the size of the city's Jewish population at about 250,000, making this the world's fourth largest Jewish collective as well as Argentina's third largest ethnic group, after Spaniards and Italians.

Jews in Buenos Aires are commonly referred to as "*los rusos*" — the Russians. The label has stuck from the times of the first

massive Jewish immigration to Argentina a century ago, when Jews fleeing the pogroms of czarist Russia first arrived. They came as part of an ambitious colonization scheme financed by a German philanthropic Jew, Baron Maurice Hirsch. In all, about 70,000 Jews settled in agricultural colonies, mostly to the north of Buenos Aires in Entre Rios.

Jews constituted the first Jewish peasantry in this hemisphere, and by most accounts mixed well with the gauchos who inhabited the region. "We learned the language of the gauchos," recalls Maximo Yagupsky, one of the first Jews born in the colonies. "And then

some of the gauchos learned our Yiddish, and even some of our songs and cooking."

Like most of the "Jewish gauchos," Yagupsky ended up in Buenos Aires. "If your aspiration is to advance, you go to the city—there you have civilization and culture," says Yagupsky. By the 1920s, almost all immigrant Jews settled in Buenos Aires. They worked as street peddlers, craftsmen, and shopkeepers, largely keeping to two large neighborhoods crossed by Avenida Corrientes.

One of these "ghettos" is **Once**, a largely commercial area between Callao and Pueyrredon. It is the garment district, with street after street lined by fabric shops that sell both wholesale and retail. Many are closed Saturdays. "Kosher" signs appear in the display windows of some meat markets, and small shops known as *rotiserías* offer Jewish pastries, breads, and smoked fish. The **Taam Tov Bakery** at Pueyrredon and Corrientes is a magnet for gourmets.

Another landmark in Once is the **Jewish Cultural Center**, known as the SHA (on Sarmiento, between Uriburu and Pasteur). One half operates as a repertory cinema, the "Cinemateca" where both avant garde and classic films are shown in the evenings. Alongside is a cultural center with a library and cozy theater.

Several blocks over from the SHA, at Pasteur 633, is the headquarters of **DAIA**, an umbrella organization for the many Jewish associations in the country. Part of the center operates as a school where Hebrew and Yiddish are taught.

The other major Jewish neighborhood is **Villa Crespo**, along Corrientes between Estado de Israel and Dorrego. It is mostly residential, although there too, tasty Jewish food can be found. **Dorin** (Corrientes 5542) is reputed to have the best bagels and challah bread in town (this claim is disputed by the patrons of **Berny's** at Pueyrredon and Las Heras, a New York-style deli featuring machine-made bagels).

expected to live at home until marriage. High costs for setting up a new abode partially account for the reluctance to cut the umbilical cord, but perhaps more decisive is the unpleasant fact that in Buenos Aires, leaving the nest "early" (that is, unmarried) still raises scandalous questions about filial loyalty.

Ninety percent of *porteños* consider themselves Roman Catholics, and the president of Argentina is still required to be a member of the church. Yet if you look inside any one of the city's many churches on a Sunday morning, you will find plenty of available seats. Older people, and especially older

growth and fulfillment. Many hold down several jobs simultaneously, racing from one to the next in six-hour shifts. Paychecks normally come only once a month—if the streets seem less crowded than usual, it's probably been a spell since the last pay day.

It is leisure, not labor, that defines the *porteño:* where he takes his vacation, how he spends his weekends, which movies he's seen. Well-established amusements are the rule. *Porteños* crowd like lemmings to the Atlantic beaches during summertime, battle each other in ticket lines for the symphony, and patronize restaurants that invariably offer the standard fare of beef and pasta.

women, seem to comprise the bulk of parishioners. The rest of the population is Catholic when it's time to get married or buried.

Buenos Aires is regarded throughout Argentina as a frenzied city where people have forgotten the art of relaxing. Yet for all their activity, work remains a sore subject with most *porteños*. Surveys show that people tend to regard employment more as a means of survival than a source of personal

Left, deli owner poses with fresh challah and bagels. Above, mother and daughter enjoy a snack in San Telmo pub.

Ethnic roots: For all their cultural homogeneity, *porteños* are a people with diverse ethnic origins. As Argentina's principal port, Buenos Aires was always the first stop for waves of European immigrants, many of whom went no farther. First came Spaniards, later Britons and Italians, then Eastern European Jews, Arabs, Irish, Welsh, and Germans. The most recent arrivals are Koreans and Argentina's neighbors from Uruguay, Chile, and Paraguay. While the Spanish cultural heritage prevails, Italian influences abound. You'll remember listening to the soaring and dipping nuances of *porteño* Spanish. Buenos Aires also has the fourth largest Jewish community in the world, although its conspicuous presence is far less than its size. Virtually no blacks and few traces of Argentina's indigenous peoples remain in the city; dark complexions prevail but fair skin and light hair are also commonplace.

Notwithstanding their strong links with Europe, *porteños* are surprisingly irreverent towards the large ethnic groups from the Old World. Ethnic jokes portray Italians as humorless drudges, Spaniards as simple-minded country bumpkins, Englishmen as cunning exploiters, and Jews as culturally unadaptable. Such chauvinism is often the

product of resentment towards hard-working immigrants for their upstaging work ethic. This resentment too may account for the *porteños* admiration for what's known locally as "*viveza criolla*"—native cunning used to swindle unsuspecting outsiders. Such con-man attitudes have prevailed not only towards foreigners: as early as the 1820s an Argentine observer wrote that "the *porteño* mentality may be summed up roughly as the inner conviction that Argentina exists for Buenos Aires."

Proud city of the middle class: Latin American neighbors of Argentina take umbrage at what they regard as swaggering airs of superiority put on by *porteño* visitors. Such arrogance in Buenos Aires, however, is seldom tolerated. A table waiter may not earn much more in a month than the bill he presents at a dinner party, but he expects the guests to treat him respectfully. In a city where nearly every worker belongs to a trade union, menial jobs in general are better paid than elsewhere in Latin America. Some bus drivers even consider themselves members of the middle class, an unthinkable status for their colleagues in neighboring countries. City buses, in fact, may be one of the best places to observe the coexistence of social classes in Buenos Aires. Women wrapped in opulent furs sit primly next to factory workers clad in dungarees. It is a sight almost inconceivable in most other large Latin American cities.

This is not to say there are no class divisions in Buenos Aires. High society has survived the spread of the middle class. The slurred nasal speech of the *gente bien*, or beautiful people, can be heard at the Colón Opera House and at polo matches as well as in the city's best private schools. These are frequently members of the landed gentry, descendents of the military heroes of the wars for independence who were rewarded with giant tracts of land. Their offspring are among those who can still take fabled shopping excursions abroad and who bury their dead in the exclusive crypts of Recoleta Cemetery.

At the other end of the *porteño* economic spectrum are the slum dwellers who live in the tenements of *barrios* like San Telmo and Monserrat. Often they are recent arrivals to the city who live in former mansions that have been divided into *conventillos*. They are the table waiters, the housecleaners, and construction workers of Buenos Aires.

But this is primarily a proud city of the middle class. There is an atmosphere here of egalitarianism seldom found elsewhere in Latin America. The *porteño* relishes the city's epicurean delights as one of many rather than as part of an elite.

Left, girls having some fun while waiting for the bus in La Boca. Right, *porteño* families tend to be close-knit and affectionate.

THE BRITISH

Scattered throughout the suburbs of Buenos Aires are little pieces of England.

Cricket is a regular weekend event over summer at the Hurlingham Club—or "the Hurlo" as it is affectionately known. The gentle 'thwack' of bat on ball drifts across perfect lawns to an ivy-covered clubhouse where gin and tonics are sipped in leather armchairs. This is followed by proper English tea with jam and toast at five.

The local English-language newspaper, *The Buenos Aires Herald*, appears daily on the newsstands. During the military government, the *Herald's* firm pro-democratic stance elevated it from a community newsletter to a respected general newspaper. However, its social pages still focus on community happenings such as the dates of the bridge nights at St. Michael's, literary talks at the Pickwick Club or the St. Thomas

Tucked away in various corners of the city are various meeting spots such as the **Dickens Pub**, **John Bull Bar**, **Queen Bess** and **Fox Hunt Café** .

Argentina has always had a large and influential English-speaking community. The Anglo-Argentines carry on in their eccentric habits, although life is certainly not what it was in the past. "It's like a small Edwardian society fixed in time," says Roy Gooding, the secretary of the Hurlingham Cricket Club.

Born in Buenos Aires but educated in Britain, Gooding speaks with a strong, distinct Eton accent.

More Society's annual *asado* or barbeque.

The Anglo-Argentines gather at the summer polo, rowing regattas in Tigre and the grand Caledonian ball with Scottish dancers in full kilt and sporran. They select their books from the English language bookshops **ABC**, **Rodriguez** and **El Ateneo**.

And they take a decent pot of tea at the **Café Ideal** or the **Richmond** on Florida—where in Graham Greene's novel on Anglo-Argentines, *the Honorary Consul*, Dr. Plarr would watch his mother gorge herself on sweet cakes.

The British were established in Buenos Aires as smugglers long before Commodore

Sir Home Popham decided to capture the city during the Napoleonic Wars. Although the British soldiers were rudely expelled, London was able to take over Argentina in the 19th century with the more gentlemanly weapon of the all-powerful pound sterling. Britons owned and managed the country's entire gas, water and telephone systems. Railways were designed by British engineers, financed by British bankers, worked by British technicians and even powered by British coal.

Tens of thousands migrated to Buenos Aires to work in the banks or headed to Patagonia where they set up sheep stations. Even President Alfonsín's grandmother was English-born.

A world apart: The community today is a pale shadow of its "golden age" earlier in the century. The decline was confirmed when Perón nationalized many of the British interests at the end of World War II. Anglo-Argentines, who had numbered about 100,000 in the 1920s, fell quickly to 40,000 and are now about 17,000.

"Forty years ago you could still live in a little British world," laments Roy Gooding, "a little cocoon where you didn't even have to learn to speak Spanish. Now there's no doubt about it, the community is breaking down very rapidly and I think will soon collapse completely."

One enduring Anglo-Argentine figure has been Charlotte de Harting, who has observed the fading of Empire from a small and shadowy flat in central Buenos Aires. Now 83 years old, she reminisces cheerily about the community's heyday: sipping champagne at the races, playing tennis at the club and dancing until the wee hours of the morning at black-tie parties.

"Life was very boring then," she laughs, "but one didn't realize it was boring. I don't feel any sadness that those days have passed. We knew nothing of Argentines or the outside world—and comforted ourselves that the feeling of isolation and meaningless would pass."

More English than the English: Today some of the local St. Andrew's Scottish pipers are experts at the highland jigs but cannot speak a word of English. Even in the hallowed grounds of the Hurlingham Club, many of the younger cricketers cannot call a bat a bat.

"My children have always wondered what the hell I'm talking about," admits Gooding. "They ask: 'What is all this about Britain? Why do we have to speak English?' For them it's all a curious anachronism."

His son Alex, 23, has always spoken to his sisters in Spanish but to his father in English.

"We feel that our father's more English than the English," Alex explains in an accent that is difficult to place. "But if he went to England and saw all those funny-looking punks, he'd be a little disappointed.

While the process of time has forced the British community's integration, it was the Falklands War that sealed its fate. Many found themselves admitting that they were more Argentine than Anglo. For the 50-year-old Brian Reynolds, who holds a British passport but served in the Argentine Navy during the war, those weeks only heightened the sense of Anglo-Argentine rootlessness depicted by English novelist Grahame Greene in *The Honorary Consul*.

"I feel that I don't belong anywhere," he sighs, looking out over the yacht club he now manages. "Argentines call me *El Inglés* (the Englishman) but in England I would never be accepted as one."

Today the British, like every one else in Argentina, would rather forget the brief but bloody war.

Meanwhile, as the Anglo-Argentines continue to integrate, cricket secretary Gooding is looking forward to many a happy innings: "They play very well, the Argentines, I'm happy to say."

Left, anglophile *porteño* enjoys tea in the London City Café while brushing up on his English with the *Buenos Aires Herald*.

THE PORTEÑO—AS SEEN BY A PROVINCIAL

EDITOR'S NOTE: The writer of this article, Roberto Fontanarrosa, is the author of several collections of cartoons and short stories. His drawings appear regularly in the newspaper Clarín. He lives in Rosario.

While vacationing in a coastal town in southern Brazil, I went to the local tourist office in search of information. Among the group of people clustered around the counter, I noticed an Argentine (decked out in vacation togs, a cigarette stuck to his lower lip) with a Brazilian who evidently worked there as a guide and interpreter. Attempting to make the wait more pleasant, the Brazilian said to the tourist, "I know a bit of your country—Salta, Jujuy, and a few other places in the north. What part of Argentina are you from, sir?" "Pompeya," (a neighborhood of Buenos Aires) the *porteño* replied.

This anecdote pretty well sums up the image *porteños* have in the interior of their country. For them, the country *is* Buenos Aires. That immense, formidable city is enough; an abstract of everywhere else.

I often get the impression that the *porteño* is one type of person in Buenos Aires and another type outside. Within the city limits, he's a splendid fellow: cordial, hearty, happy to help out a passer-by. Once outside, he becomes sarcastic, biting and scornful, not above abusing his ability to push himself to the head of every queue—an ability at which one becomes daily adept while struggling to survive in a hostile city of 10 million inhabitants.

His sense of superiority is not without a certain logic. For the *porteño*, the vast majority of cities in the provinces (and in South America) are towns with squat buildings, few cars, and dark, dull nights.

Personally, I have nothing but affection and sympathy for a large number of those

Porteños feel more kinship with Parisians than they do with their compatriots in the provinces.

long-suffering inhabitants of Buenos Aires. Some of my best friends live there, especially after the flowering of so many *porteño*-provincial romances along the Ramblas in Barcelona, during the recent Argentine diaspora. Since I first began making trips into the city to visit publishers or solicit advice from established cartoonists, (now some 15 years ago), I have always been received with hospitality and warmth. This openness says something about the city's tremendous ability to incorporate foreigners from all latitudes, whether they come seeking wealth, fame, notoriety, or mere subsistence.

The typical inhabitant of Buenos Aires, who likely as not holds down two full-time jobs, leaves home at six in the morning and doesn't return until midnight. The provincial, on the other hand, goes home for lunch, takes a siesta, and invests the two hours that the *porteño* spends in the *colectivo* or behind the wheel of his car, chatting with friends in the corner café. As the mongoose is the natural enemy of the cobra, so is the siesta the natural enemy of stress. Yet to utter that word in Buenos Aires is to open oneself up to jokes about yokels. I have sometimes suggested to *porteños* that we arrange to meet "at the hour of the siesta" and have been given disconcerted, condescending looks.

And in that judgemental glance, which one cannot help but elicit, lies the power which *porteños* wield and the rest of us accept: the need for approval from the Big City.

You can write marvellously in La Rioja, act to perfection in Corrientes, or sing like an angel in La Pampa, but none of it counts until you "pass" in Buenos Aires. Perhaps that qualifying power of Buenos Aires stimulates the insecurity, respect and irritation the rest of us feel with regard to the *porteño*. That *porteño* who is indifferent to the rest of the country, for whom the city is more than sufficient. The man who lives within the confines of Capital Federal—in Pompeya, perhaps.

THE PORTEÑA

The *porteña* walks the streets of Buenos Aires with the bearing of a queen. She is followed by the glances of *porteño* males who, however hurried they might be, comment on her passing in the best Italian manner. Meticulously groomed and annointed with shampoos, creams and perfumed bath salts, she always seeks to emphasize her best physical features. She tends to follow fashion but is not enslaved by it. Chic and conservative at the same time, she usually disdains extreme styles which might make her the center of too much attention. She wears her skirts a bit shorter or longer than the prevailing whim. If brilliant colors are the mode, she'll wear a bright scarf or necklace, but will find it hard to dress in a way that announces her presence flamboyantly.

Caught halfway between a Roman Catholic past in which the Church imposed its regulations on love, sex and family, and a present greatly influenced by psychoanalysis, the *porteña* has overcome the old-fashioned prejudices of a few decades ago and lives more in the style of an American or European woman. Today, it's possible to say that the *porteña* is liberated. She is able to make her own decisions about what work she will do and how many children she will have, or even whether she wants to be a mother at all.

Guilt, sex and melancholia: Given to introspection, she reads everything she can get her hands on about the female character, about parent-child relationships, about love. Introverted and melancholic, she has a tendency to feel guilty, especially with regard to her children. If she works outside the home, she'll try to arrange a schedule which permits her to be there when her children get home from school. If she divorces the father of her children and finds another partner (until quite recently Argentine law did not permit divorced people to remarry), she will try to compensate her children for the pain she believes she has inflicted on them.

Her introspection, her demands on herself, and her propensity for melancholy often lead her to psychoanalysis. There are very few *porteñas* who have not had some experience with psychotherapy, whether it's orthodox Freudianism, Freudian-Lacanianism, or simply brief American style therapy such as Gestalt.

Her behavior with regard to men is comparable to that of most Western urban women, although many Spanish and Italian men say she is not typically Latin; that she is more direct, less wily and seductive. She may embark on a sexual adventure without the requisite long flirtation, the *paseos* and romantic dinners other Latin women expect. Although she's shy about expressing emotion, and tends not to exclaim over music or landscapes, the *porteña* is capable of saying to a man, without blushing: "I'd like to make love with you."

Generally, she has a lot of women friends. Day and night, the restaurants and cafés of Buenos Aires are full of tables of women talking about films, politics and clothes, but above all, about relationships. Using a language which is proof of her contact with psychoanalysis, the *porteña* will speak of sexual frustration, somatization, repression, etcetera.

French women, American men: The society and culture she most admires is that of France. She likes French films, literature, and the language itself. She admires the discretion and elegance of French women, their capacity for séduction. Catherine Deneuve is perhaps the *porteña's* ideal.

She is somewhat ambivalent about American women. She finds them attractive, and irresistible to men, but a bit obvious. American men, on the other hand, fascinate her. She tends to see them as efficient and capable of making decisions in difficult moments, unlike her brooding male counterparts in Buenos Aires.

Mother and daughter admire lingerie on elegant Avenida Santa Fe.

PROFILE OF ADELINA DALESIO DE VIOLA

Few Argentine women have risen to prominence in the male-monopolized world of politics. Those who made it almost always did so on the coattails of a famous father or, as with Evita and Isabel Perón, a powerful husband. But Buenos Aires city councilwoman Adelina Dalesio de Viola insists it is sheer hard work, not family connections, that has made her one of the shiniest political stars of Argentina's democratic springtime. That success has more than startled the old boys club who have always dominated Argentine politics. "Rising by my own merit has made it more difficult for me," she says, "because in a macho country, a woman who makes it in politics with the help of a man is pardoned, but not so if she rises alone."

As she talks curled up at the foot of her living room sofa, an image of De Viola's face flickers across the family television from a program taped earlier in the day. Her golden hair and cheerleader-fresh face get instant recognition throughout Buenos Aires, making her the darling of producers seeking sparkle for political talk shows. The newspapers call her "dazzling," the politicians call her bold and driven. She is matter-of-fact when asked about her political ambitions. "Next I want to be mayor of Buenos Aires, and later I want to be president."

Heady aims these may seem for a woman only recently elected to the Buenos Aires City Council, but then no other council member has ever achieved the kind of instant fame De Viola has garnered in office. In the *villas miserias* (shanty towns) around the city, mothers name their babies Adelina in gratitude for her visits and help; long lines of people come to her office daily seeking work; radio talk shows barrage her with phone calls every weekday morning. Her glamor, tenacity, and compassion for the poor all invite comparisons with another famous blonde Argentine politician. But De Viola says she is by no means another Evita Perón. "Evita was motivated by grudges. I work to restore the capitalistic-liberal theory that's been abandoned for so many years in this country," she says. "I want the poor to realize that there's somebody on the Argentine political right who cares for them."

De Viola is one of the founders of the Union of the Democratic Center, or UCD, Argentina's sole conservative party. As a university student during the early seventies, she says she was attacked verbally and physically for expounding her faith in private enterprise and was eventually barred from attending classes in the law school by Perónist militants. De Viola's political thinking developed growing up in the Buenos Aires *barrio* of San Telmo as the daughter of a prosperous family. "This typical acceptance of Argentines that things are the way they are and that's it just never washed in my household," she says. "Everything had to have a reason, an explanation, unlike the rote learning that goes on in the schools here."

Hovering around De Viola as she talks and keeping an eye on their four children is her husband, Carlos, who owns a security agency. Like a growing number of Argentine men, he is accustomed to having a wife who works outside the home. During the last military government, De Viola ran a boutique on Calle Florida featuring dresses and leather handbags she herself designed. Her youngest child, Francisco, was born 16 hours after she was elected to the city council in 1985. De Viola was on the job 20 hours later, taking Francisco along in a cradle. "This is the kind of job that can't wait for a maternity leave," she explains. Francisco has been going with her to work ever since, becoming something of an office mascot. "If we conservatives want to lift up the image of the family and the values attached to it, we can't divide our lives between our families and our work. I'm proud of my family and I take my children and husband with me whenever I can," she boasts.

Left, City Councilwoman Adelina Dalesio with two-year-old son Francisco in her San Telmo office.

PROFILE OF ERNESTO SÁBATO

The neighborhood just on the western edge of the city of Buenos Aires is definitely middle-class. It is a clean, plain, old-fashioned neighborhood in a suburb called Santos Lugares. This is where famed Argentine writer Ernesto Sábato has made his home for several decades.

Everybody in the neighborhood knows where "Don Ernesto" lives. Step up to Sábato's gate to ring the bell and you can bet that you'll be accosted by some neighbor who will ask politely, if somewhat suspiciously, if he can help you. Everyone takes good care of Sábato and his wife, Matilde.

At age 76, when he prefers to be puttering about in his library or dabbling in his painting hobby, Sábato finds himself more in the spotlight than ever before. Various times a year, one finds him tensely preparing for a trip somewhere, to receive a prize for literature or for public service.

"They start giving you prizes and medals when they think you're going to die," Sábato says drily.

While Sábato's fame worldwide is second only to that of the late Jorge Luis Borges, his recent return to the limelight is probably more a result of his concern for human rights, than of his writing. Throughout the former military regime in Argentina, Sábato was an outspoken denouncer of human rights abuses and as such the target of threats and ultra-rightist terror.

When Raúl Alfonsín was elected president in 1983, he asked Sábato to head a commission his government had formed to gather evidence of human rights abuses to be used in the trial of top military officers of the former regime.

The commission Sábato headed (CONADEP) gathered the most comprehensive information to date on the nightmare of counterterror operations from the mid to late 1970s—a period now referred to by many as "the dirty war."

The information on thousands of cases of kidnapping, torture and murder was published in a book called *Nunca Más* (Never Again), which immediately sold out four complete editions, as Argentines, anxious to break the silence of more than seven years of repressive military rule, dug into their recent, tragic history.

While the average Argentine knows Sábato as a novelist, he has written only three novels: *El Túnel* (1948), *Sobre héroes y tumbas* (1961), and *Abaddon el exterminador* (1974).

When asked about this relatively low output of literary works, Sábato smiles and replies rather offhandedly, that he is "self-destructive."

"I've burned most of what I've written," he explains.

Despite his small but painstakingly crafted output of fiction, he has also written several books of essays on man faced with the crisis of modern times. He is also the author of a number of scholarly articles published in Argentina and abroad.

Now, except for answering an occasional request from friends in magazines and other publications, Sábato has all but retired as a writer.

"My sight isn't good anymore," he complains, but then adds rather surprisingly, "so now I paint."

"My poor vision keeps me from writing, but the size of my paintings permits me to paint," he says.

He said that as a child he was torn between painting and writing but that for almost 40 years he devoted himself entirely to writing.

"If you're going to do something seriously you have to devote all of your energy to it," he says.

Sábato differs with those who insist that the writer must be a mere observer: "You can better observe the human condition by getting into the action than by sitting apathetically in a corner."

Novelist Ernesto Sábato likes to paint in his spare time.

PROFILE OF LUIS PUENZO

Luis Puenzo wasn't much more than a kid when he began his career in moviemaking. Brought up in middle-class Floresta on the West Side of Buenos Aires, Puenzo started working for an advertising filmmaker while he was still in high school. He learned the trade quickly, and by 19, was directing his own commercials.

That was back in the '60s. But it wasn't until nearly 20 years later that he made Argentine film production history by winning the Academy Award for best foreign film with his first real feature-length picture, *The Official Story*. That was when he realized that he had something to say—to Argentines and to the world.

In the midst of a brilliant career in advertising filmmaking, Puenzo tried his hand at movies for children in 1973. The resulting shots were, he says, unsatisfactory. He found them stiff and unnatural and he went to work immediately on improving his camera technique.

Shortly afterward, intrigued by several short stories written by Argentine author Antonio Di Benedetto, he decided to make a film trilogy of them which, combined, would be of feature length.

But the results of this new experiment in serious picture-making also disappointed Puenzo and made him decide to give up all attempts at feature filmmaking until he was in a position and had material to create a work of real excellence.

With this in mind, Puenzo returned to producing and directing commercials for nearly a decade, until the tragedy of the 1970s in Argentina and the apathy of the public at large changed his thinking and his life. Puenzo says that he woke up one day to find that he was living in a country "full of people who lived as if they had no idea what was going on."

To his horror, he found that he was one of those people.

"None of my four children was old enough to have been involved in politics. I was doing well in advertising. It was as if the torture and disappearances since they hadn't affected me, weren't my concern."

But he realized with sudden clarity that the horror of the 1970s in Argentina was indeed part of his life—that the phenomenon was the result not merely of a cruel regime but of a whole social attitude.

He decided then that he had to speak up. It was a risky commitment. The year was 1983 and although the military regime was on its last legs, it was still in power.

In early 1983 Puenzo got together with Argentine television and film writer Aida Bortnik. He says that the working atmosphere between him and Bortnik was excellent, but that the climate in general was tense and foreboding.

"Aida kept getting telephone threats while we were here at my house working on *The Official Story*. The threats had to do with a series she was doing for television that was critical of the regime. But the calls were coming to my house."

Witchhunt: Suddenly, Puenzo was finding himself in the thick of the witchhunt that he had long avoided, and although it added to the tension, it also added to the veracity of the filmscript.

"We were writing the story as the story was taking place," he recalls. The regime was on its way out. Denunciations were becoming more frequent and much bolder. Bodies were turning up. Clandestine detention centers were being uncovered and the children of the missing were being trailed by grandmothers and other relatives who had discovered the *modus operandi* of paramilitary kidnappers: When a victim of the regime gave birth in captivity or was with her child when kidnapped, the baby was later "adopted" by some childless friend of the regime.

This is the story told in *The Official Story*: not the story of a struggle between leftwing terrorism and rightwing counter-terror that ripped through the Argentine social fabric in the 1970s, but of the most innocent of victims of that struggle and the horrific search that followed for the orphaned children of the "missing."

"At first," says Puenzo, "I was writing the script from the point of view of the grandmother of the child."

But he found this too impassioned a view, a standpoint which would appeal only to the opponents of the military regime without being able to touch the sector of Argentine society that had little or no sympathy for the "missing" or their families.

"The lesson," says Puenzo, "is that politics is not some abstract, but the result of how each of us behave as individuals. That we are, all of us, responsible for what happens in society."

The Official Story won awards at Cannes, New York, Los Angeles, Cartagena, Toronto, Chicago, Havana and Tashkent, which testifies to the universality of the story's appeal.

"It's like in chess, says Puenzo. "When I can't see my next move from where I'm sitting, I get up and walk around the chessboard. Sometimes seeing it from another angle helps me plan what to do next."

The final script turned out by Puenzo and Bortnik told the story from the point of view of a woman who learns the terrible secret that the child she has illegally adopted is the daughter of a missing person.

Luis Puenzo, Oscar-winning director of *The Official Story*.

Puenzo, 41, has ambitious plans for the future. Currently he is working on a filmscript for a movie version of Mexican author Carlos Fuentes' novel *The Old Gringo*, a fictional account of the last days of American writer Ambrose Bierce. He will direct the picture which is to star Jane Fonda. He also has two other major film projects in the works.

What they all have in common is the theme which Puenzo made part of his life with the creation of *The Official Story*: human dignity and the important role the individual plays in the shaping of a political society.

PROFILE OF QUINO

His birth certificate reads Martin Lavado, but everyone knows him as Quino. Beloved in Europe and Latin America, he is Argentina's major exporter of humor. His best-known creation is Mafalda, a precocious little girl who asks unsettling questions. Small and slight, with a faint smile always hovering about his lips, Quino has the distracted air of someone who doesn't like what he sees around him and has turned

fore, it dealt more with ordinary daily life.

Q: Which country's humor attracts you the most?

A: I always laugh a lot in Spain. I once saw a man on a street in Madrid tearing down a wall with his hands. He wasn't using any tools! A friend of mine got into a taxi over there and said to the driver, "Quick, take me to the airport." The driver didn't move. A long time passed before he turned around

inward. He could easily be one of his own cartoon characters: he looks like an overly wise child.

Q: A French writer who dedicated 44 years of his career to writing about humor finally wrote a book called, *Why Can't We Define Humor*? What do you thin humor is?

A: I'd quote another humorist, Mordillo, who said, "Humor is the gentle side of fear."

Q: Do you think that humor changes over time?

A: Yes, humor has changed, but don't ask me why, because I don't know. All I know is that it's evolved. Graphic humor, for example, is almost always political now. Be-

and said, "You don't look like someone who's going to the airport."

Q: Your humor seems to be pretty universal. Your books are sold everywhere in the world.

A: Not in the two biggest parts of the world—Asia and Africa. My humor sells well in Latin America and Europe. In North America too, but not quite so well.

Q: Is it difficult to be funny on deadline?

A: Yes, sometimes I dream that I'm drawing pages and pages. In my dream everything is lovely, but when I wake up I see it's not so lovely. On the other hand, when I'm asleep, I'm suddenly attacked by an idea. I turn on the light and write it down. I can't understand it when people say you can learn mechanisms for coming up with ideas.

Q: What would you compare cartooning to?

A: I feel as though it might be like directing a film. For example, in one drawing of a wedding in a laboratory I spent two days wondering from what angle to draw the scene.

Today they're usually slim, and they might wear jeans and running shoes.

Q: Let's get back to the question of what makes people laugh.

A: Well, I roar with laughter at the Bible. There are so many comic things. There are two angels whom God sends to Sodom to see if the rumors about the place are true. The Sodomites see the angels and begin to chase them. So the angels go to Lot's house for

Q: Where to put the camera...to an outsider, those difficulties are unimaginable.

A: Not only those. There are others. For example, how do you draw a safe these days? Now they don't have dials and those big handles. And a millionaire? How do you draw one?

Q: With a big belly, a cigar and a gold chain across his vest.

A: Where are there millionaires like that?

Left, cartoonist Quino at home. Above, a recent drawing.

protection. Lot comes out in despair and says to the pursuing Sodomites, "Cool it, I have a 16-year-old daughter who's a virgin. You can have her." But the Sodomites don't want the 16-year-old virgin. "We want the angels," they say. I think that's pretty funny.

Q: When did you first discover your vocation as a cartoonist?

When I was little and my parents went to the movies, my uncle (who I lived with after my parents died) came to babysit us and he'd entertain us by drawing. For me, it was like a musician laying his hands on a piano for the first time: a revelation. So I began to bug everybody about becoming a cartoonist.

PROFILE OF MARÍA ELENA WALSH

María Elena Walsh is one of Argentina's most beloved poets. Thousands of adults in Argentina remember singing along to the children's poetry she set to music—poetry that captured a child's sensibility with subtlety and humor. Now in her sixties, her outspokenness on feminism and human rights have put her more in the limelight than ever.

She doesn't like interviews. Before we begin, she asks, with a child's impatience, how long it's going to last. Later, she keeps asking if it's almost over. When the interview ends, everything changes. She smiles and her gruffness evaporates. But at the first question that sounds like an interview question, the other person returned.

Q: What made you come to see so early and so clearly the way society differentiates between men and women?

A: *The Second Sex*, by Simone de Beauvoir, confirmed something I already knew. I was already aware of the difference.

Q: Did you change your conduct after reading that book?

A: I was a rebel before reading it. It confirmed that my rebellion was justified.

Q: What did you rebel against?

A: It's all in my book ... I rebelled against my father, who like all fathers of that time tried to impose an established and acceptable role on me. I had poet friends. Poets were not considered serious or acceptable.

Q: Your parents had typical middle class attitudes?

A: Not exactly. They were quite open-minded and cultured for middle class people. They were people of humble origins who enjoyed a comfortable position economically, and who hadn't become collectors of objects.

Q: Do you think there is such a thing as feminist literature?

A: I believe so. In general, women have a very different view of the world than men. I'm thinking of Virginia Woolf, Simone de Beauvoir, Doris Lessing. A woman's view of the world is very particular. Gentle, pained. Women see details, complexities, things that most men don't notice or pay any attention to.

Q: What roles do love and work play in your life?

A: They are the two pillars of my life. And although it sounds affected, my work is based on love.

Q: Ingmar Bergman once said that "all works of art involve not only political action but ethics." I believe this is especially true in your case.

A: I don't like the word ethics. It is used by the least ethical people in the world. Think of the military, how they talk about equality, democracy, and ethics too.

Q: In your work there is always a position taken towards various types of conduct. What could we call this besides ethics?

A: Humanism.

Q: What do you try to do when you write?

A: I try to make people happy. Perhaps I often don't achieve it, but it's what I always hope and aim for.

Q: A deliberate and conscious attempt?

A: No, not deliberate or conscious. But after I write this or that, I discover that the desire to give happiness is always present.

Q: Could you say that in your work there are ideas and images that always emerge? The artist is always trying to say just one thing, make one point.

A: I agree. But don't ask me what it is in my case, because I don't know.

Q: At no point during this interview did I feel that you were comfortable or relaxed. Why?

A: Your questions make me think of the psychoanalyst, or of the police. It's over now, right?

Q: Yes.

A: Ah, how wonderful. Would you like a cup of tea? A piece of cake? I have some delicious cake.

Poet, singer, feminist and activist María Elena Walsh.

Profile Of Celeste And Sandra

Folk singer Sandra Mihanovich and rock singer Celeste Carballo have brought their acts together. The two young Argentine stars have quite a few things in common: long wavy hair, casual clothes, and even a similar vocabulary.

Sandra's charm lies in her mystery; in her self-contained and often distant manner. Celeste's charm is quite the opposite. She seeks out other people like a matador going

suerte que viniste (How Lucky That You Got Here), a song I wrote for my father, I sang like any other, without the personal touch the song needed.

Q: What, specifically, did Sandra teach you?

C: Watching her day after day I understood how she made each song into a story. How she aroused the audience and tried to reach them.

after a bull. Both women are, above all, seductresses.

Q: In what sense has this collaboration enriched both of you?

CELESTE: Sandra is a great performer. Through Sandra I've become aware of what it means to be a performer. I'd never paid much attention to that before. My career was always one of a composer.

Q: You saw what it meant to be a performer?

C: Yes; I used to sing my songs as if they were all part of a great whole. Listening to Sandra I understood that each song is a unit, different from any other. For example, *Que*

SANDRA: I think Celeste's contribution to me was information. I'd always lived a bit in isolation. Celeste brought me closer to the Argentine music of today and made me lose my fear.

Q: In that sense this unit is very positive.

S: Yes, although we are very opposite, up on stage we're complementary. Celeste, for example, has rhythm that I lack.

Q: Are you referring to an internal tempo?

S: Yes, and also to the rhythms when she sings. I think that's what she brings to the act, while I contribute a certain calm and serenity that she lacks. I think it's important that we're the same age. We both come from the generation born in the late 1950s.

Q: Why do you think drugs and rock and roll are so frequently related?

C: I don't think the relationship is more frequent than in other circles; what happens is that other groups try not to appear tied to drugs, while the rock movement has never hidden the things that plague it.

Q: Sure, in the tango world there were often drugs; not just alcohol as we tend to believe.

C: With tango, there were, are, and will be drugs. The same goes for politics. Nevertheless, people don't realize it. Rock was an explosion of frankness among young people.

Q: A gesture which led people to accept themselves as they were.

C: Sure. Anyway, drugs are not part of my world. I got into rock because of my generation, because I liked listening to it. But I was never in rock groups. When I started in 1980, '81, people thought I was on drugs.

Q: Why?

C: Because of the way I sang and moved. I was considered the Argentine Janis Joplin. Nevertheless, I didn't have anything to do with drugs.

Q: How would you characterize the world of your generation?

C: I think young people of our generation were attacked on all sides. In the mid-seventies I was in high school.

Q: When the dictatorship began?

C: Yes. And the dictatorship set out to squash all youthful rebellion, both directly and subliminally.

Q: Do you think young people were broken by the dictatorship?

C: That was the intention, but the consequences were the opposite; sometimes repression brings about greater rebellion.

Q: What part did rock play in all this?

C: For many of us it was a sort of salvation.

Left, folk singer Sandra Mihanovich and her rock-and-roll partner Celeste Carballo.

We couldn't read the books or see the films we wanted to. We were left with (Argentine rock singer) Charly Garcia's rock, whose lyrics nobody understood except us.

Q: In that way you didn't suffer censorship. Sandra, what do you think of your generation?

S: I think it's a very repressed generation, although it's hard for me to see myself as part of a generation since I'm very solitary. I think fear made a big mark on us in the seventies. We grew up with fear.

Q: Who were your musical influences?

C: In my case I'd mention folk music along the lines of Joan Baez and Bob Dylan. Also Joni Mitchell, Rickie Lee Jones, and, above all, the Rolling Stones. Even now for me Mick Jagger and the Rolling Stones are like parents, godparents.

Q: More than the Beatles?

C: Yes, much more. The Stones shake me up. They are true rockers to the core; authentic, without makeup.

S: In my case I'd have to mention my father's family. They had a basement where all the great jazz musicians who came to Buenos Aires got together. After they left the theater they'd play at our house until dawn. Later I was influenced by American musical comedies. I went to the U.S. when I was 14 and I saw everything that was playing, and I bought all the records.

Q: What was playing then?

S: *Promises, Promises, Applause*, and another with Danny Kaye and one with Barbra Streisand, who was my idol from that moment on. Later when I began to sing and realized people didn't get it, I began to be interested in local musicians.

Q: What do you think is the basis of your popularity?

C: People feel we represent them. Not only by what we sing and what we wear, but what we say in interviews.

S: I agree with Celeste and would add that perhaps the most important thing is that we're for real. We don't put on an act to be popular.

PROFILE OF RAÚL ALFONSÍN

Having a conversation with the President of the Argentine Republic, Dr. Raúl Alfonsín, is not an easy matter. You need a good deal of patience and plenty of free time in which to run after his friends, family and secretaries. And when the interview is granted, you generally have to share it with urgent phone calls, papers that need to be read and perhaps signed, and some other journalist—usually foreign—who has not merely caught a taxi but who has just flown thousands of miles.

Q: Do you have nerves of steel?

A: Steel? I don't know if they're made of steel.

Q: At least they are very steady. I don't know about inside. But outside, you are the image of composure.

A: I'm not an impetuous man.

Q: I don't mean that. I mean that one always has the sensation that you are in control of yourself. In control of time.

A: I'm in control of myself. Not of time, unfortunately.

Q: Do you ever lose your composure?

A: No. Don't think I'm vain, but I believe this has to do with the fact that I respect people.

Q: Even your opponents?

A: Yes. I rarely explode. When I do, I say what I have to say slowly, bit by bit.

Q: Tell me about your childhood. Your earliest memory.

A: An employee of my father's put me on a horse. Somehow I slipped off. I remember my mother being frightened and running towards me. I was laughing because I thought the fall was meant to be part of the fun.

Q: You were born in 1927. When the Spanish Civil War broke out, you were a child. Do you remember how your family reacted to the war? Which sides they took?

A: They were Republicans. And well... so was I. Later, as an adolescent, I went to the Liceo Militar (military academy). There, almost everyone was on the side of the Nazis. Of course, I was on the side of the Allies.

Q: Having gone to a military secondary school didn't make you want to join the army?

A: Never. My decision was between philosophy and law. I chose law because it seemed like a better way to earn a living.

Q: Have you ever thought about why you were elected, why people chose you to be the President?

A: I believe there is one fundamental thing: I don't lie in order to improve my image. I am what I am and that's it. Why are you making me talk about myself? I don't like it.

Q: Unfortunately, I can't oblige you. Do you usually listen to the people around you? Do you ask for opinions?

A: Constantly. I like to play the devil's advocate with my own ideas. I argue with myself and usually laugh at myself.

Q: In other words you aren't a fanatic. What men of the 20th century do you most admire?

A: In Argentina, Irigoyan. (Radical party President elected in 1912 and overthrown by the military in 1930.) Outside Argentina, I admire Franklin Roosevelt. I believe he fundamentally renewed the United States. He took office when the country was in a situation very similar to what we are experiencing in Argentina today.

Q: In the middle of a depression.

A: Yes. He had great empathy, imagination, and original ideas. He got things done.

Q: How did you feel when you were elected? Were you afraid?

A: No, I wasn't afraid, but I didn't have a great feeling of success. Nor of euphoria. The responsibility was too great.

Q: What would you like future generations to say about you?

A: He was honest. He had courage.

Argentine President Raúl Alfonsín has overseen the country's transition from dictatorship to democracy.

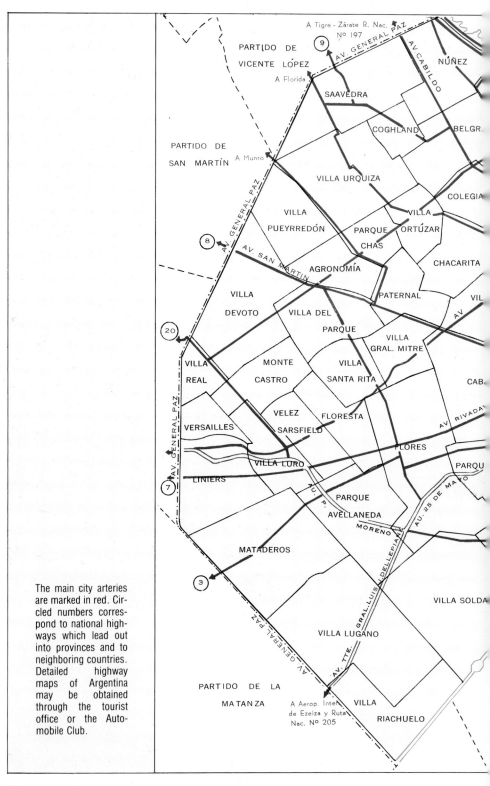

The main city arteries are marked in red. Circled numbers correspond to national highways which lead out into provinces and to neighboring countries. Detailed highway maps of Argentina may be obtained through the tourist office or the Automobile Club.

BUENOS AIRES: CAPITAL FEDERAL

THE CAPITAL

About a third of the nine million inhabitants of Greater Buenos Aires live in the district known as **Capital Federal**, whose borders are **General Paz Avenue** and the Rio de la Plata, or River Plate. The avenue border might strike some observers as imaginary, since blocks of tidy residential streets stretch for miles on both sides of General Paz. But for *porteños*, the symbolic demarcation is crucial, for it separates the sophisticated urbanites from the less privileged provincials.

Within the confines of General Paz, the city is a cluster of *barrios*, each one with its own strong loyalties and sense of identity. The *barrio* originally grew up as a parish, centered around the neighborhood church and the Spanish-style plaza which were the two poles of the community. Urban growth melded the *barrios* together but the divisions remain: celebrated in poetry and tango lyrics, reinforced by neighborhood football teams, political affiliations, ethnicity and tradition.

For most visitors, the easternmost sections of the city along the riverbank will be the center of attraction. Hotels, museums, government buildings, shopping and entertainments are generally located in Recoleta. Retiro, San Nicolás, Monserrat, San Telmo and Boca.

As for the outlying areas, the most interesting are: **Villa Crespo**, a traditional Jewish neighborhood and a center of wonderful delicatessens; **Chacarita**, a location of the world's largest urban cemetery (it's considered to be a less elegant eternal address than Recoleta Cemetery, but it contains the tombs of General Perón and tango crooner Carlos Gardel); and **Flores**, a cosy neighborhood of old-fashioned colonial houses traversed by a colorful tramway on Sunday afternoons.

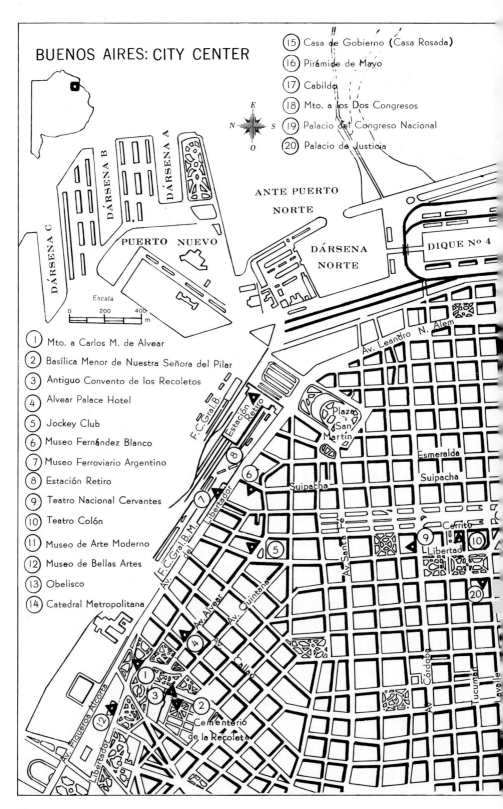

BUENOS AIRES: CITY CENTER

1. Mto. a Carlos M. de Alvear
2. Basílica Menor de Nuestra Señora del Pilar
3. Antiguo Convento de los Recoletos
4. Alvear Palace Hotel
5. Jockey Club
6. Museo Fernández Blanco
7. Museo Ferroviario Argentino
8. Estación Retiro
9. Teatro Nacional Cervantes
10. Teatro Colón
11. Museo de Arte Moderno
12. Museo de Bellas Artes
13. Obelisco
14. Catedral Metropolitana

15. Casa de Gobierno (Casa Rosada)
16. Pirámide de Mayo
17. Cabildo
18. Mto. a los Dos Congresos
19. Palacio del Congreso Nacional
20. Palacio de Justicia

ANTE PUERTO NORTE

DÁRSENA B

DÁRSENA A

DÁRSENA C

PUERTO NUEVO

DÁRSENA NORTE

DIQUE Nº 4

Escala
0   200   400
m

Plaza San Martín

Av. Leandro N. Alem

Esmeralda

Suipacha
Suipacha

Cerrito
L. Libertad

F.C. Gral. B. M.

Estación Retiro

Libertador

Av. del Libertador

Av. Alvear

Av. Quintana

Av. Santa Fe

Figueroa Alcorta

Libertador

Córdoba

Tucumán

Lavalle

Calle

Cementerio de la Recoleta

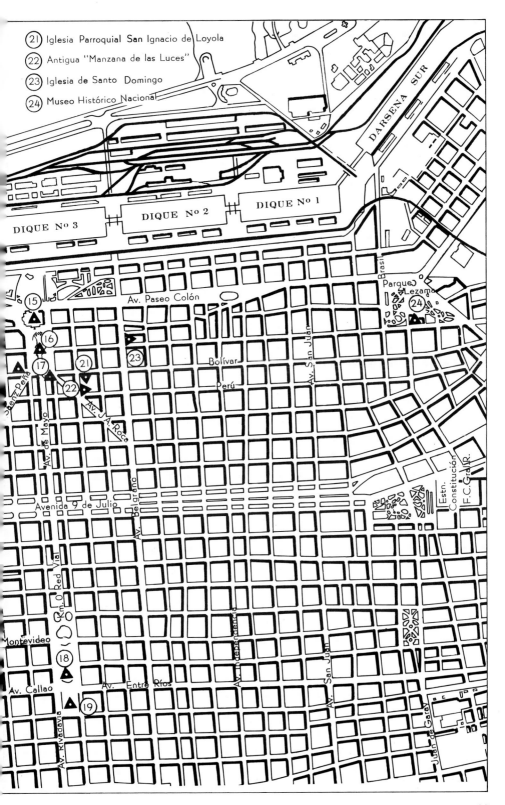

21 Iglesia Parroquial San Ignacio de Loyola
22 Antigua "Manzana de las Luces"
23 Iglesia de Santo Domingo
24 Museo Histórico Nacional

95

A WALKING TOUR TO
BUENOS AIRES

*Buenos Aires was a wonderful city for walking, and while I was
walking I decided it would be a pleasant city to live in.*
 —Paul Theroux, *The Old Patagonian Express*

In addition to her nostalgic, Old-World beauty, there are two
fundamental reasons why Buenos Aires is so inviting to those who
enjoy exploring on foot. First, it's a city which evolved as a cluster
of almost self-contained villages, each with its own particular airs
and ambience. And it's a place where the walk or *paseo* is woven
into the fabric of everyday existence. Strolling through a particular
quarter will give visitors more than a glimpse of *barrio* life.

This section of the book is divided according to neighborhoods.
Each *barrio*'s main interests are highlighted: these include not only
museums and monuments but the no less venerable shrines of
pastries, wine and pasta.

The first stop is the **city center**, the hub of hotels, steak houses and
foreign exchange. The Casa Rosada (Government House) is the
area's heart; nearby are the Congress Building, the Colón Opera
House, and some of Buenos Aires' stateliest coffee houses, cinemas
and bookstores, many of which are open all night.

The *barrio* of **San Telmo** is the city's Soho, a charming quarter
where old architecture serves as a backdrop to postmodern art and
attitudes. It's a neighborhood of cobbled streets and crumbling
villas, of tango and jazz clubs and "underground" theater.

La Boca is the old port area, settled by Italian dock workers at the
turn of the century, renowned for its pizza parlors and flashy
cantinas. The corrugated tin houses painted in bright primary colors
give the neighborhood a carnival atmosphere, but it's a residential
neighborhood still strongly influenced by its Italian heritage.

In glittering contrast is **Barrio Norte**, an elegant neighborhood
built around a cemetery. This *barrio* of Parisian-style houses,
boutiques and continental restaurants was built at the height of
Argentina's Gilded Age, and retains a good measure of its aristo-
cratic grandeur. Adjacent is **Palermo** the home of Italiante villas,
parks, a turn-of-the-century racetrack and a world-class polo field.

The **Costanera** is the river coastline at the edge of the city. It's too
long to walk the entire route; a pleasant way to see it is to spend a
late morning strolling on the old-fashioned promenades, then taking
a taxi to one of the riverside restaurants for lunch.

Suggested day or weekend trips from Buenos Aires include an
excursion out to the villages and ranches of the **pampas**, to the river
delta at **Tigre**, or to neighboring **Uruguay** by river ferry.

**Preceding pages: the bright lights of Avenida Corrientes, the
Broadway of Buenos Aires; map of the Capital Federal; map of the
City Center.**

CITY CENTER

Inside every *porteño's* head is a picture of Buenos Aires which resembles the famous *New Yorker* drawing of Manhattan. Looming large in the foreground is his *barrio*, his favorite *café* and the 24-hour *kiosko* (sweet shop) nearest his front door. On the horizon is **Avenida General Paz,** the city limit, beyond which are endless pampas and foreign countries. In the middle distance is **El Centro**, the city center, where he spends a large amount of his spare time.

Buenos Aires is a city of fervent neighborhood loyalties, but the center belongs to everyone. No matter what the *porteño*'s political persuasion or economic situation, there are certain landmarks—the bright pink **Government House,** the gilded and crumbling **Café Molino,** the closet-sized bookstores on Corrientes—which he loves passionately. Never try to tell a *porteño* who is showing you around downtown that the landmarks do not belong to him personally, or that there are other citizens of Buenos Aires who love them equally. He will only smile at you in disbelief. He is not just pointing out buildings, he is telling you his version of the city's history, which is as vivid and as intimate as a wonderful, recurring dream.

The following walking-tour encompasses four important aspects of life in the city center: politics, entertainment, cafés and shopping. Begin at the Plaza de Mayo, follow Avenida de Mayo to the Plaza de los dos Congresos, then double back down Corrientes and Lavalle to Florida, the main shopping promenade. The walk takes about two hours, but you should allow a bit more time for coffee and pastry in one of the old *confiterias* along the way. This tour also takes advantage of the flow of traffic. So if need be, you can take a taxi or *colectivo* up Avenida de Mayo and then back down Corrientes to Florida.

The Plaza de Mayo: Buenos Aires began with the Plaza de Mayo. Today it's a strikingly beautiful plaza with its tall palm trees, elaborate flower gardens and central monument, set off by the surrounding colonial buildings. The plaza has been and continues to be the pulsating center of the country. Since its founding in 1580 as the *Plaza del Fuerte* (fortress) many of the most important historical events have had physical manifestations here.

The most eye-catching structure in the plaza is unquestionably the **Casa Rosada** (Pink House), the seat of the executive branch of the government. Flanking it are the Bank of the Argentine Nation, the Metropolitan Cathedral, the City Council and the **Cabildo** (Town Council).

Pink House: The Casa Rosada was originally a fortress overlooking what is now the **Plaza Colón,** but was at that time the river's edge. When the Indian attacks subsided, the plaza became

Plaza del Mercado, a marketplace and social center. The name and role of the plaza changed again with the British invasions of 1806 and 1807, when it became the Plaza de la Victoria. Finally, following the declaration of independence, the plaza assumed its present name, in honor of the month of May, for it was in May 1810 when the city broke away from Spain and became an independent democracy.

The date also marks the first mass rally in the plaza, when crowds gathered to celebrate independence. Subsequently, Argentines have poured into the plaza to protest and celebrate most of the nation's important events. Political parties, governments (de facto and constitutional), and even trade unions and the Church, use the plaza to make addresses or appeals to the people, and to gather support for their various causes.

Salient events in the history of **Plaza de Mayo** include the 1945 workers' demonstration organized by Eva Perón to protest her husband's brief detention. Ten years later, the airforce bombed the plaza while thousands of Perón's supporters were rallying to defend his administration from the impending military coup. In 1982, Argentines flooded the plaza to applaud General Galtieri's invasion of the Malvinas/Falkland Islands. A few months later, they were back, this time threatening to kill the military ruler for having lied to the country about the possibilities of winning the war with the British. More recently, on Easter Sunday, 1987, the population responded to President Alfonsín's call to defend democracy with a turn-out of more than 300,000.

The mothers' vigil: But the most famous rallies have been those of the Mothers of Plaza de Mayo, whose Thursday afternoon protests, demanding information on the whereabouts of their "disappeared" children, and punishment of those responsible for the kidnappings, still go on today. Their presence in the plaza is perhaps the best

Demonstrators gather outside Casa Rosada.

illustration of the symbolism of rallying here. During the last years of the military regime, young people accompanying the mothers would chant at the menacing army and anti-demonstration units: "Cowards, this plaza belongs to the mothers..."

Leaders traditionally address the masses from the balconies of the Casa Rosada. This building was constructed on the foundations of earlier structures in 1894. Sixteen years earlier, President Sarmiento had chosen the site for the new Government House. There are several versions of why he had it painted pink, the most credible of which is that it was the only alternative to white in those days. The special tone was achieved by mixing beef fat, blood and lime. Some insist that Sarmiento chose pink to distinguish the building from the U.S. White House. Still others say that pink was selected as a compromise between two feuding parties whose colors were white and red.

The Grenadiers Regiment guards the Casa Rosada and the President. This elite army unit was created during the independence wars by General San Martin. They wear the same blue and red uniforms that distinguished them during those times. At sunset each day these soldiers lower the national flag in front of the Government House. On National Holidays the Grenadiers often parade on horseback. They also accompany the President during his public appearances.

The other major historic building in the Plaza de Mayo is the Cabildo (Town Hall), located at the western end of the plaza. This is perhaps Argentine patriots' greatest attraction. School children are brought here from various parts of Argentina to hear the story of how their forefathers planned the nation's independence in the Cabildo.

The Town Council has been at this site since the city's founding in 1580, although the present building was constructed only in 1751. Originally, it spanned the plaza with five great arch-

ontime anging of guards the government use.

ways on each side. In 1880, when Avenida de Mayo was built, part of the building was demolished. Again, in 1932, the Cabildo was further reduced to its current size with two archways on either side of the central balconies.

The Cabildo also has an historic museum, exhibiting furniture and relics from the colonial period. The city government runs an outdoor theater in the interior patio in some seasons.

Across Hipolito Iriqoyen, to the south, is the **Consejo Municipal**, (City Council) an ornamental old building known for its enormous pentagon-shaped clock on the tower.

The cathedral: The **Metropolitan Cathedral** is the next historic building on the plaza. The seat of Buenos Aires' Archbishop, it lies at the northwest corner of the plaza. The cathedral's presence in this highly political plaza is appropriate. The Catholic Church has always been a pillar of Argentine society, and since the city's founding, the church has shared the Plaza de Mayo. A mural at the northern end of Avenida 9 de Julio illustrates the founding of the city, with a spade representing the military, and a priest representing the church.

The cathedral, built over the course of several decades, was completed in 1827. It was built, like the Cabildo and the Casa Rosada, upon the foundations of earlier versions. There are 12 severe neoclassical pillars in the front of the cathedral that are said to represent the 12 apostles. The carving above portrays the meeting of Joseph and his father Jacob. This section is considered to be the work of the cathedral architects, yet legend persists that it was created by a prisoner, who was then set free as a result of his beautiful carving.

Inside are some important artworks, including oil paintings attributed to Rubens and beautiful wood engravings by the Portuguese Manuel de Coyte.

For Argentines, the most important aspect of the cathedral is the tomb of General Jose de San Martin, liberator of

Left, on the steps of the Cathedral on Flag Day; right the tomb of General San Martin, father of Argentine independence.

Argentina, Chile, Peru, Bolivia and Uruguay. San Martin, who died during his self-imposed exile in England, is one of just a handful of national heroes revered by Argentines of all political persuasions. Remains of two of his military friends, Generals las Heras and Guido, as well as those of an "unknown soldier" who died during the struggle for independence are also kept in the cathedral.

At the north eastern corner of Plaza de Mayo is the **Banco de la Nación Argentina** (National Bank of the Argentine Nation). The old Colón Theater was on this site before it reopened on Lavalle Plaza in 1908. The imposing marble and stone bank was inaugurated in 1888. On the first floor, there is a marvelous fountain called "The Athletes" sculpted by the Uruguayan Zorrilla de San Martin.

The Plaza de Mayo has a central pyramid that was constructed on the first centennial of the anniversary of the city's independence. It serves as the centerpiece for the Mothers of Plaza de Mayo's weekly rounds.

A Spanish avenue: The view from Plaza de Mayo down Avenida de Mayo to the National Congress is spectacular, and the fifteen block walk is a wonderful introduction to the city. The avenue was inaugurated in 1894 as the link between the Executive Branch and the Congress, most of which had been completed by 1906. It was originally designed like a Spanish avenue, with wide sidewalks, gilded lamp posts, chocolate and *churro* shops, and zarzuela theaters. Today, however, there is a superpositioning of influences and style. No art terms adequately describe the special combination of influences seen here. Nor is there a traditional pattern or coherence from one building to the next; ornate buildings stand side by side with simple and austere ones.

There are several well-known restaurants along the way. One of the oldest is **Pedemonte**, which dates back to the

uminated untain on leve de lio.

turn of the century. This is a favorite lunch spot for government functionaries and politicians.

Farther down is the **Café Tortoni**, an historic meeting place for writers and intellectuals. Apart from the famous customers said to have frequented the café, the ornamental interior makes the place worthy of a leisurely coffee-stop. Marble tables, red leather chairs, bronze statues and elaborate mirrors create an almost regal atmosphere. A jazz band plays in a back room at night.

Traditional Spanish restaurants are also a feature of **Avenida de Mayo**. At the 1200 block, on the left, is **El Globo** best known for its *paella valenciana* and *puchero* (boiled stew). There are similar restaurants one block to the right towards Rivadavia.

World's widest avenue: You could not have missed Avenida 9 de Julio at the 1000 block, which at 140 meters, is what the Argentines claim to be the world's widest avenue. Everything about it is big—big billboards, big buildings, looming *palo borracho* (drunken trees) laden with pink blossoms in summertime, and, of course, the big **Obelisk**.

The military government of 1936 demolished rows of beautiful old French-style mansions in order to build this street. Much of that central block is now occupied by parking lots. The only mansion to survive was the French Embassy; its occupants refused to move, claiming it was foreign territory. A barren white wall facing the center of town, testifies to the disappearance of its neighbors.

Obelisk jokes: The Obelisk, which marks the intersection of **Diagonal Norte Corrientes**, and 9 de Julio, was built in 1936 in commemoration of the 400th anniversary of the first founding of the city. Because of its phallic appearance, it became the subject of much public joking. Three years after its creation, the City Council voted 23 to three to tear it down. But apparently even this decision was not taken seri-

Inside the venerable Café Tortoni.

ON THE TELEPHONE

"Am I glad you called me, because I've been trying to call you all week!"

That's an excuse that one hears a lot in the city of Buenos Aires. Sometimes it is a white lie used by a *porteño* when in fact he has forgotten to call altogether or never had the intention of doing so in the first place. But quite often it is true. And even if it isn't true, it doesn't matter because it is, after all, a totally credible excuse for not making contact.

Exasperated business people sometimes refer to the city of Buenos Aires as being *incommunicado*. It is not quite that bad, but telephone service in Buenos Aires is notoriously deficient.

Service in the downtown area was improved somewhat in the 1970s to handle the heavy traffic resulting from the 1978 World Cup Soccer Championship, which Argentina hosted that year. And home telephone services are being very slowly bettered under a system called Megatel by which those interested in having a phone, participate in the financing of line installment. But no matter how you look at it, extensive use of the telephone in Buenos Aires can be a truly nerve-jangling experience.

Lines are often "fuzzy" and full of interference so that if you have to make several calls in a row, you might end up hoarse from shouting into the receiver.

Phones are also scarce. Although most offices in the downtown area have at least one line and many have several, someone opening a new office may have to pay an exorbitant fee (as much as $10,000 to $15,000) to get a line installed in a relatively short time— sometimes through illicit means.

The Megatel system can mean waiting several years to get a phone for a private home. But at least it is a slight improvement on the old system—there were horror stories of people who had been renewing their request for a phone every year for 30 or 40 years with no

luck. That's why real estate ads in the major dailies advertise the telephone (beautiful brand new luxury flat, with phone!) as a major sales attraction.

To make a call from a payphone, you will need to buy tokens, called *cospeles*, which are usually available at *kioscos*. During peak hours (8 a.m. to 8 p.m.) a *cospel* will last you two minutes. At other times it will last six minutes.

Long distance calls are subject to international rates, and can be made either from Entel offices or from hotels which have IDD (International Direct Dial) service.

Don't try to place an overseas call on a private phone unless it is equipped with IDD. Trying to get an international operator can literally take days, although they are quite helpful once you have them on the line. If you are visiting Buenos Aires on business, you may want to choose a hotel which offers IDD, although hotels do place stiff surcharges on international calls.

phones
ern but
n don't
k.

ously, for the Obelisk is still standing.

Like Obelisks, statues by Auguste Rodin seem to lend a centain air of solidity to the cities of the world. Visitors will be reassured by the familiar sight of "The Thinker," who in Buenos Aires furrows his brow in **Plaza Lorca**, two blocks before Congress at the end of Avenida de Mayo.

The next block is **Plaza de los dos Congresos** (Plaza of Two Congresses). The plaza is a wonderful place to watch people on warm summer evenings. Old and young eat pizza and ice cream on the benches, feeding the pigeons and enjoying the civilized atmosphere. There is a dramatic fountain with sculpted galloping horses and cherubs and, at night, classical music booms out from below the falls. There is a monument above the fountain that honors "two congresses"—the 1813 assembly that abolished slavery, and the 1816 congress that declared the country's independence.

The Congressional building houses the Senate, on the south side, and the House of Representatives on the north (Rivadavia entrance). Congressional sessions are open to those with press credentials or a pass provided by a member. The interior is decorated with appropriate pomp: important paintings, bronze and marble sculptures, luxurious red carpets, silk curtains and wood paneling.

Across the street is a new wing of the House of Representatives. Construction began in 1973, but halted with the military coup of 1976. With the return to democracy building resumed, and it was inaugurated in 1983.

A delicious respite: On the corner of Rivadavia and **Callao** is the old **El Molino Café**. The building dates from 1912, and since that time it has been famous as a meeting place for congressmen and their staffs. Along with the requisite coffee and pastries, the café has a gourmet carryout counter.

Rivadavia is a key street in Buenos Aires. It divides the city in two; street

Schoolchildren on field trip to city center

names change at its crossing and numbering begins here. *Porteños* claim that they not only have the widest street in the world, 9 de Julio, but the longest, Rivadavia, which continues west into the countryside and out towards Luján.

About 12 blocks up Rivadavia from Congress is the neighborhood known as **Once**. This is the cheapest shopping district in town, particularly for clothes and electronic goods. A traditionally Jewish neighborhood, many of the businesses are owned by Orthodox Jews and immigrants from Korea. The area marked by **Puerreydon**, Corrientes, Rivadavia and **Urquiza** is filled with one-room shops that sell at wholesale prices.

Eating places near the Congress include **Quorum**, located directly behind the Congress on **Calle Riobamba**. This is a big meeting place for congressmen. Another famous restaurant in the area is **La Cabaña** at 436 **Entre Rios**. La Cabaña is unfortunately recognized as one of the best steak houses in the city and therefore somewhat overpriced and touristy. Still, they have wonderful salads and baby beef.

Movies and books: Four blocks down Callao (the continuation of Entre Rios) is **Avenida Corrientes**, another principal street in the lives of *porteños*. It is often introduced to foreigners as the "street that never sleeps" or the "Broadway of Buenos Aires".

Indeed, there are neon lights, fast food restaurants, and movie theaters on Corrientes. But the atmosphere is exceedingly intellectual, rather than gaudy like New York's Broadway. There are tiny bookstores everywhere, newspaper stands with a wide selection of newspapers, magazines and paperbacks, and old cafés where friends gather for long talks. The selection of international and national films reflects the serious interests of the moviegoers.

The bookstores are traditionally one of Corrientes' greatest attractions. They are single rooms open to the street, selling both secondhand and new

books. Some come to hunt for old treasures or the latest best-seller. Others use the bookstores as a meeting place. They stay open way past mid-night, and, unlike many other Buenos Aires shops, one may freely wander in and out without being accosted by aggressive salespeople. There are even *porteños* who claim to have read entire books during successive visits to the bookstores.

One of the first points of interest walking east again on Corrientes is the **San Martin Municipal Theater** at 1532. This chrome and glass building was inaugurated in 1960. It is the largest public theater in Argentina, with five stages and an estimated half a million spectators each year. It has a never-ending agenda of free concerts, theater, film festivals, lectures and musical performances.

San Martin Center: In the block behind the theater, at 1500 Sarmiento, is the **San Martin Cultural Center**, a sister building with an equally important flurry of cultural activity, including film festivals, art exhibits, puppet shows, poetry readings, round tables, and seminars and conferences on every imaginable subject. In addition, the center is used for big press conferences, international meetings and inaugurations. The City Tourism Bureau is on the fifth floor, where one can pick up free invitations to city tours.

The great number and variety of free concerts, seminars and other cultural activities is one of the most striking aspects of life in Buenos Aires. If anything, the activity has gained momentum in recent years, despite the economic crisis, and has undoubtably been bolstered by the freedom that has come with democracy. For visitors, both these centers are an introduction to the contemporary cultural scene found in the city.

Plaza Lavalle is another center of activity in the area. It is two blocks north of Corrientes at 1300. The **Federal Justice Tribunals** are located at one end of this historic plaza, and the **Browsing in an all-night bookstore.**

Colón Opera House is at the other. The plaza was initially used as a dumping ground for the unwanted parts of cattle.

One block from the Colón is the **Jewish Museum** at 773 **Libertad**. The museum is dedicated to the history of Jewish immigration to this country. The Jewish population in Argentina today is over half a million, making it the largest Jewish community in Latin America.

Crossing 9 de Julio takes you into the *minicentro*, an area limited on the other three sides by Rivadavia, **Leandro Alem** and **Córdoba**. Traffic here is restricted to public transportation during working hours, but do not let this lull you into pedestrian complacency: *colectivo* and taxi drivers are, in the opinion of many, the wildest in the Western hemisphere.

For this reason it is worth going one block over to **Lavalle**, which is a pedestrian walkway. Lavalle is also a moviegoer's paradise: there are 18 theaters in a four block stretch. Pizza parlors, cafés and ice-cream shops provide sustenance between shows.

Lavalle intersects with **Calle Florida**, also closed to motor vehicles. This promenade is packed with shoppers as well as folk musicians, mimes, preachers and others passing the hat. There is a leisurely pace here, and because of the crowds, it is not a good route for those in a hurry.

Issues of the day: Most intriguing of all are the heated political debates taking place on the avenue. Sometimes they are intentionally provoked by party activists who have set up campaign tables, but just as often they are begun by groups of old men who seem to have made these discussions their retirement hobby, or they are simply spontaneous arguments over the news of the day. In all cases, crowds gather around to hear the central players shout their opinions. Even for visitors unable to follow the conversation fully, it is worth pausing to observe these frequent episodes, for they provide an insight to

...ffee and ...nversa ...on in Café ... Paz.

and an understanding of, the Argentine political scene.

The shopping on Florida is slightly more expensive than other districts outside downtown. As elsewhere, most shops are one-room boutiques, many on interior shopping malls that exit onto adjacent streets. They sell clothes, leather goods, jewelry, toys, and gifts. Leather continues to be the best buy for visitors.

One of the most famous malls is the **Galeria Pacífico** between **Viamonte** and Cordoba. It is part of a turn-of-the-century Italian building that was saved from demolition because of the frescoes on the interior of its great dome. Five Argentine painters: Urruchua, Bern, Castagnino, Spilimbergo and Colmeiro, contributed to this vivid, lurid mural of social realism.

The **Ateneo Bookstore** is at 340 Florida. The largest bookstore in the country, Ateneo has a good and extensive collection of English paperbacks in the basement.

There are two traditional cafés along Florida: the **Richmond**, beloved by middle-aged *porteñas* for its English tea and homemade scones, and **Florida Garden,** a haven for journalists and politicians.

What to take home: Harrods, one of Buenos Aires' few department stores, is just past **Paraguay** on Florida. The U.S. Embassy **Lincoln Library** is on the next block. Here you can read the *New York Times* and the *Washington Post,* as well as major international periodicals and books written by American authors.

Below Florida, on the 300 block of **Calle Paraguay**, is **Kelly's**, the best-stocked and cheapest Argentine handicrafts store. It sells traditional artisans' goods from different provinces, including double-layered sheepskin slippers (the inside layer is to wear to bed), bright-colored wool scarves, leather bags, wooden plates for barbecues, gaucho belts and smaller souvenirs made of native materials.

Spontaneous discussion of current events on Calle Florida.

EATING OUT
DOWNTOWN

The variety of choices open to somebody searching for a bite to eat downtown is quite overwhelming. From elegant and sophisticated French cuisine (sort of) to down-to-earth grilled meats to fast food to simple sidewalk cafés, Buenos Aires' shopping and financial center offers the lot. Like in any other city, the quality and the prices vary greatly: at midday, however, almost all the places are full.

Any selection of restaurants must necessarily be subjective, as it is impossible to enumerate all those available. If you start at the southern end of Florida (behind the Cabildo) you could visit **La Veda**, a "lunch only" basement restaurant specializing in grills plus a few specialities such as breast of turkey Sultanne and sweetbreads Jean Bart. Above it, on the third floor, is **Cámara de Sociedades Anonimas**, a businessman's lunch hideout, with a menu of international cooking including some South American specialities. It is another very agreeable option.

On Florida, with a moving staircase which whisks you up to the first floor, **Deck Grill** offers one a wide option of grilled beef, chicken, salads and desserts for a most reasonable price. It is self-service and most popular at midday. Almost underneath it, below street level, **Blab** is quite a different affair: a luncheon restaurant with an extremely popular bar, it is open from midday to late evening, but not for dinner. A bit cramped at midday, it provides a good meetingplace and good food. Behind Harrods is one of the most interesting establishments in the city. Run by a genial Iranian ex-civil engineer, **Au Bon Air** is basically a French restaurant with strong Oriental overtones; the cooking is personal and the food, especially the rice dishes, is frequently outstanding. Close by is **Catalinas**, a really top fish and seafood place whose chef-in-chief Ramiro Rodriguez Pardo wields a mean skillet. A taste of turn-of-the-century Buenos Aires can be found at the **Restaurante de la Vieja Panadería**, above one of the city's oldest bakeries. The old-style decor goes hand in hand with honest cooking, including a really recommendable speciality: pork and spareribs baked in bakery ovens.

For those nostalgic for pub beer and meals, **Down Town Matias** could well be the answer. Described by an Irish journalist as "a typical New York-Irish pub," Matias is unique to BA.

For Spanish food, the option must certainly be **El Figón de Bonilla**; its old-time architecture and authentic cooking make it a fun place and a serious eating establishment.

Across from the BA Sheraton is **Las Nazarenas**, one of the innumerable *parrillas* infesting the city, but also one of the better ones, serving top beef, pork, mutton, chicken, kid and organ meats.

BEEF AND WINES OF ARGENTINA

Two Argentine taste experiences that should not be missed are its wines and beef.

Argentina is justly famous for its beef—generally grilled over coals—and Buenos Aires is full of restaurants devoted to preparing it to its best advantage. Nearly every tourist has heard of **La Cabaña**, probably one of the most famous steak houses in the world. Although it has changed its style in recent years, a visit there is still a must. Excellent grills are also served along the north riverside drive. Originally just a row of open air food carts, these cavernous beef emporia are still called *carritos*.

Little separates one from another, but if someone in your party is not all that beef crazy, a good choice is probably **Look**, because it offers more than just grills. The riverside location is an attraction by itself in warm weather.

A matter of terminology: A steak may be a steak in many parts of the world, but in Argentina it is many things under many guises. Making head or tail of the menu in a local *parrilla* (steak house) may be child's play for locals, but it can be bewildering to visitors. Herewith are a few tips to ensure carefree eating.

Local cuts differ greatly from what a US or European butcher would recognize. Argentines don't, for example, distinguish between sirloin, porterhouse and club steak, prime rib and short ribs the way a US butcher does. Rump and round are handled quite differently, and tenderloin has only a passing resemblance to *lomo*. Identifying Argentine cuts according to US and European classifications can thus lead to confusion.

Bife means a steak prepared from any of the recognized roasting cuts; *churrasco* refers to a steak prepared from a cut not usually used for roasting (e.g. chuck, brisket or shank). *Bife de chorizo*, the most popular cut, is a steak cut off the rib and roughly rump or sirloin in context. A *bife de lomo* is sirloin and a *bife de costilla* corresponds roughly to a T-bone steak. After the *bife de chorizo* the most popular cut is the *tira de*

asado, which is a strip of rib roast. If the *tira* is off the grill, it will be a long, fairly thin cut; if it is off the spit, it will be a shorter and much thicker cut.

Two other cuts that will figure on almost any menu are *vacio* and *matambre*. The former is a cut which comprises the bottom part of what in the U.S. is designated as sirloin porterhouse and the flank. Correctly grilled, it is perhaps the most favorsome and juicy of all the cuts. The latter can come in various guises: cold and rolled up like a Swiss roll, with a vegetable and egg filling. Sometimes this is also served hot right off the grill. The more usual way to serve this cut is hot and with no filling. Other cuts such as *peceto* (the upper part of the round) and *cuadril* (rump) do not normally figure on the menus of a *parilla*. If you like your beef rare ask for it *jugoso*; if medium, ask for it *a punto*; and if you like it well done, ask for it *bien hecho*.

No matter how you eat your beef, have it with some Argentine wine. The two complement each other well.

Although Argentina is the world's fifth largest producer of wine, it is relatively unknown outside its own borders. This is because until recently, Argentina has been drinking all its own wine—a whopping 91 liters per head per annun in the 1970s! The recent decline in consumption (59 liters per head in 1986) combined with an almost uniform level of production (an overage 20 million hectoliters per annum), has allowed Argentina to begin to seek foreign markets for its surplus wines.

To enjoy the many good wines (and a few exceptional ones) that Argentina makes, you must go to Argentina. To discover the best, it is necessary to know a little about how the country's wine market functions and how Argentines qualify their wines. Argentine wines are divided into two main types: *vino común* or *vino de mesa,* and *vino fino*. There is also a third insignificant classification called *(vino reserva,)* usually regarded as a *vino común*.

A *vino común* is a table or jug wine which can be modest or dreadful. Unless you are advised by a knowledgeable local, it is best to pass up this type. *Vino fino* is a fine wine and as such is the one which will demand your attention. A good number are generic wines (blends) but many varietals are now making their debut, with great success. In Argentina a varietal must contain a minimum of 80 percent of the base grape, a rule

ing about 80 percent of Argentina's fine wine, originates in the province of Mendoza, tucked in the Andean foothills. Mendoza cultivates its vines on desert flatlands made fertile by irrigation water from the icy, crystalline snow which descend from the Andes. Other wine regions of importance are San Juan, La Rioja and Salta in the Andean foothills, and the valley of the Rio Negro river, to the south.

which is in line with that of all other leading wine countries. In the case of white wines the percentage is generally 100. Red wines are more flexible.

Argentine grape varieties are almost entirely of European origin: Chardonnay, Chenin blanc, Riesling, Cabernet Souvignon, Merlot and Malbec which are only a few of the 50-odd varieties cultivated. Almost 75 percent of the total wine production, includ-

A typical lunch in Buenos Aires *parrilla* or steakhouse.

Although made from European grapes, Argentine wines have a local flavor. This is due to the climate, soil and irrigation methods. In the case of many noble varieties, such as Cabernet, Riesling, Chardonnay and Merlot, the typical flavor is easily distinguishable. However, there are two varieties which can be considered exclusively Argentine for their quality if not their origin. The first is Malbec, a grape which in France is not particularly distinguished but in Argentina makes what many consider its finest red wine. The second is the Torrontes, an unpopular grape of Spanish origin, which makes a superb, full, fruity, rich white wine.

"MEET ME AT THE CAFÉ"

The social life, and to a great extent the business and cultural life of Buenos Aires revolves around cafés, or *confiterías* as they are called in Argentina. "Meet me at the *confitería*" is the typical response to an invitation to go to the cinema or the opera as well as to talk over a deal or to simply get together for a chat. A coffee or a cognac in a favorite *confitería* is also the standard ritual for ending a night out on the town.

There are cafés on almost every corner and they range from the most elegant to modest and cosy gathering places where neighbors exchange greetings or employees from nearby offices take a break to read the daily paper. Visitors often comment that only Paris rivals Buenos Aires as a true "café society."

The importance of the café in daily life probably has roots in the necessity of creating meeting places outside the home, which in the Latin vision, is a private sanctuary. Another reason for the development of the café as an institution was the high proportion of male immigrants, either single or whose womenfolk had stayed behind. Lonely and living in hotels and pensions, these men found companionship, and, in some cases, domino or parchesi partners in the corner café. The *confitería* as a refuge was not just limited to humble immigrants. In one of Argentine literature's most famous novels, *El hombre que está solo y espera,* (The Man Who Is Alone and Waiting), published in 1931, author Raul Scalabrini Ortiz situates his melancholy protagonist in a café on the corner of Corrientes and Esmeralda, site of the old café Royal Keller, a famous meeting place of the era, where Scalabrini Ortiz himself as well as other literary figures often went.

But whatever the social class, the early cafés were definitely a male preserve. In

fact, a '*Salón de familia* ,' which used to be found in some *confiterías*, was a concession to the female population given that it was thought improper for respectable ladies to be directly exposed to men's public habits, such as loud discussions and smoking.

So intimate was the connection between *porteños* and their cafés that many of them became associated with specific clientele. Each political, artistic, literary, student and

social group laid claim to its own café. From the turn of the century up to the present, many of the events that mark Argentine political and intellectual history were first discussed among friends or foes over a *confitería* table.

The café was, and is, a place to be alone. Its association with loneliness has made the café the setting of many tangos; it is there late at night that the abandoned lover sings of his despair as he drinks " the last coffee" (Tango *El Ultimo Café* with lyrics by Catulo Castillo and music by Héctor Stamponi). One of the most famous tango lyricist, Enrique Santos Discepolo, immortalized the

Left, solitary gentleman takes coffee in the Café Tortoni. Right, gilded lamppost in the Café El Molino.

café in his *Cafétín de Buenos Aires* recalling it as "a school of all things" where he learned "philosophy, gambling and cruel poetry, and to think no more of me."

Preserving the past: A few of the most famous cafés still exist, little changed from their golden era. In the city center are four *confiterías* that evoke the Belle Epoque, each with its own special flavor and history.

One of the oldest, most historically well known and best preserved of the Buenos Aires cafés is the **Tortoni**, on Avenida de Mayo and Piedras. Its deep red leather chairs and beautiful painted skylights, the luminous billiards room, *salón de familia* and

Aires made an appearance at *La Peña*.

The autobiographies, biographies and histories of the period are replete with anecdotes that take place in the Tortoni.

The Tortoni is still a center of musical and artistic life, with poetry readings and recitals, particularly of local jazz groups, taking place every weekend. And debates over literature, politics and the meaning of life, spiced by frothy *café con leche* or a cold beer, take place every day, just as they have for more than a century. Not far away, on Suipacha just off Corrientes, is the **Confitería Ideal**.

Right in the heart of the theater and movie

onyx chess and domino tables evoke the epoch, celebrated in the portraits and photographs on the walls, when the Tortoni was a gathering place for the most famous and infamous in the city's active cultural life.

Founded in 1858 by a Frenchman named Touan, the Tortoni became the epicenter of intellectual life on May 12, 1926, when the painter Benito Quinquela Martín presided over the founding of "*La Peña*" (the Circle).

Throughout the 1920s, '30s and '40s— every distinguished and avant garde figure in Argentina frequented the Tortoni. In addition, every well known intellectual or cultural personality that visited Buenos

district, it is a legendary meeting place for high tea. More than that, for the price of coffee and cake, you can have a taste of life in Argentina's Art Nouveau past. Elaborate brass fittings embrace the marble columns and in the late afternoons, an organist plays a medley of classic tunes—waltzes, tangos, ballads—giving tired shoppers and expectant theatergoers a rest from the crowded downtown streets.

Tea at five: Staying close to the city center, another café that has escaped destruction and/or audacious remodeling is the **Richmond**. Located on Florida between Corrientes and Lavalle, the Richmond has been the place to take tea and scones since the early days of the century. At one time it was, like the Tortoni, a center of literary life, with authors and public figures holding court in its anglophile atmosphere.

Politics and pastries: Politics was always the theme at the other great monument to the Argentine café—**El Molino**. How could it be otherwise? The Molino is just across the street from the Congress and, of course, the Senators and Deputies often go there to meet with associates and friends.

'**Molino**' is the Spanish word for 'mill' and the café's name derives from the fact that its original location, at Avenida de Mayo and Rodriguez Peña, just a block away, was across from a flour mill. This is also the explanation for the landmark neon windmill on the building's lovely cupola.

El Molino's owner, Cayetano Brenna, saw an opportunity for expansion when work began on the Congress building in 1905 and bought the corner property. By 1914 the Molino was "the place to go," leading Brenna to undertake a vast remodeling that was completed in 1917. Not only did the refurbished *confitería* boast of the latest Belle Epoque decor in its imported Walter Scott-inspired Vitreaux, porcelain and marble fittings, but it also had three underground levels for the preparation of pastries, wine storage and ice making.

In 1979, after four difficult years caused by the closing of Congress by the military government, it was announced that El Molino and the entire building was to be demolished. After months of public outcry, a new corporation formed by descendents of Cayetano Brenna was able to negotiate the landmark's salvation. El Molino's turn-of-the-century beauty is sadly faded, with its delicate glass mosaic lanterns and windows broken and inoperative, its walls unpainted and its upper floors badly in need of restoration. But one can hope that with more years of active constitutional government, it will prosper and the owners can return it, once again, to the splendor of past decades.

In addition to the above 'grande dame'

Teatime in the Café Ideal is a time-honored custom among older *porteños*.

cafés, there are dozens of others with some special element. At the corner of Rivadavia and Medrano in the heart of Caballito, is the hundred-year-old **Las Violetas** which is a more modest version of El Molino. Or if you'd like to try your coffee in the open air, there is **La Biela** in the Recoleta area and **El Rosdal**, set across from one of the lakes in Palermo Park.

There are also cafés which appeal to the anti-establishment factions of Buenos Aires intellectual society. A long favored haunt of "café revolutionaries" is the Café **La Paz** on Corrientes, across the street from the San Martin Cultural Center. Decorated in a no-frills 1930s style, the neon-lit café often resembles a library reading room, as patrons pore over recent purchases from nearby bookstalls. La Paz offers a snack menu as well as the requisite thick black espresso, but it's perfectly acceptable to spend several hours at a table over a single cup of coffee. During the military government, police routinely raided places like La Paz for "subversive elements," but in these more tranquil times, families and dapper elderly couples join the ranks of bearded young *porteños* discussing the state of the world.

Another delightful bohemian spot is **La Giralda** on Corrientes, whose rich Spanish-style chocolate and *churros* (fritters) are famous throughout the city.

If you are out in Belgrano, there is the **Steinhauser Café**, famous for its German pastries. If you're curious about where journalists and political "insiders" meet to exchange information, stop in at the **Florida Garden** at the corner of Paraguay and Florida. The **St. James** at Cordoba and Maipu is one of the cafés where Jorge Luis Borges used to be seen, although, to defend Borges' good taste, it was a much lovelier place before it joined the long list of cafés ruined by "remodeling." For tango lovers, there is the **Café de los Angelitos** at Rivadavia and Rincón, where Gardel sang. It, too, is more than a little shabby but perhaps that will just add to its tango aura!

Of course, you can adopt the old *porteño* custom and choose your own special café. Then when making plans with friends, you too can say, "As always, meet me at the café..."

ARGENTINE CINEMA

The *porteño* passion for cinema has filled Buenos Aires with an overwhelming variety of theaters and supported a new Argentine film industry which is taking prizes at festivals the world over.

Over 70 cinemas are operating in the city center alone. They radiate from two main centers: the pedestrian walkway Lavalle, which clogs with departing audiences after evening sessions until it is almost impossible to move; and Avenida Corrientes, where queues a block long can be seen at 1:30 a.m. every Saturday or the *trasnoche* session.

Every day, the cinema pages of the newspapers eagerly follow the latest releases in the United States and Europe, which quickly make their way to Buenos Aires. Spanish critics assess their quality, and gossip columnists follow their stars.

Movie houses: Some of the old theaters on Corrientes are worth visiting for themselves. They include cinema palaces of the 20s which nobody has had the money or the heart to knock down, with marble staircases and chandeliers. The art deco **Gran Rex** is an old favorite, opposite **El Opera** with its elegant balconies and statues where, when the lights go down, tiny twinkling stars appear on the ceiling.

Besides the commercial chains are a whole range of art-house cinemas which show classic re-releases. The daily *Guía de Espectáculos* in the center of **Clarin** is the best place to check the latest offerings: the **Leopoldo Lugones** in the San Martin Cultural Center shows cycles of old films, as does the **Hebraica** in Sarmiento, **Auditorio de Buenos Aires** in Florida, **Cosmos 70** and **El Arte** in Corrientes, **Empire**, **Sala Uno** and **Sala Sec**.

Most bohemian of all are the meetings at the · **IRCA** (Instituto de Realización Cinematográfica Argentina) cinema, where nearly everyone has to sit on the floor. Film reels are changed by hand on the sole projector available, and every screening is followed by an audience debate on the artistic, social, psychological, political and other aspects of the movie.

Porteño film buffs have been catching up on world cinema after years of film censorship under the former military government. Classics such as *Last Tango in Paris* had to wait until democracy returned, to be screened. Even today, many films from the 1970s, once considered 'unhealthy,' are being premiered in Argentina.

A bizarre side-effect of this sudden free-

dom is the tendency to translate foreign film titles more suggestively. *The Sound of Music,* for example, ran under the titillating name of *The Rebel Nun.*

Artistic freedom: The lifting of censorship under democracy has also been a major impetus behind the Argentine film industry. A burst of creativity in recent years has pushed the country's cinema onto the international stage.

"The opening-up after censorship allowed us to experiment with new themes," says critic and Argentine cinema expert Jorge Couselo. "We were able to expose and analyze what had happened in these last years:

the repression, the exiles, the lack of freedom of expression."

This process of revealing the hidden history of the dictatorship was recognized overseas when Luis Puenzo's *La Historia Oficial* (The Official Story) won the Academy Award for Best Foreign Film in 1986. It told of the experience of a *porteño* couple who thought that they had escaped the traumas of the 1970s—only to find that their

Paris desperately trying to hold onto their identities through fragile tokens such as *mate* and the tango.

The two other great successes of the new cinema should be seen when they are being re-screened. *La Pelicula del Rey* (The King and His Movie) is "a tribute to all failed heroes." It is about a director's colorful but doomed attempt to make a film about a 19th-century Frenchman who declares himself

adopted daughter's real mother was 'disappeared' by the military for political reasons.

New films dealing with the dictatorship continue to appear—after all, Italian cinema was still obsessed with fascism 35 years after the war. A highly entertaining classic that regularly reappears in Buenos Aires cinemas is *El Exilio de Gardel* (The Exile of Gardel), which looks at Argentine exiles in

Left, moviegoing crowds on Lavalle. Above, scene from the popular film, *The King and His Movie*.

king of the Patagonian Indians.

El Hombre Mirando al Sudeste (Man Facing Southeast), is about a psychologist whose patient believes that he came from another planet.

Despite its international success at film festivals, Argentine cinema is still struggling to compete in its small local market with the flood of overseas films, and to overcome its shortage of funds.

"You cannot separate the cinema's problems from the economic problems of the country," says Couselo. "But the artistic ingredients are certainly there to ensure continuing success of the industry."

A Night At The Opera

Even those who don't usually make a point of hearing classical music while traveling, should not miss a night at the **Teatro Colón**.

Settling back in a turn-of-the-century armchair as the great hall reverberates, you can soak up the atmosphere of what has been for 80 years one of the world's great opera houses. At the Colón, every performance is still a grand event.

asts queue for last-minute tickets at *precios populares*, usually gaining fine seats for only a few dollars. But even the most impecunious must never forget that men are refused entry to many performances if not appropriately attired in tie and coat.

After lingering for a suitable spell on the theater's outside steps, the audience make their way into the entrance foyer. Here they savor the splendor which inspired dancer

Whether or not they have actually set foot inside, *porteños* universally invoke the Colón as proof that their city's remoteness from Europe is a question of geography rather than of culture or style.

The building takes up a whole city block at **Plaza Lavalle**, in the middle of Avenida 9 de Julio. At night it is floodlit, providing an irresistible backdrop for Argentine elegance. Taxis and limousines glide to the doorway bearing gentlemen in tuxedos and pomaded hair, and suntanned ladies in fur coats, where they are met by uniformed doormen who furtively pocket their tips.

Meanwhile the more humble arts enthusi-

Mikhail Barishnikov to call the Colón "the most beautiful of all the theaters I know."

The performance hall within is even more spectacular. The orchestra consists of 632 individual wooden armchairs laid out in careful rows, each padded with mauve velvet. The theater is ringed with six tiers of curtain boxes and gilded gallery seats, allowing the Colón to seat 2,400 or stand 4,000 if a great artist is performing.

At the base of the stage are *baignoires* where *porteños* once heard performances. It now houses the radio equipment used to broadcast every performance live to Buenos Aires. The domed ceiling boasts a mural by

Raúl Soldi and a vast chandelier holding 700 light bulbs.

The extravagant plans for the Colón were first drawn up at the end of the 1880s. The Italian architect Francisco Tamburini hoped for completion within three years. Eighteen years and two architects later, the theater was ready, displaying its curious mix of German 19th-century, Italian Renaissance and French classical styles.

and more recently, María Callas, Plácido Domingo and Joan Sutherland.

The museum also contains relics from the 1920s, when European opera groups would spend their off-seasons in Buenos Aires. An original faded tutu is preserved beneath glass, along with a portrait of Argentine composer Héctor Panizza. The conducting baton of Arturo Toscanini remains the museum's prized possession.

A small museum attached to the entrance foyer pays homage to the famous and forgotten artists who have performed in the Colón since *Aida* was first presented in 1908. Vaslov Nijinsky and Ana Pavlova have bounded across its stage. Stravinsky, Strauss and Bernstein have conducted here; while *porteño* audiences have thrilled to the voices of such greats as Italian tenor Enrico Caruso, Australian soprano Nelly Melba

Yet now as in the past, over a month of preparations are needed before the curtain is raised on any production. Beneath the Colón's stage are three floors of underground workshops, where tens of thousands of costumes and wigs are stored. Carefully filed are 30,000 pairs of shoes, including the proudly displayed leathers worn by Rudolf Nureyev in *The Nutcracker*. In these workshops, the entire 1,000-square meter backdrop to each opera is handpainted by teams of craftspeople. Elsewhere, a subterranean rehearsal room is an exact replica of the stage upstairs, allowing artists to practise while another work is being performed.

Left, the Colon Opera House. Above, applause at the Colon Opera House.

THEATER

On a Saturday night as you walk down Corrientes in Buenos Aires' main entertainment district, someone might well approach you and thrust a slip of paper into your hand. If the piece of paper is not advertising a new vegetarian restaurant or courses in parapsychology, then it's probably promoting some new play or other. Many of these plays offer free admission to those who bring five friends along.

anything about foreign debt, Argentina built playhouses and a world-famous opera house as monuments to its European past.

The very first theater in Buenos Aires was a large straw-roofed storehouse called *La Rancheria* or The Settlement, because of its proximity to many new settlements.

Early Argentine theater often covered rural themes and later the lives of those who lived in the city's famous *conventillos* or

The "Broadway" of Buenos Aires: Corrientes itself is lined with theaters, but the street hawkers are usually selling "off-off Corrientes" productions. There is plenty of both in Buenos Aires, but, as is happening worldwide, theater is losing out to the video age; and in a country where cinema production is also experiencing a national revival, many theaters are having a difficult time. Not just the audiences are vanishing. Directors, too, complain they are losing good local playwrights to the more lucrative cinema and television industries.

Of course, theater has not always struggled. In the days before anyone knew

tenements. In this century, Argentina's theater became particularly well-known for its *Teatro Independiente,* a movement which adapted Miller-style realism to local themes.

Today, Argentine theater often suffers from self-censorship. Restrictions imposed by past military governments made such an impression on artists that they have yet to completely shake themselves out of their own mental self-censorship.

"On Corrientes" offers popular plays and musicals by well-known local, Spanish or international playwrights, while the "Off Corrientes theaters," such as the historic **Cervantes**, tend to offer more serious productions. Some of the less commercial theaters are also an excellent way of getting to know the city's cultural scene in general.

San Martin Theater: The best example of noncommercial theater is the state-run San Martin Theater in the heart of Corrientes Street. It not only has the excellent resident dance and theater companies, but also a photographer's gallery, a bookshop and a ground floor entertainment hall offering free concerts on a regular basis. Tickets to dramatic productions are very cheap, although popular shows sell out quickly. The best way to obtain information is to drop by the Center and pick up a free schedule. Tickets for most events may be purchased in advance.

Linked to the theater is the **San Martin Cultural Center** in Recoleta. There, too, you can find a wealth of theater productions, cinema and community events and courses open to the public. Almost all are free.

San Telmo Theater: Following the example of the two San Martin complexes, several small "off-off" Corrientes theaters have opened their doors to artistic events in general. **La Gran Aldea** in San Telmo is one which now offers not just theater, but poetry readings, recitals and music. There are some 20 theaters in San Telmo, many of them offering either free or inexpensive theater. Some of them even offer several productions a night in imaginatively converted *conventillos,* houses or warehouses.

Many of San Telmo's productions are put on by what are known as actors' cooperatives. These are groups of semiprofessional actors who earn their living in other full-time jobs, but are members of the actors' union and often perform several nights a week year round. San Telmo is the best place to find imaginative new theater, as well as performances of works by more established local playwrights such as Eduardo Pavlosky

Left, innovative, quality theater productions are offered continuously at the Centro Cultural San Martin. Right, mime entertains crowd.

or international playwrights such as the Argentine favorite, Berthold Brecht.

San Telmo is also home to two theaters unashamedly geared to the tourist. The **Casa Rosada** and the **Casa Blanca** offer a quick tour of Argentine culture from gaucho dancing to folk music, as well as the tango shows for which they are famous. Tickets are definitely tourist-priced (around $20 as opposed to the $5 or $10 tickets for most other thea-

ter), but they do attract some of the best local talent. Just two blocks away, you can find a decided change of pace: behind graffiteed wooden doors is the Centro Parakultural, which offers more offbeat theater as well as music, art exhibitions, and pop video shows.

Live drama may be struggling to make money in Buenos Aires, but with at least 60 theaters in the city, there is no shortage of plays concentrating on Argentinian themes, such as military rule, exile, and psychoanalysis. One-man shows are also becoming popular and street theater on Florida's pedestrian malls, squares and parks, is booming under the new artistic freedom.

SAN TELMO AND MONSERRAT

If any place in Buenos Aires confirms that this city has been around for much more than the last century, it's the neighboring *barrios* of **Monserrat** and **San Telmo**. To the south of Plaza de Mayo, these historically colorful *barrios* were once the heart of city life and are where virtually all of the pre-20th century buildings can be found. A project to demolish these ancient structures that was dreamed up in the 1950s happily never reached fruition, and since 1979, the area has been protected as a historical zone.

Monserrat, which borders the south side of Plaza de Mayo, is where *porteños* once gathered to watch bullfights before the sport was outlawed at the end of the last century. Today locals go there to buy computers or industrial machinery. But the *barrio*'s legend as a hangout for bigtalking knifefighters— *cuchilleros*—lives on, as in this popular verse:

"*I'm from the barrio of Monserrat,*
where steel flashes
what I say with my mouth
I enforce with by hide."
(Soy del barrio e' Monserrat
donde relumbra el acero
Lo que digo con el pico
lo sostengo con el cuero.)

Long knives no longer hold sway in Monserrat, and a stroll through the bustling *barrio* during the daytime should prove quite safe and give a revealing glimpse of another era in the city's life. As always on the city's narrow one-way streets, stick to the sidewalk nearest the passenger side of vehicles to avoid exhaust fumes.

Block of enlightenment: A good starting point is Plaza de Mayo. From there, head up **Diagonal Julio A Roca**, the diagonal street that begins to the left of the old white Cabildo. The big equestrian statue dominating the traffic circle at the end of the block is of General Roca, who distinguished himself massacring the nomadic Indians who resisted westward expansion in the 1860s. The **Ministry of Labor** is to the right, a site of frequent boisterous workers' demonstrations. To the left, on the corner of **Alsina** and **Peru**, is the historic **Manzana de las Luces** or Block of Lights, earlier known as the Block of Intellectuality. Most of the buildings on this block date back to the 18th century. A theater complex run by the municipality occupies the side of the block along Peru. This area once housed the lower house of congress and was earlier headquarters for the Jesuit missions in Argentina.

Turning down Alsina and walking toward **Bolívar**, you'll find the oldest building in Buenos Aires, the **Church of San Ignacio**. This "temple of lights," as it was called by its Jesuit founders, was begun in 1710 and finished in 1734. Like all the other churches in the area, San Ignacio was sacked and burned by Peronist mobs in 1955. But its gilded

carved wood altar survived the attack and is virtually the only baroque decor to be found in all of the city's churches. Next to the church on Bolivar is the prestigious **Colegio Nacional**, a highly selective staterun school where many of the country's business and political leaders got their secondary education. It also happens to be the alma mater of imprisoned Montonero terrorist leader, Mario Firmenich.

Crossing Bolívar and continuing along Alsina brings you to some fine examples of old residential architecture. At 463 Alsina begin the crumbling remains of a circa 1840 residence, whose wrought-iron railed balconies reflect the Italian architectural lines in vogue at the time. The *casona* was once occupied by the widow of the 19th-century dictator Rosas. On the corner is the oldest house in the city, built in 1812. (Older structures collapsed from the boring of termites). Across the street, at 412 Alsina, is the **Museum of the City**, one flight up. Its historical

exhibits are changed every other month, and are housed in what used to be a family dwelling.

Next to the museum, on the corner, is **La Farmacia de la Estrella**. The etched shop windows and dark wooden cabinets inside recall turn-of-the-century Buenos Aires, as do the porcelain chamberpots on display, relics from "when *porteños* refused to leave the bedroom." A ceiling fresco inside allegorically portrays "the triumph of pharmacy over disease."

On the corner across Defensa Street are the **San Francisco Church** and convent, completed in 1754. An enormous tapestry (exceeded in size only by a tapestry in Great Britain's Conventry Cathedral) that portrays the Virgin Mary hangs where the main altar stood before it was incinerated in the 1955 Peronist riots. On the right-hand side of this Franciscan church, towards the back, is a statue of San Benito de Palermo, "the black Franciscan saint," patron of the needy. (Monserrat was

Wares at Sunday Antiques Fair in Plaza Dorrego.

once heavily populated by emancipated black slaves, whose descendants have now virtually disappeared from Buenos Aires).

If you wish to linger in Alsina, stop in at **La Puerto Rico** (number 422), a simple and traditional teahouse.

Argentine handicrafts: From Alsina, turn right, up **Defensa**. This street was once the ox-cart thoroughfare for products coming from the south. A block and-a-half up the street, at 372 Defensa, is the **National Handicraft Market** (Mercado Nacional de Artesanías), housed in an early 9th-century home with its stone slab floors and heavy wooden ceiling beams still intact. This state-run market claims to have the only collection of traditional handicrafts for sale from all of Argentina's 22 provinces. The work is handsomely displayed, reasonably priced, and includes weavings, ceramics, silverwares, masks, carved wood and leather. (Open Mon-Fri 10 a.m.-7p.m., Sat & Sun 12-7p.m.)

Half-a-block further up Defensa, crossing **Belgrano**, is the **Church of Santo Domingo**, built in 1751. The courtyard is dominated by a bier on which rest the remains of General Manuel Belgrano, a hero in the fight for independence and the creator of the Argentine flag.

The upper portion of the belltower on the left side of the church is studded with 19 wooden plugs. Like wounds carefully kept from healing, these plugs supposedly mark where patriots' bullets struck when fired at British troops holed up there in 1806. (It is from this episode, incidentally, that the street Defensa got its name). Inside the church, behind a shrine to the Virgin on the left-hand side, are four faded and tattered Union Jacks, captured from the British who had tried to seize the city. One of the flags once flew over what was later to become Plaza Britannia (in front of Retiro train station)

From Santo Domingo Church, walk down Belgrano past the old convent

and turn right up **Balcarce**. This wide, quiet flagstone street takes you past the former mint, now the **Army General Archive**. Jog left on **Chile** to keep following Balcarce. You are now entering **San Telmo**, once the swankest part of town and now home to an eclectic mix of artists, construction workers, journalists, politicans and waiters.

San Telmo: Until the harbor was moved upstream in 1888, San Telmo was a riverport neighborhood, rising above shoals of the River Plate that almost reached what is now **Paseo Colón**. (The incline going down to this broad thoroughfare was once the old riverbank). Both high and humble society lived here—great landowners and traders in imposing mansions; fishermen, stevedores, and black slaves in adobe huts. As late as 1838, blacks made up a third of the *barrio's* population and had their own social center, *La nacíon conga*. White dwellers were, almost without exception, of Spanish birth or descent.

All this changed drastically in 1871, when a ferocious plague of yellow fever killed more than half of San Telmo's inhabitants— more than 13,000 people died during the three-month epidemic. At the time, nobody realized that this disease indigenous to the Americas was spread by the mosquitoes that proliferated along the riverbank. All who could fled the *barrio* during and after the plague. The rich abandoned their mansions and moved to the burgeoning Barrio Norte, while most of the poor relocated in Monserrat.

San Telmo was quickly repopulated by shiploads of European immigrants, arriving mostly from Genoa, Italy and the Basque region of Spain. They moved into the abandoned mansions, which got subdivided into crowded one or two-room dwellings. These squalid *conventillos* still exist in San Telmo, and are today largely inhabited by families from impoverished northern provinces and recent immigrants from Uruguay, Paraguay and Bolivia. These

Baroque church of Nuestra Señora de Belen.

THE KIOSCO

Sometimes it's little more than a hole in the wall. It can be a truly depressing sight on a wet, chilly Buenos Aires winter night: the bluish light of a neon tube illuminating a tired-looking, ageing man, with the melancholy of the tango etched on his gaunt face, a traditional beige shawl over his shoulders against the cold, a display case bearing a few dusty rolls of mints, a meager supply of chocolate bars and the ever-present rack of cigarettes and matches tilted toward the customer before him. It's the epitome of the soft-sell.

At its best, however, the *kiosco* is a veritable miniature general store, cheerfully lit with flashing advertising signs, carnival-like strings of colored bulbs, and with a supply of just about anything you could possibly think of.

As far as is known, the *kiosco* is a *porteño* invention. While the word kiosk is used in Britain, for instance, to describe the corner newsstand, only in Buenos Aires does the word conjure up images of a place where one can buy anything from a pack of cigarettes to a sachet of shampoo.

Your typical well run *kiosco* is glass-fronted, or simply an open window, with two lateral walls and a door at the back through which the owner enters and leaves. The door may lead into a grocery, a restaurant, an ice cream parlor, a stationery store, a barber shop, a toy store or a private home. Or the *kiosco* might, if it is, say, on the platform of a train or subway station, be an independent lean-to structure made of metal sheeting. What is important is that its window opens out onto a public thoroughfare—preferably a busy one.

The interior of the *kiosco* is seldom larger than a medium-sized closet. Business is transacted through the window over the candy case. The sides of the *kiosco* are generally lined with cigarette racks and shelves within easy

reach of the *kiosquero*.

The well-stocked *kiosco* is a cornucopia of little items one is bound to need at any hour of the day or night. (Although *kiosqueros* tend to be very bohemian about keeping regular hours, a good *kiosco* is open 24 hours a day, or at least attempts to be open when other types of stores aren't).

So what can you buy in a *kiosco*? Perhaps a better question would be what can't you buy?

Kioscos stock candy, cigarettes, shoestrings, razor blades, soap, shampoo, deodorant, shaving cream, combs, aspirin, lottery tickets, ballpoints, paper (writing and toilet), five-and-ten-type toys, batteries, penlights, key chains, glue, bug-spray, stomach salts, condoms, hip-flasks and, if the operator can squeeze in a small fridge, beer, cider, soft-drinks and ice cream.

If you don't see what you want, ask! *Kioscos* are full of surprises.

...ndy is ...ly one of ...e items ...r sale at a ...enos ...res ...osco.

people tend to use the front stoops and sidewalks as an extended living room in warm weather, giving the *barrio* a lively street life, especially in the evenings—a refreshing change from the somber streets wending through concrete canyons elsewhere in Buenos Aires.

Since being declared a historic zone in the early 1970s, San Telmo has gone through both a commercial and real-estate renaissance to become one of the trendiest neighborhoods in Buenos Aires. Decaying 19th-century homes have been transformed into cozy restaurants and shops that preserve many elements of the original structures.

You can see the inside of a restored *conventillo* by turning up from Balcarce onto quiet, charming **Calle San Lorenzo**. **Patios de San Telmo**, at San Lorenzo 319, was until 1970 a *conventillo*. Presently it's divided into 35 artists' studios, with a bar at the entrance where you can hear live Argentine folk music on weekends.

Tango shrines: Up the street are **Patio Mio**, **El Ultimo**, and **La Cueva de San Telmo**, all of them tango nightclubs. Like churches in a holy land, this neighborhood is populated with such clubs, being part of that sentimentally sacred terrain of Buenos Aires known loosely as "El Sur" (which includes just about anything south of Plaza de Mayo). Here is where sharply dressed *guapos* (dandys) adorned with forward-tilted fedoras and long white scarves used to lean against lamp posts and pick their teeth, slyly waiting for passing women to swoon below their gaze. Or at least that's how the slice-of-life paintings of the era remember them.

Reaching Defensa, turn left. At Defensa 788, up a flight of stairs, is **Yuchán Artesanía Aborigen**, where you can peruse or purchase handicrafts made mostly by indigenous tribes from near Paraguay. The creatures carved from rock heavy *palo de rosa* wood are especially interesting. ′

Farther up Defensa, on the other side

Playing *truco* in Lezama Park.

of **Independencia**, is **Pasaje Giuffra**, another charming side street worth exploring. In the evening, stop in at **La Gran Aldea** (Giuffra 330). It's a handsome complex of cafés, theaters, and courtyards, just across the street from a Franciscan nunnery.

Further up Defensa is the antique shop zone, which runs on for several blocks. These places are usually open after 3 p.m. and their negotiable prices tend to undercut those prevailing in the U.S. and Europe.

Don't miss the block-sized turn of the century indoor market between **Estados Unidos** and **Carlos Calvo**. This is one of the last great holdouts of a kind of shopping space that has become increasingly rare in Buenos Aires.

The restored colonial-era home of "the poet of the Revolution," **Capitán Estéban de Luca**, is now a pleasant restaurant and cafe on the corner of Defensa and Carlos Calvo. The food is good and reasonably priced.

Sunday fair: Continuing up Defensa brings you to **Plaza Dorrego**. During the week this is a rather unremarkable square sorely lacking benches. But on Sundays, from 10 to 5, it's transformed into a colorful antique and curio fair where you can buy anything from satin underwear to copper-plated milk cans. The "Feria de San Telmo" is a popular destination for both foreign tourists and jet-set *porteños*, who are also entertained in adjacent streets by bards, dancers, mimes, and itinerant singers and musicians.

A couple of peanut-shells-on-the-floor bars facing the plaza are inviting: **Bar Pedro Telmo**, which by night is a gay hangout, and **Cafe de la Feria**, where the tap beer far outflows the coffee. Take a table on the terrace on warm evenings.

Morbid museum: Near the plaza, just down **Humberto Primo**, is one of the more ghoulish attractions Buenos Aires has to offer. It's the **Penitentiary Museum**, housed in a mid-19th century prison that functioned until the late

t, man ⋅s on hat street r. Right, ⋅ng ⋅teño.

1870. Here you'll find leg-irons attached to cellblock walls and mournful looking mannequins sporting prison garb from centuries past. All this is explained in numbing detail by cheerful young Spanish-speaking guides from whom you can pick up a surprising number of euphemisms for the word 'prisoner.'

Just down the street from the jail museum is a San Telmo landmark, the graceful **Church of Nuestra Señora de Belén**. Its construction, which began in 1805, took another 71 years to complete, mostly for lack of adequate funds from the tight-fisted parishioners.

Not all the locals gave up on San Telmo after the 1871 yellow fever scourge. The Eseiza family took advantage of rock-bottom land prices when the plague's victims had barely been buried. The large patio-centered home they built on Defensa between Humberto Primo and **San Juan** is now the **Pasaje de la Defensa**, an attractive array of shops selling artisan and manu-factured goods. There's also a pricey cantina that serves dinners on Fridays and Saturdays and lunch on Saturdays and Sundays. As are most establishments in San Telmo, it's closed on Mondays.

Farther up Defensa, at **Calle Brazil**, you'll find **Parque Lezama**. This is where the Argentine author Ernesto Sábato opens his renowned novel, *On Heroes and Tombs*. The park has seen better days, but remains a popular gathering place for children and the aged. During summer there are often free evening concerts in its open-air amphitheater. Here is where mimes and actors made the first stabs at public performances during the former military regime. All were arrested for their efforts, but they have since flourished under Argentina's civilian government.

From Parque Lezama, you can either plunge onward to La Boca, the riverside Italian *barrio* splashed with color, or return by Defensa or Paseo Colón to downtown Buenos Aires.

Antique clothing store in Pasaje de Defensa.

THE COLECTIVO

Elsewhere in South America, buses are called just that: bus or omnibus. But in Buenos Aires the bus is called a "*colectivo*" (short for *transporte colectivo* or collective transport).

If you are the kind of person who demands comfort and courteous service, the *colectivo* is definitely not for you. If you want to see the entire city of Buenos Aires and the surrounding suburban and industrial area for a few cents, the *colectivo* is what you want.

The minimum fare—which will take you about 30 blocks—costs about a dime. And unless you travel to the ends of the earth, it's pretty hard to spend a dollar aboard a *colectivo*.

There are over 140 *colectivo* lines serving Buenos Aires and the greater Buenos Aires area and they run about once every five or 10 minutes throughout most of the day. A number of them run slightly less frequently at night and those that don't, only rest between about midnight and 5 a.m.

If you don't insist on taking the *colectivo* at peak hours of the day—8 to 10 a.m. and 5 to 9 p.m.—you can plot your own daily tour of different parts of the city. By combining *colectivos* you can reach practically any point of the Greater Buenos Aires area and get from there to just about any other point you choose. And all points lead to the center of the city—eventually.

Taking a bus at rush-hour is an experience that is only for the hardened Buenos Aires resident—a bone-crushing free-for-all in which seats are fully occupied and commuters squeeze three-deep into the narrow center aisle. At this time of day, men and boys hang precariously out the doors of the vehicle and drop running to the pavement as the driver slows, but does not completely halt at stops.

The typical *colectivo* driver (colectivero) is a surly, rude, bossy man who will leave you behind if you don't hop on board as soon as he stops. These men (women *colectivo* drivers could probably be counted on the fingers of one hand) fight snarled unruly Buenos Aires traffic all day, with many of them driving shifts of up to 14 hours. They sell tickets, keep track of their own intake and ticket sales, make change and live with inspectors breathing down their necks about the schedule. They could hardly not be surly.

But it is the *colectivo*—with its varied and flashy color combinations which distinguish one line from another—that mobilizes the *porteño*.

It's also surprisingly efficient. For the traveler with a minimal command of Spanish, it can be an interesting, exhaustive way to see the city.

When you board the bus, tell the driver your destination and he will compute the fare. Approach your local fellow passengers regarding directions—most *porteños* are helpful.

POPULAR EATERIES

For those with expensive tastes, Buenos Aires has plenty of four-fork restaurants where the menus are in Spanish and English and the prices are geared for expense-account living.

But there are also many places for those who prefer good food with few frills.

Probably the most popular eatery in Buenos Aires is **Pippo's**. Actually, there are three Pippo's, all on the same block—one at

and soda water (as *porteños* are wont to do), makes a refreshing spritzer. Unlike many other restaurants in Buenos Aires that have more rigid schedules, at Pippo's you can order a meal any time from late morning until after midnight.

Another popular eatery in the same district, but slightly more upscale, is **Chiquilín**, at Montevideo and Perón. The immortal tango crooner, Carlos Gardel, grins under

356 Paraná, and the other two side by side on the other side of the block at 345 and 346 Montevideo. They're all the same—brightly lit, pale green *trattorias* with white-jacketed waiters rushing around teetering stacks of dishes. Patrons sit at paper-covered tables (on which waiters used to scribble the bill until printed receipts became mandatory) often elbow-to-elbow with strangers. The food is economical and dependable—"ours is export meat," says the sign; the pasta is made on the premises. Try a steaming platter of *vermicelli mixto:* pesto and tomato sauce on plump noodles. The hearty red house-wine comes in carafes and, mixed with ice

his fedora from a portrait hung at one end of the dining area. Gazing proprietarily from the other side is a brass bust of Anibal "Pichuco" Troilo, the squeeze-box "monster" (as *porteños* call their heroes) who made this restaurant legendary in the tango "Chiquilín de Bachín." Cured hams hang from the rafters, wine bottles line the walls, sheets of paper cover the tables, and the cloth napkins will protect the most generous girth. There are no table menus—just a lighted sign hanging in the middle stating the eating options and their reasonable prices. Grilled beef and pastas are the house specialities. As an appetizer, try a *provoleta*—a

140

thick round slice of provolone cheese grilled with a topping of garlic, oregano and olive oil. The *flan* (egg custard) with whipped cream and *dulce de leche* (a caramel topping) is edible sin.

For a more intimate setting, there's **La Payanca** at 1015 Suipacha, near Santa Fe. You can eat at the long counter and banter with the waiters, or you can sit at a table in the small dining area. The restaurant special-

lar in Buenos Aires, where *pizzerias* abound. One that's especially enticing is **Guerrín**, on Corrientes. Its garish panoply of multi-colored wall tiles complements perfectly the amazing variety of pizzas you can order there. Among the more than ninety options is one that comes with muzzarella, hearts of palm and strawberries; another is muzzarella, asparagus and hard-boiled eggs; and there's a camembert cheese pizza topped

izes in foods from the north of Argentina— *empanadas, tamales, locro* (a corn chowder) and, of course, beef.

Across the street is **Los Chilenos**, where fish and seafood are prepared by people who, unlike most chefs in this carnivorous city, don't cook fish as if it were a cut of beef. The often spicy Chilean dishes include eel soup, abalone and *gambas al ajillo* (shrimp with garlic).

Pizza is quite good and deservedly popu-

Left, young couple enjoy *vermicelli mixto* at Pippo's. Above, the ubiquitous steak— served at almost every meal.

with mouth-watering chunks of octopus.

For good pizza but also a tasty sampling of regional foods, there's **La Americana** at 77 Callao, near Bartolome Mitre. A large sign boasts this is "the queen of the *empanadas*" —no small claim in a land renowned for these snacks. The large meat-filled pastries come spicy (*salteña*) or bland (*criolla*).

Besides these locales, there are countless other good and inexpensive eateries. Unless you're dying for familiar food, avoid the fast-food hamburger franchises—why eat rubbery burgers and limp french fries when you can eat just as economically in places with considerably more character?

SNACKING

Presumably, the bad news about caffeine and sugar has not reached Buenos Aires. The typical *porteño* day is broken up by an infinite number of short breaks for strong coffee and a sweet morsel. A Spanish poet who visited Argentina at the turn of the century reckoned that the *porteño* sweet tooth was a legacy of their Spanish-Arab ancestors. In any case, you never have to look far in Buenos Aires for something delicious to eat. Virtually every street has at least one sweets and soft drinks vendor who works out of the hole-in-the-wall sidewalk stalls called *kioscos*. There you can find candy bars (both "*Shot*" chocolate and "*Mantecol*" water-covered peanut nougat bars are favorites), chewing gum (generically called "chiclets"), hard candies (*caramelos*), and lollipops (*chupetines*). A *kiosco* is also the place to get the great Argentine hunger postponer, the *alfajor*. This pastry-in-an-envelope consists of two cookies that sandwich a creamy filling, usually either chocolate or *dulce de leche,* that soft caramel which Argentines also spread on their morning toast. Although the *alfajor* is usually bathed in white or dark chocolate, eating one without a glass of milk at hand can prove a mouth-drying experience. Those made by Surchard tend to have this effect less than others and are recommended.

Candy-coated peanuts cooked on the spot in copper kettles are a common snack on street corners. Popcorn sold by the same vendors, though, tends to be rubbery.

Ice cream in Buenos Aires is the stuff fond memories are made of. To all but the most disciplined, it can quickly become addictive, and there are plenty of shops there to tempt you. Almost all churn out their own ice creams on the premises, and they can offer a bewildering variety. If you visit one of the trendy Freddo shops, try a cone (*cucurrucho*) of the house specialty, a nougat cream called *torrocino*. The mint-chocolate chip is also compelling. Other local flavors include *sambayón* (eggs and rum), *dulce de leche* (caramel, and *crema rusa* (nuts and cream). It's all right to ask for several flavors even for a single scoop.

In winter months many ice cream parlors offer thick hot chocolate and *churros,* deep fried ridged fritters about the size of a fat cigar. (Try the *churros* injected with *dulce de leche.*) A cozy establishment specializing in these treats, Chocolate con Churros, is at Corrientes 1453, near Parana.

For in-depth snacking, there are innumerable cafés, tea-houses, and bars.

Argentines tend to fill these places as the afternoon wanes and their stomachs whine. This is the hour of *la merienda,* the secret to how Argentines make it from mid-day lunches to late night suppers. If you only want coffee, remember it comes in a *demitasse* unless you request a *café doble*. If you want it with a bit of milk, ask for a *café cortado,* or with a lot of milk, a café *con leche*. With the latter, try the local version of croissants: *media lunas,* or half moons. *Media lunas* usually come in threesomes and are more compact and chewy than their French cousins. They are made either of butter (*de manteca*) or lard (*de grasa*).

Sandwiches tend to be on the dainty side. There are the sandwiches *de miga,* pre-fabricated crustless squares stacked high on counter tops for your inspection. Try them toasted (*tostadas*).

There are also more substantial sandwiches in buns called *pebetes*. Proscuitto (*jamon crudo*) and slices of meat rolled with vegetables (*matambre*) are popular fillings.

For a variety of salty snacks, request a *picada*. This is a tray full of treats that usually includes cheese cubes, salami slices, olives, pretzels, pate, and peanuts.

Sweet pastries called *facturas* are also served for *la merienda,* as are plates of little cakes called *masas*. Don't let the mound of sweets intimidate you—you only pay for what you eat.

A coffee break in a sidewalk café.

142

MATE: ARGENTINA'S NATIONAL DRINK

Mate, the green Paraguayan herb which is drunk as an infusion in a variety of different ways, is something of a national passion, especially among the less affluent portion of the population, and particularly so in the country, outside the more sophisticated and bustling cities. (And if Argentines think they are *mate* fans, they should see how the Uruguayans treat it! Uruguayans are seldom seen without a thermos flask under their arm and a *mate* gourd in their hands.)

To drink *mate* the traditional way you require four things: a hollow gourd, a long metal pipe or straw called a *bombilla, yerba mate* (the dried leaves and stalk which provide the infusion) and hot but not boiling water. The gourd is filled to two thirds with *yerba*. The *yerba* is moistened with a little cold water and the mixture is allowed to stand for a minute. The hot water is then poured in until the gourd is full to the brim. A generous froth should cover the surface. Sugar can be added or not. If it is used it is placed in the gourd first, before the *yerba*. On being poured the *mate* is sucked up through the *bombilla* until the water has gone. The gourd is then filled with more water and passed to the next drinker, who repeats the process and passes on the gourd to the next person. Everyone uses the same *bombilla,* which has a perforated bulb at the end which acts as a strainer. *Bombillas* can be simple metal straws, or they can be elaborate objects of silver or silver and gold.

The gourds can be plain hollow dried squashes or they can be ornately embellished affairs of silver artistry. The Fernandez Blanco Museum contains an exceptional collection of silver gourds and *bombillas*.

Mate contains about the same amount of caffein as a cup of coffee; it is refreshing and stimulating and helps stem the pangs of hunger. It is also a great remedy for mild stomach and intestinal upsets.

Young family drinking *mate* in traditional manner.

TANGO

The tango is a paradox in Buenos Aires: it is both everywhere and nowhere. Visitors who have their hearts set on spending every night in dark, glamorous clubs enthralled by local couples dramatically reenacting the tango's primitive ritual are likely to be disappointed. On the other hand, those who are attentive to the city's more muted melodies that suddenly break through a surface of urban sound to reveal its soul, will hear tangos in taxis, cafés, and floating out of upstairs windows.

The tango, which had its origins at the beginning of this century, has both traveled far and stayed close to home. A number of clubs located in San Telmo feature tango music and professional dancers who provide tourists with the variety of tango flavors which made the dance a successful exotic export. On the other hand, in some of the more plebian social clubs and dance halls, the tango can be heard and seen very much as it was 50 years ago.

Immigrant roots: As the tango is Argentina's most authentic form of popular music, its history and the history of Argentina are intertwined. Edmundo Rivera, one of the great tango singers, said: "When all is said and done, the tango is no more than a reflection of our daily reality." Tango's reality began somewhere in the 19th century, when Argentina was consolidating after a series of bloody civil wars and a frontier war against the local Indians. Buenos Aires was becoming a thriving commercial center. The growth of the city created an impression of endless opportunity. Discharged soldiers, along with *criollos* from the economically declining interior provinces, sought to put down roots in the semi-rural areas surrounding the city. They were joined by several thousands of European immigrants who arrived hoping to *"hacer la America"* (to make

it in America). Argentina, like the United States, became a great melting pot.

This polyglot immigrant mixture, composed mainly of Italians, Spaniards, Jews and Eastern Europeans, encountered the native *criollos* and descendants of African slaves in the growing number of *conventillos* (tenements) and in the outlying part of the city called the *arrabal*. Each group brought to the tenement patios and *barrio* street cor-

ners its own cultural "voice" in its most transportable form: music. The haunting laments of Spain's flamenco, the rhythms of Africa's candombles, and the lilting milongas of the creoles came together. The disparate sounds were forged into one by the shared experiences of nostalgia for an irrecoverable past and hope for a still uncertain future. The tango was the product of this fusion.

Lascivious dance: Beyond a general knowledge of its family tree, the tango's birth is a mystery: exactly when, where and which group of progenitors contributed what are questions that are still hotly de-

Left, popular 1930s tango singer and movie hearthrob Carlos Gardel. Right, elderly couple doing the tango in La Boca.

bated. What is known is that the tango was first a dance and only later did lyrics appear. Even then the words were mostly improvised and seldom written down. In part, that is explained by the shady character of one of the main branches of the tango's family tree. Bordellos played a major role in launching the tango. Brothels and rough-and-tumble cafés attracted Argentina's predominately male immigrants. There men escaped their loneliness and poverty, spending evenings listening to the bawdy lyrics of the early anonymous *tanguistas* and dancing among themselves.

By day these workmen shared the

rapid change. Not only was its audience expanding, but the configuration of instruments altered, adding the sound that marks the tango to this day. A type of accordion, the *bandoneón* (concertina) was added to the previous combination of guitar, flute, violin, and, when it was available, piano. Manufactured in Germany until the 1920s, bandoneons are only available secondhand today, and are passed from generation to generation with reverence. Its most renowned repair specialists are found here in Buenos Aires. So essential is this strange instrument with its haunting tone to the tango, that one famous lyricist, Homero Manzi, paid homage

crowded tenements in the southern area of the city with their womenfolk and before long the tango, both as a dance and as song, had also found a place in the patios, fiestas and plebian theatrical productions known as *sainetes*. By 1904, the popular magazine *Caras y Caretas* was heralding this new cultural phenomenon in an article titled "The Stylish Dance." Only the culturally conservative upper classes remained aloof to what the author called this "madness" for the "lascivious dance" with lyrics "that would redden the face of a policeman."

As the new century opened, the tango, like the city that gave it birth, was in a process of

to it in a well-known tango, *Che bandoneon*!

In the madcap days before the outbreak of World War I, the tango appeared in European cafés, scandalizing its upper classes. Kaiser Wilhelm prohibited the dance among his officials and Queen Mary refused to attend parties if there were to be tangos. But for everyone else, it was the rage. The tango's success in Europe gave it the seal of approval back home where even among the aristocracy the tango came to represent national creativity.

The magic of Gardel: With its acceptance by the monied classes and the introduction of recordings, the tango entered a new stage.

148

Fancy clubs and records made possible the appearance of tango "stars" and the development of a mass audience. When, in 1917, Victor recorded the voice of a little known singer named Carlos Gardel singing a song called *Mi Noche Triste* the tango hit the big time not only in Argentina but all over Latin America.

Gardel is unquestionably tango's biggest superstar and the symbol of its golden era. He is to tango what Frank Sinatra was to North America's swing era ballad. Like the tango itself, Gardel's origins are a matter of debate among aficionados, some of whom claim that he was born in Lyons, France.

cess in the new media—recordings, radio, cinema—that simultaneously wrenched the tango from its traditional working class and neighborhood roots. The new audiences required more romantic and sentimental tunes and a dashing vocalist to sing them. Gardel, who met all these requirements, had no equal. His fame was spread by a series of movies made from 1929 to 1935. With luck, you might catch one on television during your stay. Many tango devotees still insist that "every day he sings better" and posters of Gardel are still seen to this day all over Buenos Aires. The romance of Gardel was heightened with his tragic death in a plane

Others claim that he was born in Montevideo, Uruguay, tango's other wellspring. With exotic good looks, dubious connections in the marginal world of brothels, clubs and political bosses, Gardel was rescued from obscurity by his clear tenor voice which, by 1912, had secured him a spot on the hill in the most elegant nightspots of Buenos Aires. What catapulted Carlos Gardel into the public's heart was his suc-

crash during a 1935 tour of Colombia. Thousands of sobbing fans met the boat containing Gardel's body, at Buenos Aires' harbor. And even to this day, his shrine in the Chacarita Cemetery is always adorned with fresh flowers.

But Gardel's truest memorial is the widespread adoption of his gestures and singing style, which you will see and hear in the clubs of Buenos Aires. Gardel's success and impact was so great that it has become part of common language. If a *porteño* wants to say that someone is at a peak of achievement, they are likely to remark that the person is "Gardel."

Dancing the tango on San Telmo street corner. Right, hand-painted filete recalls a well-known tango melody.

Unfortunately, the tango itself has had a different history. Always related to the well being of its main audience, the popular classes, the tango flourished during the 1940s when Perónism provided a sense of promise and real income distribution among the Argentine masses. By the end of the 1950s the tango entered a crisis from which it has never really emerged. Competition from newer musical forms, mainly rock-and-roll-derived ballads, and its own inability or reluctance to evolve has pushed the tango to the sidelines of the contemporary entertainment world.

However, even as the great names of yester-year disappeared from the play bills and marquees of Avenida Corrientes (the Boulevard of Tango), some innovative forces were at work. Argentine musicians who have either traveled abroad or been influenced by other musical forms have created a current that could be called "neo-tango." The most important and best known of these modernizers is Astor Piazzola.

Piazzola's training as a classical and jazz musician has led him to produce fascinating experiences in fusion. Piazzola's and incidently Gardel's broad appeal was demonstrated again in 1987 by the success of his sound track for the prize-winning Argentine film, *The Exile of Gardel*.

The tango's future, especially as a popular dance form, is a question mark. Relegated to tourist clubs and dance halls of another era, the tango is not the shared social idiom of today's Argentine youth, as it was in previous generations. Tango fans are hoping that the enthusiastic reception in the United States and Europe recently given to the dance show *Tango Argentino* and the revival of tango abroad will reverberate at home. But for now, while the tango may be the very air *porteños* breathe, it is not the music they prefer to dance to.

And all the better—more room on the dance floor for the rest of us!

Where to hear and see the tango: The best introduction to the tango, and to other Argentine folk music is an evening in the **Viejo Almacén**. Founded in the early 1970s by Edmundo Rivera, one of tango's great voices, the Viejo Almacén has the best tango orchestras. The show usually includes a dance act, a bit of folk music, and several tango songs. The audience exudes a contagious enthusiasm, especially at the late shows on weekend nights.

A number of San Telmo clubs are variations on the Viejo Almacén theme. The **Casa Blanca**, the **Casa Rosada**, and **Taconeando** (whose owner, Beba Bidart, was one of the dance stars of the 1940s tango films), all offer floor shows with various types of local music. The **Bar Sur** and the **Bar Union** are a bit shabby but on weekends, a stream of tango singers and musicians transform the atmosphere from seedy, to interesting and authentic. The best place in town for authenticity is the **Club Croata** at the corner of San Juan and Boedo Avenues. No giltz, no glamor, but on Saturday nights (only) the old dance hall is filled with older folks gliding gracefully. Club Croata, with its bright lights, limited drinks menu and extremely modest devotees, is tango's natural habitat.

Another dance hall, **La Argentina**, on Rodriguez Peña just off Corrientes, has interludes of tango spliced between other kinds of contemporary music. On Saturday nights and Sunday evenings you can often see good tango dancers grooving.

La Boca, the traditional Italian neighborhood on the southern side of Buenos Aires, was for many decades a center of tango. Unfortunately, this is no longer the case. However, one cantina, as the combination restaurant/music halls are called, has a homey tango touch. At the **Cantina Feli Cudi** (Corner of Suarez and Hernandaria Streets) families of old and young alike dance and sing along with a bandoneon player, giving us a nostalgic reminder of tango's home-spun roots.

If the tango is at the top of your list, you should ask at your hotel if there are any special shows in town during your stay. Occasionally one of the big names: Susana Rinaldi, Osvaldo Pugliese, Astor Piazzola, Eladia Blasquez, will be performing and your hotel can arrange tickets for you.

Right, accordion player shows his stuff at tango club Feli Cudi.

UNDERGROUND NIGHTLIFE

Much of Buenos Aires' Bohemia was forced "underground" during military rule and retains a secretive air. Today, *porteños* are breaking out and making up for lost time, although the result can be anything from 60s hippy-style to 80s punk.

The cheapest place to start is **El Taller**, a hangout of left-wing students referred to by *porteños*, with some irony, as *"psico-bol-ches."* There is no cover charge as performers prefer to pass around the hat for contributions. The crowded and boisterous atmosphere makes it an easy place to meet people, especially since you will almost certainly be forced to sit at someone else's table.

As in all of Buenos Aires' *boliches* (bars) there is no point arriving before midnight. The main performance does not start until 2 a.m. Meanwhile, musicians will play experimental jazz and the audience will quaff copious amounts of *clerico*, white wine mixed with fruit.

Saturday night is often reserved for cabarets or stand-up comics such as the popular MacPhantom: his mimes, with sound effects, of B-grade American films are hilarious, no matter how little Spanish you know.

Similar *boliches* where *porteños* go to nurse a *café con leche* or glass of wine for hours are **La Cama** and **Café del Jazz** in San Telmo. Regular appearances are made in both places by the comic trio Los Vergara and the musician Fontova, who invents obscene lyrics to accompany his classic *salsa* tunes.

More upmarket is **La Verduleria** on Avenida Corrientes, a mariner's hangout renovated to attract a wider clientele. A dwarf in a doorman's uniform guides guests to their tables, where they must first endure a solo performance by an Argentine version of Frank Sinatra. At around 3 a.m., a band starts up with *cumbia* or *samba*, to roars of approval.

Singing group Gambas al Ajillo satirize *porteño* notions of propriety.

For Western rock, one of the most "in" discotheques is the **Paladium**. The huge converted warehouse offers foreign music with film clips as well as *el rock nacional*. **Cemento** remains the classic hangout of Buenos Aires' small and exclusive punk set, although it is dark enough to allow the inconspicuous participation of those whose dress and haircuts are not quite to standard.

The *porteño* punks have taken their style and studied ennui from their British counterparts, remaining a subculture still trying to find its feet in a society which views them with amusement. The elegant art-school atmosphere is anything but threatening, with almost up-to-date dance music playing until a live punk band starts up at around 4 a.m. playing regular favorites such as *los Viola-dores* and *Licor de Semen*.

But the most famous and accessible underground nightspot is the **Centro Parakultural**. Having progressed from Bohemian obscurity to relative respectability, the Parakultural can still receive a ritualistic police raid at opening time, persumably in search of forbidden substances. The walls of the vast and rundown building are covered with graffiti and changing exhibitions of paintings by local artists. Sawdust is sprinkled over the floor, cheap wine is sold by the bottle and silent eight mm experimental films are shown in one corner.

Live rock bands during the week lead up to cabarets on Friday and Saturday nights. The Parakultural's greatest success has been with regular performers comedian Omar Viola and the cabaret group *Las Gambas al Ajillo*. Taking their name from a Spanish shrimp dish, the four women of Las Gambas poke fun at every local sacred cow from religion to motherhood, and dwell at length on the sexual hangups of *porteño* males.

Some of the cabaret may be difficult to follow as it relies on colorful Argentine slang but this is compensated by the English music which follows soon after the show, and which invites the audience to dance on until dawn.

LA BOCA

The working class neighborhood of La Boca is at the southern tip of the city, along the **Riachuelo Canal**. The *barrio* is famous for its sheet-iron houses painted in bright colors, and for its history as a residential area for the Genovese sailors and dock workers in the 19th century.

La Boca came to life with the mid-19th century surge in international trade and the accompanying increase in port activity. In the 1870s, meat salting plants and warehouses were built, as well as a tramway to bring workers into the area. With the expansion of the city's ports, the Riachuelo was dug out to permit entrance of deep water ships. La Boca became a bustling dock, and sailors and longshoremen, most of whom were Italian immigrants, began to settle in the area.

The sheet-iron houses which can still be seen throughout La Boca and across the canal in **Avellaneda** were originally built from materials taken from the interiors of abandoned ships. The idea apparently came from Genoa. The style, as well as the bohemian play on colors so unusual in the rest of decorous Buenos Aires, became a tradition in this part of town.

Local artist: The famous Argentine painter Benito Quinquela Martin also influenced the use of color in the neighborhood. Quinquela was an orphan, adopted by a longshoreman family of La Boca at the turn of the century. As an artist, he dedicated his life to capturing the essence of this working class neighborhood. He painted dark stooped figures scurrying like ants against the florid background of the docks. In one painting, which, according to legend, Mussolini unsuccessfully tried to buy with a blank check, men hurriedly unload a burning ship against an immense background splashed with bright or-

eceding
ges:
ffee
ndor on
minito in
Boca.
ft, young
ers
neath
saic of
gentine
l Carlos
rdel.

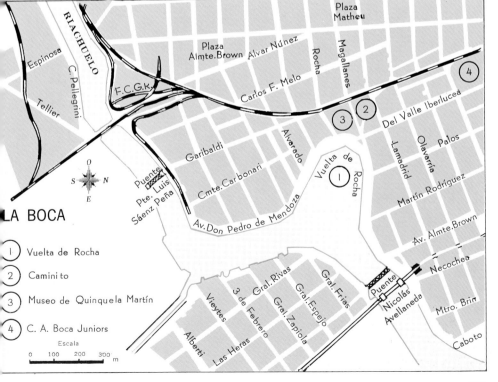

LA BOCA

1. Vuelta de Rocha
2. Caminito
3. Museo de Quinquela Martín
4. C. A. Boca Juniors

Escala
0   100   200   300 m

ange, blues and black. In later years, Quinquela used whimsical pastels to represent the fabric of life in La Boca, making a subtle social protest.

Neighborhood residents took pride in their local artist, and were influenced by his vision of their lives. They chose even wilder colors for their own homes, and a unique dialogue grew between residents and the artist.

Quinquela took over an alleyway known as **El Caminito**, decorated it with murals and sculpture, and established an open air market to promote local artists. The brightly painted houses and strings of laundry and hanging bird cages give the Caminito the look of a stage setting, but the modest lives of the people here are quite real. There is an uncomfortable contrast in this *barrio* between tourists with their cameras, gaudy souvenir shops and humble local stores, and small children begging for coins.

A stroll through La Boca begins at El Caminito. Heading north from the river on the alley, it is worth walking around the block and back to the riverside to get a sense of a residential street. The colorful houses look like toys, but they are in fact solid homes. Most have long corridors leading to interior apartments, and are lined with wood paneling. The cobblestone streets are lined with tall sycamore trees; elevated sidewalks foretell rainy season flooding.

Ship's graveyard: La Vuelta de Rocha where El Caminito begins, consists of a small triangular plaza with a ship's mast. It overlooks the port area, which might be more accurately described as a decaying shipyard. More boats lie half sunken on their sides than upright and functioning. Depending on which way the wind is blowing, visitors may be accosted by the rude odors coming up from the canal which is so polluted that reputedly there is no life in its waters. Residents blame the old slaughterhouses upriver, which in the past dumped wastes into the canal.

East along **Pedro de Mendoza**, the

La Boca is splash of color in a city of otherwise muted tones.

avenue parallel to the canal, is the **La Boca Museum of Fine Arts** (1835 Mendoza). The top floor was used by Quinquela as an apartment studio. Many of his most important paintings are here, and you can also see the flat he used in his last years. The museum is an interesting stop if only to get a view of the shipyard from the window of the studio, the same shipyard depicted in his paintings.

Further down Pedro de Mendoza is the **Nicolas Avellaneda Bridge**, used by commuters living south of the city. There is a rickety old escalator that takes local pedestrians and game visitors up to the bridge, where you can experience a rush of acrophobia and get a view of the neighborhood.

A night on the town: Just past the bridge is **Calle Necochea**, whose rowdy cantinas provide an atmosphere that seems part gameshow, part eatery and dancehall. These were originally sailors' mess halls and are enjoyed by both locals and visitors for their garish decor, fresh seafood, and corny floor shows.

Bright flashing lights, speakers set out on the sidewalk blaring loud music, and the aggressive doormen may remind some visitors of San Francisco's North Beach strip joints, but the scene is not as seedy as it appears. Families from the interior of the country are there for a festive night out. Old people are singing their favorite tunes and dancing amidst balloons and ribbons. The idea that a night out on Necochea is a celebration of sailors returning home is definitely preserved. Most of the action takes place on Necochea between Calle **Brandson** and **Calle Suarez**.

Pizza break: Two blocks west is **Avenida Almirante Brown**, the main thoroughfare in La Boca. The avenue holds no particular charm except for its excellent pizzerias. *Porteños* come from all over the city to eat pizza *a la piedra,* a thin dough pizza baked in a brick oven and *faina,* a chick pea dough which is eaten on top of pizza.

raditional alcony on orrugated n houses.

FOOTBALL

Towering above the wood and corrugated metal dwellings and old brick warehouses of La Boca is the giant stadium of one of Argentina's leading professional soccer clubs, Boca Juniors.

La Bombonera (the chocolate box) is an imposing and austere rectangle of concrete about 180 feet (60 meters) high that covers two full blocks and becomes a cauldron of working class passion on match days, marked by the famous ticker-tape welcome the fans give their team and by off-the-cuff verses chanted to the tunes of pop songs, sung to their glory or to the damnation of their team's rivals.

Boca Juniors and archrival River Plate are clubs founded on the waterside at the turn of the century, when British immigrants spread the game throughout the country.

River Plate moved out in the 1920s and went on to become a middle class club with a wide range of sports. Financially successful, it is nicknamed the Millionaires. Boca Juniors stayed behind, rooted in the working class harbor area.

Both have vied for dominance ever since, and their rivalry overshadows all others. Boca claims to belong to "half the country plus one," enjoying a following that spreads from the northern tropical provinces to the vast Patagonian wasteland in the south.

Passionate loyalties: Many ardent fans who grew up supporting big teams in the capital have seldom seen them play and have never been to the Bombonera, or to River Plate's **Monumental** stadium, where the 1978 World Cup final was played.

It does not matter. The passion of soccer in Argentina knows no boundaries, pervading family and *barrio* life. Every member of a family roots for a team, and not always for the same one.

Essentially, in a city with eight first division clubs, four more in the suburbs and twice that number in the second division, the neighborhood in which a fan is born or raised, is the decisive factor in choosing which team to support.

But the passion takes root at an early age, and the choice can be influenced by many other factors, such as which team is the champion at the time, or a persuasive older kid next door: "You're for Boca or else!" ... "Never mind if your Dad supports San Lorenzo."

Soccer is something you learn as a natural part of growing up. The traveler will find no published procedure for going to matches, and ticket information and recommended games are most easily obtained by word of mouth. But Argentines are very willing to help with advice on one of their favorite topics. A visitor naturally would like to see good soccer in a packed stadium full of atmosphere. Anyone, from the hotel concierge to the waiter at the corner café, is likely to be well-informed about what good derbies are on at a given weekend or if one of the teams is playing an important cup match against another South American country.

The average weekend game is easy. There is seldom a full house, but the uninitiated must go armed with words such as *tribuna visitante* (visitors' stand) or, if you feel you will be safer among the home crowd and are prepared to pay extra to rub elbows with the club members, ask for the *tribuna local.*

The teams: Boca have traditionally been noted for their strength of spirit and physical commitment rather than technique. River Plate tend to favor open attacking football and have the money to sign the best soccer players.

Independiente, just across the murky Riachuelo in the city suburb of Avellaneda and owners of the oldest concrete stadium in the country, are ball artists like River. Their neighbors and archrivals, Racing Club, built a beautiful stadium a stone's throw away. Unfortunately, structural damage and lack of funds to make the necessary repairs, has kept fans away.

San Lorenzo, which hails from Almagro, sold their stadium on a site now occupied by a huge supermarket. They rent other grounds, usually Boca's Bombonera or

Velez Sarsfield for their home games.

Argentina's soccer fortunes have gone the way of the country, but the game has survived the worst economic crises and a well-managed Argentine Football Association has in the past decade been responsible for Argentina's success at the international level.

Fame and fortune: It is on this foundation that Argentina gave the world Diego Maradona, out of poverty is through professional sport.

Argentina is an endless conveyor belt of soccer talent. Half the boys tried out by the clubs fail to make the grade, but not so much for lack of skill as for temperamental reasons, especially those from the provinces, who cannot stand the loneliness of the big city and return home.

Maradona entertained crowds at half-time with ball-juggling feats when he was barely

dona. Maradona, like so many Buenos Aires kids, was discovered by a scout for the small first division club Argentina Juniors, while playing in games on vacant lots in a poor working class district of the city, Villa Fiorito, on the fringes of Lanus borough.

Maradona is exceptional in having made his first division debut at the age of 15, and having played his first full international match at 16. But his story is like that of so many Argentine youngsters whose only way

Above, star player Diego Maradona celebrates another goal.

in his teens, but this sort of extra act is rare nowadays. However, there is the atmosphere to be savored, provided it is not turned sour by fighting between rival fans or between fans and the police.

Maradona is not exceptional in having pursued a more lucrative career abroad. Especially during times of economic crisis, when professional sportsmen's salaries are well below those on the world market, it has become common for the best soccer players to move to teams in Europe for huge fees.

But Argentina always manages to produce equally talented replacements to keep the fans' interest alive.

PAINTING AND PRINTMAKING

Buenos Aires has a great deal to offer visitors interested in the visual arts; there are probably more painters and schools of painting here than anywhere else on the continent. The city that proudly calls itself the Paris of South America has traditionally looked to Europe for technique and inspiration. Nevertheless, the geography and social realities of Argentina have added a rich dimension to the lessons of the old world masters.

In the 1830s, as soon as Buenos Aires had established itself as the main and most southern port in South America, the first painters emerged. A young Italian engineer, Carlos Enrique Pelligrini, decided to become a painter when his first portraits and landscapes became successful. Until his death, his paintings, portraits, and lithographs of the city of Buenos Aires were acclaimed and sought after. They are fascinating documentation of the society and customs of that period.

In the middle of the 19th century another painter, Pirilidiano Puerreydon, stood out. His paintings, portraits and landscapes are of a profound professionalism. Puerreydon's portrait of *Manuela de Rosas y Ezcurra* has a fine quality and the use of red tones (the color of Federalism which was imposed by her father, Juan Manuel de Rosas, governor of the Province of Buenos Aires) is superbly accomplished.

At the end of the 19th century and beginning of the 20th century, there were Eduardo Sivori, whose painting *La Pampa en Olavarria* is one of many paintings that depict the placid life in the Argentine country (the pampas) and Ernesto de la Carcova, whose paintings, in contrast, deal with Buenos Aires and its people, particularly its poor, as in one of his paintings *Sin Pan y Sin Trabajo* ("No Bread and No Work"). He used background light as did Fernando Fader in his beautiful landscape paintings.

Social realism: During the 1920s Buenos Aires became an important city due to its industrial development, which consequently also gave the arts new life. The outstanding painter of this period was Benito Quinquela Martin, who was born and raised in the southern port quarter of Buenos Aires called La Boca. He himself was a stevedore when he decided to put his life and La Boca on canvas. His paintings are strong and full of vigor. La Boca has always been a place where artists lived and worked. Even now, on weekends, on a street called **Caminito**, painters can be seen working and selling their typical scenes of La Boca.

Social realism was expressed most heavily by such artists as the following: Lino Eneas Spilimbergo, known for his strong, impassioned, and expressive work, his figures, his still, and his landscapes; Antonio Berni, whose large paintings of workers and later, his painting collages of two main characters typical of the poor and neglected of the city. These collages are a major expression of Argentine art. Both of these artists were also accomplished printmakers. The work of Juan Carlos Castagnino, another expression of this style gives a lighter and more beautiful treatment to this subject matter (the poor). Perhaps the largest and most expressive work of these three artists are their 1946 murals which can still be seen in the **Galeria Pacífico** (now called **Las Malvinas**) on Calle Florida.

Another artist of a slightly younger generation is Carlos Alonso. Painter, printmaker and illustrator, with a different lyrical and poetic touch, Alonso's characters include both those that populate the city of Buenos Aires as well as the gauchos in the countryside (as in his illustrations for *Martin Fierro*.)

Surrealism influenced many Argentine printers, including Xul Solar, one of the first surrealists; Raquel Forner a few years later, and Roberto Aizenberg, known for his neo-surrealist works.

There is also a significant Argentine group of non-figurative artists, Vicente Forté, Leopoldo Presas, and Luis Seoane, to name a few; as well as the more contemporary neo-figurative artists like Antonio

Segui, Romulo Maccio, and Felipe Noe.

Printmaking: As in the rest of South America, printmaking is an important visual expression in Argentina. Woodcuts, linocuts, lithographs, etchings, silkscreens and even experimental printmaking have strong traditions and dedicated contemporary practitioners.

The first prints and woodcuts to be found in what is now Argentina were done by the

duced an amazing quantity of work: the first illustrated newspapers, a series entitled "Picturesque Customs of Buenos Aires" (see pg. 35) as well as the official list of all the important cattle brands for the Rosas government.

At the end of the 19th century, a new period emerged with the etchings of E. Argelo and Eduardo Sivori. Both of these artists are the pioneers of Argentine etching.

Guaraní Indians who lived in the Jesuit missions in the northeast of the country. They were excellent craftsmen and their prints depicted mostly religious themes due to their Spanish Jesuit education.

In 1828, the first important lithographic printmaking workshop, called "Bacle and Company" was established in Buenos Aires. C.H. Bacle and his wife, E. Pellegrini (who printed a series called "Remembrances of the River Plate"), Onslow, and others pro-

Their work deals with life in the countryside as the titles suggest: *Ombues* (typical tree-like plant of the pampas), *Las Carretas* (The Ox-carts), and others.

Giving graphic arts a new spirit, in 1915, was a group called "The Artists of the People" formed by Hebequer, Arato, Vigo, and Belloca, among others. Their images dealt with the social reality of the poor and neglected, of rebellion and of hope.

At the time of this writing, works of Argentine printmakers are being organized and will constitute the basic collection of the **Museo del Grabado** (Museum of Printmaking) of the city of Buenos Aires.

Sin Pan y Sin Trabajo **(No Bread and No Work) was one of the first Argentine works to portray social conflicts.**

BARRIO NORTE

In Buenos Aires, **Barrio Norte** is where the rich people live. But this wasn't always the case. In the city's early days, a large slaughter house occupied the northern part of the *barrio*, the **Recoleta**. It was said that a ravine filled up with cattle heads and that people dreaded the rainy season on account of the floating heads.

Barrio Norte acquired some much-needed tone when a yellow fever epidemic hit the city in 1870. Wealthy *porteños,* convinced that the river fogs were causing the deaths, fled from the southern lowlands near San Telmo for the higher ground to the north.

Over the next few decades, Argentina's upper classes spared no expense in making Barrio Norte into a miniature Paris. Here, more than anywhere else in the city, it's easy to imagine what Buenos Aires was like when it was capital of one of the richest countries on earth. At the ever-fashionable **Café Biela**, you may see a handsome businessman in a well-cut Italian suit. His head may be tilted back to take advantage of the sun as a white-jacketed waiter takes his order, another man shines his shoes and a third, a street artist, sketches his likeness on a drawing pad. The thought may cross your mind that this is a wonderful life.

A wonderful death: However, to do a proper walking tour of Barrio Norte, you should postpone the cafés for an hour and begin where privileged Argentines end, at **Recoleta Cemetery**.

In a city that devotes itself to distinctions of class and military rank, the Recoleta is Buenos Aires' marble heart. To be buried in one of these ornate crypts, you must be related to one of Argentina's "name" families. A general or two in the family tree would also help. The allure of the necropolis is such that even mourners have the air of

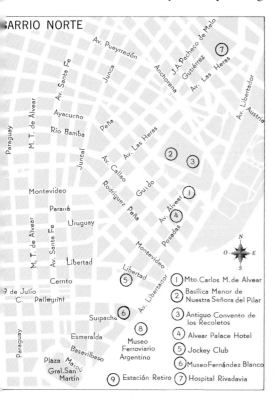

ARRIO NORTE

Av. Pueyrredón
Av. Santa Fe
Junca
Anchorena
J.A.Pacheco de Melo
Gutiérrez
Av. Las Heras
Av. Libertador
Av. Austria
Ayacucho
Río Bamba
Peña
Paraguay
M. T. de Alvear
Juncal
Av. Callao
Rodríguez Peña
Guido
Av. Las Heras
Montevideo
Paraná
Uruguay
M. T. de Alvear
Av. Santa Fe
Libertad
Cerrito
9 de Julio
C. Pellegrini
Supacha
Esmeralda
Basavilbaso
Plaza Mari. o
Gral.San Martín
Paraguay
Montevideo
Libertad
Av. Libertador
Av. Alvear
Posadas

① Mto.Carlos M.de Alvear
② Basílica Menor de Nuestra Señora del Pilar
③ Antiguo Convento de los Recoletos
④ Alvear Palace Hotel
⑤ Jockey Club
⑥ Museo Fernández Blanco
⑦ Hospital Rivadavia
⑧ Museo Ferroviario Argentino
⑨ Estación Retiro

apartment hunters, doggedly searching out immortality with a view. As one Argentine writer put it, the inhabitants of Recoleta are "more dead and less dead than the ordinary deceased." This is true of no one more than Eva Perón, reviled and revered wife of the dictator Juan Perón, whose body disappeared for 16 years before it finally came to rest in a black crypt marked simply, "Eva Duarte." Her inscriptions reads *"Volveré y seré millones,"* (I will return and be millions), a populist sentiment that does not sit well with many of the families who pay respect at the neighboring tombs. Although Evita expressed scorn for Argentina's oligarchy, she was hurt when the society ladies did not invite her to become head of an exclusive charity organization, the *Sociedad de Beneficiencia,* as was the usual prerogative of Argentine First Ladies. She lies among them now, in a supposedly unrobbable grave under six feet of concrete.

Next door to the cemetery stand the

Basilica of Nuestra Senora del Pilar and the **Convent of the Recoletos,** both completed in 1732 by the Recoletan monks (a Franciscan order) who give the area its name.

For anyone familiar with the imposing stone exterior of the Latin American cathedral, the Basilica's mustard and white stucco seems almost cheery. Children play in the nearby playground and on Sundays, artisans gather to sell *mate* gourds and handmade leather goods. The Basilica houses a Baroque silver altar and woodwork attributed to the Spanish artist and mystic Alonso Cano, yet on a sunny day at Recoleta, you could imagine that they fold the Basilica into a box when the circus gets ready to leave town.

The russet-red Convent is no longer a convent but a cultural center which displays aggressive examples of contemporary Argentine art. In one recent exhibition, *Las Historietas de Hierro* (Cartoons of Iron), visitors were greeted by a highly realistic representa-

Tomb of Eva Perón in the Duarte crypt, which belongs to her father' family.

tion of a dead steelworker crumpled in the entrance hallway. The Center's young artists often traffic in images that are violent, grotesque and explicitly sexual. Consequently you may see older Argentines jogging through the exhibitions as if pursued by a bad smell.

Sinful ice cream: Sex, death and religion all have their own shrines at the Recoleta grounds. After you have paid your respects, walk south across grassy **Plaza Alvear** towards the large billboards that advertise Calvin Klein or some other good thing. You will have arrived at cafés Biela and **de la Paix**, which face each other on **Avenida Quintana**. They are portals to the posh neighborhood of Recoleta. The most economical thing you could do at this point would be to go down Quintana one block to **Ayacucho** to have a *chocolate amargo* (bitter chocolate) ice cream at **Freddo**. Go south on Ayacucho one block to Alvear and you will witness a sumptuousness that has faded from many quarters of Buenos

Aires but which lives on in retail at the **Galeriá Alvear** (1777 Alvear) and the **Galeriá Promenade** (1885 Alvear inside the **Alvear Hotel**). The Alvear's newly restored, gleaming lobby is a favorite spot for afternoon tea. (Along the opposite cemetery wall, on **Calle Azuenaga**, you may have spotted a row of hotels called *hoteles transitorios* or *telos*. These are not student pensions but Buenos Aires' highly discreet answer to indiscretion.

Jockey Club and old silver: Walking southwest down Alvear, you will pass a number of the city's finest apartment buildings, scrupulously copied from the French. There is no choicer spot in Buenos Aires than this (for the living; the dead have Recoleta). You may gaze upon the French and Brazilian embassies, and, more importantly, the **Jockey Club**, the citadel of Argentine anglophilia. The doors of the Jockey Club open for no man who cannot produce impeccable references and an equally impeccable suit; women are allowed

only in the dining room. If you choose to postpone your membership bid, continue down Alvear which becomes **Arroyo** and then crosses **Avenida Nueve de Julio**. Gape at Nueve de Julio's obscenely large obelisk on your right but press on to the next cross street, **Carlos Pellegrini.**. There on the left is **Plaza Cataluña**, a striking piece of urban redesign consisting of a mural by Josep Niebla painted in great slashes of color across the sides of several Dickensian-looking houses.

Plaza San Martin: There is one proper way to enter Plaza San Martin and that is to enter from **Avenida Santa Fe**. Described by one Argentine writer as a "prolongation" of New York or Paris, Santa Fe offers everything imaginable in leather and will satisfy a reasonable number of other desires as well. Because of the generally enervated state of the Argentine economy, the cost of high fashion here is medium or low for the tourist. *Porteños* spend a lot of time looking in shop windows. Some

of these windows hold only the nylon-covered legs of mannequins, suspended in mid-air, a disturbing sight if you haven't grown up with such things.

Browsing southward on Santa Fe, the avenue opens up into the Plaza San Martin, a palm-fringed greensward dominated by the bronze statue of San Martin upon his horse. Built in 1862, the statue is Argentina's monument to a lost cause. The general had left his base near the present-day Plaza to wage a war of continental liberation from Spain. He returned to Argentina triumphant, only to discover that internal bickering had undone his vision of a liberal, unified South America.

The area around the Plaza is an upscale mix of travel agencies, government buildings and expensive restaurants. It's pleasant but a little dull. Since you know that San Martin will not unfreeze in mid-gallop to restore Argentina to glory with one mad dash down Avenida Sante Fe, you head southeast, downhill to the enormous

Perusing a sinister show at the San Martin Gallery in Recoleta.

C. A₁₀

ilustrador

thoroughfare, **Avenida del Libertador**. Along the way, you will pass the Sheraton Hotel, a true *yanqui* vision, with its shopping gallery enclosed in an inflated fabric tunnel.

Farther up Libertador is the **Museo Ferroviario Argentina** (Railways Museum, Liberator 405), worth a quick stop, and then on Avenidas Libertador and Callao, the **Ital Park Amusement Park** which should be worth a roller-coaster ride. In any event, the rollercoaster's airy architecture is a nice visual counterpoint to the Greco-Roman mass of the **University of Buenos Aires Law School** still farther up the road.

Fine arts: You may take the pedestrian bridge in front of the Law School, cutting back over Libertador which has branched off to the west. Now you will be hard upon the **Musco de Bellas Artes** (National Fine Arts Museum, 1437 Libertador), red bulging-columned classical building. A minute's walk away is the **Cultural Center**.

On the first floor are nudes by Rodin, Gauguin, Manet and others.

The second floor of the Bellas Artes is more interesting than the first since you won't find its likes in London or New York. There are portraits of the Argentine aristocracy, painted with all the solemnity of imported European convention; in another room folkloric canvases romanticizing the hard men of the pampas; and in another, panoramic paintings by Cándido Lopez (1840-1902) detailing the glorious carnage of military campaigns against South American neighbors. Back on Libertador, continue your northerly walk for several more blocks alongside pleasant parklands. You will come to **Calle Austria** on whose southwest corner is the desolate **National Library**, which was abandoned for lack of funds. Two blocks up the street at Austria and **Las Heras** the well-to-do ladies of Buenos Aires—*las gordas* (the fat ones)—congregate at the **Café Fontaine** for chocolate cake..

enager
lks
rebred
gs in
coleta.

DINING OUT IN RECOLETA

It is not very frequent that a cemetery is connected with fine eating, but in the case of La Recoleta—one of the leading attractions of Buenos Aires—restaurants and side-walk cafés go hand in hand with artistic and historical tombs and mortuary architecture.

An enormous number of restaurants and eating establishments, many shoulder to shoulder, are concentrated in a very small area which comprises mainly the pavement looking onto the cemetary, the Pillar church and the Cultural Center and a couple of side streets. Perhaps the most outstanding is **Lola**, a beautiful restaurant with a better than average standard of French cooking. A bare two blocks away, around the corner is **Au Bec Fin**, which functions in an old and elegant turn-of-the-century mansion. The cooking is also French in style but with a personal touch which makes it stand out from its competitors. Of a different cut is **Hippopotamus**, a night club with an international veneer and reputation and a restaurant which can be very good. **El Gato Dumas** is probably the best known of these restaurants locally, mainly because of the flamboyant character of its owner Juan Carlos "Gato" Dumas. A top professional who can cook with the best, Gato Dumas leaves much of the cooking to subordinates, with uneven results. Many of the dishes are personal creations of his and show considerable imagination and skill. Almost next door is **Harper's**, a delightful restaurant, also strongly orientated in the French tradition, with an attractive decor and superb food.

Perhaps the most popular restaurant of this group is the **Munich** whose pseudo-German style menu is nothing to write home about but amply satisfies those who are in search of a filling meal rather than sophistication. Much the same can be said of **Norte**, perhaps the least attractive (visually) of all, but which provides sound and solid fare.

The maitre d' of Fileto shows off appetizers.

A SHORT HISTORY OF SILVER

Scattered among the Cacharel and Benetton shops in the fashionable Santa Fe and Florida districts are a preponderance of jewelry stores specializing in silver objects. At the **Sunday Antiques Market** in San Telmo, it's still possible to find (often for reasonable prices) old-fashioned pieces such as silver-handled daggers, (*facones*), horn-shaped water canteens (*chifles*) and *mate* gourds.

Americans and the Spanish conquistadors had in common. Spanish priests found Indian silver smiths skilful and intelligent in their use of silver, and accustomed to treating it as a sacred metal. Native motifs combined with Catholic imagery and Spanish plateresque style created a colonial religious art that was truly hallucinatory. While much of Argentina's mission art was lost in the colonial wars with Portugal, two splendid

Silver has long had a totemic importance in Argentina. The wealth of silver in the humblest colonial chapels helped underscore the power of the Catholic Church, while on the pampas the jingling silver ornaments, bridles, stirrups and spurs proclaimed the gaucho's worshipful love of his horse. Silver *mates* are now collector's items rather than tableware, but this unique and elaborate art emerged at a time when Creole settlers were anxious to make the Indian habits they'd acquired in the New World appear more elegant and European.

An obsession with precious metals was perhaps the only thing the native South

relics of that period remain: the votive lamp and sacrarium in the **Museum of Spanish American Art**.

As with many South American capitals, the Spanish thirst for silver was the impetus behind the founding of Buenos Aires. Juan de Mendoza's settlement on the banks of the Rio de la Plata (literally, the River of Silver) was meant to be the first leg of an expedition into the Andes to find a legendary mountain of silver. As it turned out, there was almost no silver in Argentine soil, but the Bolivian border was a mere symbol until 1776, and the richest silver mines in the world were on the other side.

European silversmiths began settling in Buenos Aires; by the beginning of the 18th century there were 38 silversmiths serving a population of 20,000. During the struggle for independence the lavish use of silver was a means of patriotic expression, but as it became more common it fell out of fashion; rich *porteños* didn't want locally made silver plates and goblets but rather, imported crystal and china.

Mechanization and art deco dealt a final blow to silversmithing in the first half of this century, but during the 1960s there began a revival of interest in silver.

The Pallarols workshop: Through seven generations of changing fortunes and fashions in Argentina, the Pallarols family has maintained its silver workshop in Buenos Aires, using many of the same tools and methods brought from Barcelona in 1804.

The silverwork of Juan Carlos Pallarols, now in his 40s and the head of the family business, is very much in demand. In recent years he has been commissioned to design a *facon* for King Juan Carlos of Spain, a silver and gold chalice to commemorate the Pope's visit, and the presidential baton for Raul Alfonsin. When Pallarols was learning his trade in the 1950s, however, he never imagined he'd be able to make a living as a silversmith. "But I didn't want to do anything else," he says. "I believe every human being has the soul of an artisan." The workshop, with its 19th-century lathes and chisels worn silky by generations of use, is completely self-sufficient. Here they twist their own silver wire, heat the furnace with coal, and use the light streaming in through the french doors facing the **Plaza Dorrego**. When he moved to the neighborhood in 1970, San Telmo was far from being the South American Soho it is today, but Pallarols liked the village feeling of the *barrio,*

Left, silversmith Juan Carlos Pallarols at home in his workshop. Right, silver *mate* gourd in the form of a ñandu bird.

the plaza full of old men playing Spanish card games in the shade. Now the Plaza Dorrego is full of artisans and Pallarols' waiting list is several months long, but a sense of timelessness pervades the workshop. Pallarols and his assistants, two of which are his sons, work long but tranquil hours. They tinker with a piece for a while, sketch something and wander back and forth between the workshop and the adjoining

house. Most commissions are modest orders for christenings, weddings and birthdays. Even with a small order, such as a silver bookmark, Pallarols discusses his designs with his client. His house is filled with things he's loved making: a silver sugar bowl, a picture frame, a wrought iron staircase which throws lacy patterns against the wall. As his own father did with him, Pallarols brings home scrap pieces of metal for his four-year-old daughter to pound with a toy hammer. But she isn't sure she wants to become the first female Pallarols silversmith. "Right now," she says, "I prefer to work with bronze."

PALERMO

Palermo is a neighborhood of parks and gardens, of embassies and cattle shows, of a world-class polo field and a turn-of-the-century racetrack. Argentine writer Martinez Estrada called it "the most poetic spot in the city." Certainly its mossy cobbled streets and crumbling Italianate villas have inspired countless poets, including Palermo native Jorge Luis Borges, to meditate on Buenos Aires' frayed expectations. If neighborhoods were fictional characters, Palermo might be Dickens' Miss Havisham: a mad old lady in a musty bridal gown, who stopped her clocks when her fiancé failed to show up. The frothy marble monuments at the intersections which look like wedding cakes and the count less dowagers feeding stray cats in Palermo Park give the landscape an air of eccentricity.

Rosas slept here: Juan Manuel Rosas, a 19th-century president, was a neighborhood pioneer who built a magnificent estate in the middle of what were then swamps and thistles. Like many Argentine rulers, Rosas arouses passionate controversy long after his death: he is credited with unifying the country and accused of making death squads a grim feature of Argentine politics. One contemporary admirer, bent on demonstrating his leader's sense of humor, wrote of how Rosas enlivened one of his daughter's tea parties by letting his wild puma loose on the lawn. The women screamed and the animal fled to the river, causing the president to exclaim jovially, "How savage those women must be, to frighten my puma!"

There still are wild animals in Palermo, now safely behind bars in the 19th century **Jardin Zoologico** at the corner of **Sarmiento**, **Libertador** and **Las Heras**. At the time of its construction in 1874, it was the last word in enlightened zookeeping: the cages were built in the architectural style of the animals' countries of origin, and the grounds were sprinkled with marble reproductions of the Venus de Milo and the God Bacchus. Now, however, the buildings are sadly decayed.

Sunday in the park: The best time to visit Palermo is on a Sunday afternoon. While most of the neighborhood's residential section is resolutely upper middle class, the parks in Palermo are truly for everyone. On a sunny day porteños converge from all parts of the city to picnic, drink *mate*, kiss in the grass, jog, stare disapprovingly at scantily dressed joggers, play soccer, win political converts, and drive pedal boats recklessly around the lake. Families stroll en masse through the sumptuous subtropical gardens. Even the most casually dressed are combed and natty; children are the adored center of every group.

A tour of the area might begin with **Palermo Chico**, a neighborhood of the rich and famous just around the bend from Recoleta. In fact, you must weave around several bends to get a sense of the elegant *barrio*. This cozy nest of palaces appears to exclude the rest of the city, with its tangled web of streets and its armed guards around some of the mansions. But it is well worth winding your way through to admire the French-style houses and the spotless gardens.

The area was built in the 1880s. Many of the old palaces are now used as embassies, since the original owners could not maintain them. However, there are plenty of brand-new estates in the 20th century Southern California style, built to order by Argentine sports heroes and television stars.

Sports and suntans: From Palermo Chico, those willing to set off on a lengthy jaunt can walk six blocks along **Figuero Alcorta** into Palermo's dense green heart: **Parque 3 de Febrero**, which covers some 10,000 acres (400 hectares).

Preceding pages: park benches in Palermo; sharing a cracker at Palermo zoo. **Below** map of Palermo.

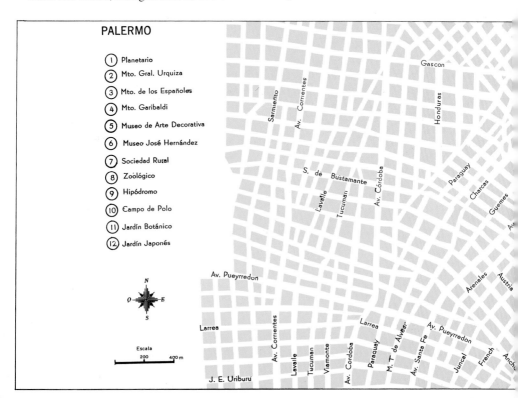

PALERMO

1. Planetario
2. Mto. Gral. Urquiza
3. Mto. de los Españoles
4. Mto. Garibaldi
5. Museo de Arte Decorativa
6. Museo José Hernández
7. Sociedad Rural
8. Zoológico
9. Hipódromo
10. Campo de Polo
11. Jardín Botánico
12. Jardín Japonés

Approaching Sarmiento, on Figuero Alcorta, is the **Cavalry** and the **KDT Sports Club**. Here, with a small entrance fee (usually around a dollar) anyone may use the excellent sports facilities. There are tennis courts, a track, an indoor pool, and a fastfood restaurant. The less energetic sprawl on the well trimmed lawn for a headstart on their tans before vacationing in the summer resorts of Mar del Plata or Punta del Este. (The latest bathing suits have reached Buenos Aires, but not the fear of skin cancer).

Across the avenue is the **Japanese Garden**, a tranquil rest spot and one of the city's most beautiful places to stroll in. Ponds full of carp and exotic vegetation create a peaceful atmosphere, and on any warm afternoon you are likely to spot half a dozen young *porteños* posing for bridal pictures among the colorful frangipani.

Sarmiento intersects with Figueroa Alcorta at an enormous statue of General Uruquiza, the president who overthrew Rosas and who made Buenos Aires the capital of the country.

To the right on Sarmiento is the **Municipal Planetarium** and a small artifical lake. To the left on Sarmiento you can take Avenida Iraola through the woods to the main lake in Palermo. Here you can rent pedal boats, wander through the pretty gardens and over quaint pedestrian bridges. There are ice cream vendors, men who sell sweet peanuts and popcorn, and others who specialize in a traditional sandwich called *choripán* (sausage on French bread). A picturesque café overlooks the lake.

Irola weaves around the lake and back to Libertador and Sarmiento, where yet another large white monument, this one donated by Spain, graces the intersection.

You are now at the back entrance to the city zoo, and may well be able to hear the voices of young *porteños* as they race delightedly from cage to cage. Argentina is a child-loving society and

dal boats lake in rk.

the children reflect it. They are self-confident and good-natured; "spoiled" in the eyes of some onlookers. They accompany their doting parents to restaurants and parties, where their high spirits are usually looked upon with benevolent amusement.

Across from the zoo on Sarmiento is a tall modern cement structure that forms part of the **Rural Society**. The Rural Society was founded in 1866 under the motto, "to cultivate the earth is to serve the fatherland." Its first president was Don Jose Martinez de Hoz, a leading cattleman and political figure. Beef made Argentina rich, and cattle breeders were a powerful interest group throughout much of the Rural Society's history. Although times have changed and the price of beef has fallen, the Rural's annual Cattle Show is still a major event on the Buenos Aires social calendar, where purebred cattle are displayed and celebrated with all due ceremony. Don't miss it if you happen to be in town in August. The Rural Society also sponsors dog, cat, and electronics shows during the rest of the year to help make ends meet.

Hippies and other traditions: Plaza Italia is at the intersection of Sarmiento, Las Heras and Santa Fe. The little plaza holds no particular charm when empty, but on weekends it becomes the center of a lively street market. On adjacent blocks is a market known to *porteños* as the "hippie fair"—the products are often made and sold by young bearded artisans and women in tiedyed dresses. It's a good spot to buy inexpensive leather goods, such as belts and handbags, as well as leather-covered *mates*. There are also ceramics, handmade jewelry, embroidered clothes, and, on the last block, secondhand books.

Political parties, particularly leftist ones such as the Intransigent Party and MAS (Movement Towards Socialism) often set up tables in Plaza Italia, or organize political cultural events such as puppet shows and street theater.

Right, Shopping for a feather duster. Below, Informal exercise class in Palermo Park.

A Day At The Races

Etiquette once required an Argentine gentleman to don a coat and tie for an evening at the movies or an afternoon at the racetrack. Today, a t-shirt and jeans suffice for the cinema, but a piece of old Buenos Aires has been preserved at the **Hipódromo Argentino** in Palermo. The racetrack still enforces its coat and tie dress code for the center grandstand, as it did more than a century ago.

The five grandstands themselves have changed little since 1882, when they were built by the Jockey Club, the bastion of Argentina's landed aristocracy.

The Jockey Club divided the grandstands into four distinct categories, thus sparing high society from rubbing shoulders with the common people. The national lottery now runs the track, but the divisions remain. *Tribuna official* has the prime location in front of the finish line. It is followed in order of price and proximity to the finish by paddock, *tribuna especial,* and *tribuna general*, where admission is free.

Despite the differences in price and location, all of the grandstands offer the same benches and a roof overhead. The gentlemen sitting on those benches share many common features themselves: tweed sportscoats, felt hats, and grey hair combed straight back with hair tonic. Any resident of Buenos Aires can be called a *porteño*, but these men at the hipódromo, like those who play dominoes in the plaza or collect the tango records of Gardel, are distinguished as classic *porteños*. In fact, prizes are sometimes named after tangos.

The racing fans of the Hipódromo Argentino also distinguish themselves as true gentlemen, according to Alfredo Rapán, who has followed the races in Palermo for 55 years. "The same guy who's causing trouble at the soccer stadium changes when he

comes here. If he bumps into you slightly he'll say, 'excuse me, I'm sorry.' If I ask to look at someone's magazine, he'll hand it to me. It's a special kind of people."

Roque Larrocca, a newcomer with only 20 years of watching the races, agrees. "At soccer they yell, say bad words — that's what the young people like today," he says, adding that horse-racing is for the more civilized. Civilized, that is, until the horses

are thundering down the home stretch.

The horse-racing season never ends in Palermo. The two most important events, the Argentine Republic prize in April and the Grand National prize in November, draw as many as 60,000 spectators, and horses from other racing countries in South America. Almost every day of the year is a racing day somewhere in Greater Buenos Aires. Hipódromo Argentino is open in the afternoon and evening of every Friday and frequently on Sundays and Mondays. The *hipódromo* in San Isidrio, an elite suburb northwest of the city, races horses every Wednesday and Saturday.

Left, at the racetrack in Palermo. Right, bettors watching the final stretch.

POLO AND PATO

Although Argentine polo players continually travel all over the world to play, they rarely do so as a team. To see the best polo in the world played by Argentine teams, one has to come to Argentina, more particularly Buenos Aires where the top tournaments are played in October and November.

Polo is played almost all year in Argentina, but the big tournaments are played in the spring. The main ones are the Hurlingham Open at the fashionable Hurlingham Club and then the Argentine Open on the picturesque polo fields in Palermo in the center of town. Games, however, frequently have to be postponed due to rain and wet fields and it is quite usual that they are still being played in December.

Polo, although originally started in India, was brought to Argentina by Britons as were most other sports. There are references to it being played in the province of Santa Fe by British farmers as early as 1875 and at the Hurlingham Club since 1888. The first Argentine Open Championship was won by Hurlingham in 1893.

The locals soon took up the game. Many Argentines, especially those living in the country, were practically born on a horse and as such, any game on horseback naturally attracted them.

By 1924, when polo was included in the Olympic Games for the first time, Argentina was represented by a team of home-born players, though some of them of English descent. The team of Arturo Kenny, Juan Nelson, Enrique Padilla and Juan B. Miles walked off with the medals.

Reigning champions: Argentina is the reigning Olympic champion. When polo was again included in the Games for the last time in 1936, they also won the title. Only once was an open world championship held—in Buenos Aires in 1949—and Argentina won that also.

The United States is the only other country whose polo is somewhere near the standard of Argentina's. A trophy, the America Cup, is occasionally played between them and this is in Argentina's hands also. Today nobody disputes Argentina's superiority in the game, although they get few chances to show it. They just do not have any rivals.

The upkeep of horses (of which a regular player needs at least 20) and playing kit is quite expensive, so the game is basically for the rich and upper middle classes. It is, nevertheless, very popular in Argentina mainly because people know their players are the best in the world and because it is overexposed in the press.

Many leading Argentine players are also in the curious position of being amateurs at home and professionals abroad.

Nobody gets paid for playing in Argentina. In fact the players have to spend quite a bit of money to be able to play. When they go to play abroad, however, they usually do so at the invitation of some wealthy player or fan who pays them to play on his team. The players also take their own horses with them and invariably sell them abroad at a far better price than they would fetch on the home market.

Argentine polo horses are much sought after all over the world. The word may still be "polo ponies," but in actual fact, ponies have not been used for the game in Argentina for a very long time. Fully-grown horses are used for speed, stamina and strength. The game has become very fast and horses must be strong to withstand the pushing which takes place during a game.

A horse needs special training for polo and nobody can do this better than certain stable hands, known as *petiseros,* at the *estancias* (ranches). The skill for this job tends to run in families and it is often said that teams depend a lot not only on the quality of their horses, but on their *petiseros.*

Polo has a set of rules designed to eliminate danger as much as possible. In spite of

Argentine polo players are undisputedly the world's best.

the vigor with which the game is played, nasty accidents to horse and rider are quite rare.

Following the game: Basically, teams of four players hit a wooden ball the size of an orange with a wooden mallet in order to shoot it into the opposing team's goal. This is formed by two posts at each end (in the middle) of the field. To avoid crashing into each other at top speed, the rules forbid a player from crossing the line of the ball (the direction in which the ball is going) and the horseman riding towards it. And when two players ride towards each other, both must give way to the left.

There are penalty shots at goal from different distances for a variety of infringements. The teams change ends after each goal and at the end of each period when a bell sounds. Other than that, play continues until a natural stoppage for a goal, an infringement or when the ball goes out of the field.

Each period is called a chukker and lasts seven minutes. Games are composed of six to eight chukkers, depending on who's playing whom.

There are over 6,000 registered polo players in Argentina today which means they have a handicap according to their standard and they play in tournaments. There are also tournaments for youngsters in various age groups from below 10 to 21. Women also play, and have their own annual tournament.

As mentioned earlier, it is a game for the wealthy. Many of them are landowners for whom rearing and keeping horses is not such an expense. There is an atmosphere of cordiality, friendship and sportsmanship among players probably not seen in any other sport. It stems mostly from long-standing friendships between the families involved.

To a large extent, the game runs in families with generation after generation playing it. Sons of leading polo players start to ride and hit a polo ball around almost before they can walk. By the time they are in their teens, they are good enough to rank among the top players in any country.

If you attend a polo match in Buenos Aires, you will rub elbows with relatives and friends of the players themselves. They are landed gentry for the most part, "beautiful people" who divide their time between the family estancia and elegant apartments in the city. Their dress code is casual elegance—sportscoats, designer jeans, crisp skirts—and they watch the matches with the reserved demanor of a crowd at a garden show. It is all a world removed from the boisterous and sometimes violent crowds of the soccer stadiums. It is a world of belonging, one most Argentines have heard about but few have actually experienced, a world where one mingles between matches with players in dusty breeches while eating finger sandwiches under the grandstand.

Pato: A cross between polo and basketball, *pato* is an authentic Argentine sport probably played by the Indians before white settlers set foot in South America, and certainly by the gauchos as far back as the 16th century. It has a colorful history, starting with its name which is Spanish for duck. The duck certainly got the worst of it during the formative period of *pato*.

A leather basket with handles and a duck inside it was placed midway between two *estancias* (ranches) or Indian encampments. Two teams of horsemen, either workers from the ranches or Indian tribes, lined up at their respective homes. At a given signal, both teams raced across the countryside towards the duck. The object was to grab it and carry it home. There was no limit to the number of participants.

The game was thus a trial of strength and horsemanship between horsemen wildly tugging at the basket's handles. As one would be pulled off his horse (with the likely fate of being trampled to death) and another would let go to avoid falling, a third would manage to get away with the duck's basket and ride at full speed for home. The rest would race after him in hot pursuit.

There were no holds barred, from lassooing an opponent to cutting his saddle free. The only unbreakable rule was that the man in possession of the "pato" had to ride holding it in his outstretched right hand, offering it to an opponent to grab if he was caught up. This would invariably produce another tug-of-war. The winning team was the one which managed to get the duck's basket back to their own farm or village.

The game was played after a feast which

would include the inevitable barbecue and which would ensure that most of the participants were the worse off for drink. It was followed by a dance at the winner's farm or village for those still able to stand.

Excommunication for *pato* players: In fact, "games" so often ended in fights and disorders that the Catholic Church tried to ban them in 1796 under the threat of excommunication for anyone who took part. The Church was not very successful, but the government was when it banned *pato* by law in 1822. The punishment was one month's hard labor and the penalty was doubled for subsequent offences.

revive the game in 1937 by first drawing up proper rules. Then he arranged exhibition games and a year later, the Argentine Pato Federation was formed.

Today *pato* is played by teams of four horsemen. The duck's basket has been replaced by a leather ball the size of a soccer ball with six handles. The playing area is approximately 650 feet by 300 feet (200 meters long and 90 meters wide). At each end is a basket, with the opening facing the field, about 10 feet (three meters) from the ground. The ball must be thrown into the basket to score a "goal." Games are played in six periods of eight minutes each.

As a result, fewer games were played, but the sport, if one can call it that, continued to flourish in the more remote areas. The passage of time did what government and church were unable to do. As people became more civilized, they turned to less dangerous sports and *pato* virtually died out.

It was left to Alberto del Castillo Posse, a great champion of Argentine tradition, to

The traditional duck in the Argentine game of *pato* has been replaced by a leather ball.

One of the few links with the past is that players wear gaucho costumes. Unlike the past though, players now wear protective head gear. Players must still ride with the ball in their outstretched hand. They punch or throw the ball to each other in team work. When it falls to the ground, they must pick it at full speed. It provides a spectacle of outstanding horsemanship.

The game is still played mostly in the provinces but major tournaments, such as the annual Argentine Open, are played either at Campo de Mayo, a military base in the western suburb of Hurlingham, or at the Palermo polo fields.

THE PORT AND COSTANERA

The European and North American tourists who traveled by ship to Argentina in the early-20th century imagined a coastal city that would greet them after their long journey. Many wrote of their initial disappointment as they approached the Buenos Aires ports, an area deserted except for the normal dock activities of a large city. Unlike Montevideo, on the other side of the river, Buenos Aires became known as the "city with its back to the river."

While the residential section of the city is still farther inland, the costal areas, over the years, has been built up as a recreational as well as a commercial district. The **Costanera Sur** and the **Costanera Norte** are both lined with *parrilla* (grill) restaurants and open spaces for sunbathers (swimming is not recommended), joggers, and fishermen. A tall stonewall prevents flooding. There are wide promenades where families set up lawn chairs to enjoy the sun, watch each other, drink their afternoon *mate* and eat *facturas* (pastries). A high-pitched whistle calls attention to the old man pushing a cart of hot sugared peanuts and bags of sweet popcorn.

There are four major ports in the city: **Riachuelo**, which includes **Barracas** and La Boca; **Dock Sud**; **Puerto Madero,** built in 1887; and **Puerto Nuevo**, the newest, built in 1914.

National ports: Historically, the ports of Buenos Aires have controlled over 70 percent of the country's international commerce. Produce is transported overland by railways built by the British in the 19th century. Those who favor the decentralization of the economy point out that the system is a holdover from colonial times and that it continues to reinforce the dominanace of the capital over the rest of the country. The subject has been of great interest recently, due to the plans to move the capital to Viedma. In fact, the possibility of constructing a new deep waterport in Viedma is a reason for moving the capital there.

Make friends: One of the best ways to see the coast is with the free tours organized by the city government's tourism office, at the San Martin Cultural Center. Most of the people who sign up are *porteños* exploring their own city. Depending on your tour guide, you may wind up singing old tangos and Spanish and Italian songs along with the rest of the passengers.

Alternatively, a taxi ride from La Boca to **Ciudad Universitaria** costs about five dollars and gives you a quick view of the port and adjacent parks.

If you begin on **Avenida Pedro de Mendoza**, there is a footbridge to the right of **Calle Brasil** leading into the Costanera Sur area. Before heading north, make a loop around to the right on Avenidas **Balbin**, **Quevedo** and **España**. Sunbathers (in season), tall palm trees, handsome statues, elegant

eceding ges: the ssissippi amboat lta een is a pular stanera staurant. ft, htening e riggings an old-shioned hooner. ght, an abian ip docked Catalinas rbor.

walkways and old stone arches covered with vines all evoke turn-of-the-century Sunday promenades. In this same block is the **Fine Arts School**, the **Naval Observatory**, and the **Arturo Dresco Monument**, portraying the discovery of America. It's also the home of **Ciudad Deportiva Boca Juniors**.

Ciudad Deportiva is a sports complex built on a series of landfill islands. In 1964, hundreds of thousands of dollars and 1,725 acres (69 hectares) of what at that time was river, were given to the owners of Boca Juniors. Only a portion of the original plan was constructed. The rest of the money was apparently pocketed by the owners.

Continuing along España to **Avenida Costanera Sur**, there is a strip of land running parallel to the promenade which serves as a bird sanctuary.

Telephones: An enjoyable stop is the **Museo de Telecomunicaciones**, near the Avenida Belgrano entrance to the Costanera. The museum is housed in an old café/bar called **Munich**. Built by a German architect in 1927, it has a fairyland look to it, with playful stained glass windows and carvings of gnomes in the walls. When it was built, the Munich was reputedly a popular spot for illicit assignations, since it was far from the watchful eyes of neighbors.

In a country where the telephone system is the object of ridicule, the museum serves an amusing as well as educational function. In one room there are dozens of different kinds of telephones laid out on bright pillows for children to play with. On the wall is a framed cartoon of a telephone from *Diario Popular* with a caption that reads: "It works, but we've decided to preserve it as a national treasure." The Avenida Costanera leaves the port area for a few blocks and returns to the riverside just past the Sheraton Hotel. Here there are warehouses, the **Customs House**, the **Air Force Headquarters**, and the **National Treasury.**

By the river: Avenida Costanera

Dock workers in Costanera Sur.

Rafael Obligado runs along the wide brown river. On a clear day you can sometimes pick out the Uruguayan coastline in the distance. There is an elegant fishing club at the end of a long dock. But most Sundays, fishermen simply throw their lines off the stone wall running along the river.

Jorge Newberry Airport, better known as Aeroparque, is across the street. Local flights and planes to border countries leave from this airport.

Opposite the airport is a private dock with a very pretty but expensive restaurant over the water. Outside is a lovely terrace surrounded by water and sun where you can have a cool drink. There is an old Mississippi style ferry called the Delta Queen docked next to the restaurant. It looks a bit strange in this South American setting, but it is a favorite spot to host private parties.

Choose your grill: The Costanera Norte is famous for its *parrilla* restaurants, dozens of which line the road about a mile north of Aeroparque. For *porteños,* a steak lunch here is a typical Sunday outing. Part of the ritual is cruising by slowly in a car to contemplate the choices, as the enticing smell of grilled beef wafts overhead. Ignore the young parking attendants waving the cars in, and look to see if there is a terrace, if you like the view of the river, if you are amused by the restaurant's name, and whether the people inside look as though they are happy with their choice. In actual fact, the restaurants are all pretty much alike. **Los Años Locos** (The Crazy Years) is the spot usually recommended to foreigners.

The last stop along the coast, before heading back down Avenida Libertador is **Ciudad Universitaria**, University City. It houses the departments of Natural Sciences, Architecture, Urban Planning and Engineering. Construction of the campus began in 1960. The original plan was to move all the university buildings to this site, but, like the National Library, the project has been abandoned for lack of funds.

ew of the
omenade
ong the
ostanera
orte.

THE PAMPA

Too much time in the big city can give both residents and visitors an overdose of neon, concrete, and smoke. The only known cure is some green grass, a wide sky, and a herd of cattle on the horizon, so many residents head for *el campo* (the country) for a day or weekend. For visitors in need of the same remedy, three especially effective prescriptions are a tour of an *estancia* (ranch) or a visit to the towns of Luján or San Antonio de Areco.

Buenos Aires is a sprawling metropolis, so the first signs of the *campo* are well outside the city limits, in the province of Buenos Aires. About 45 minutes west of the city, the concrete sprouts into grass, and paved sidestreets fade into dusty lanes. The garbage collectors here still make their rounds in horsecarts. The roadside is littered with little outdoor grill restaurants, often no more than a few card tables and a portable kitchen—a barbecue trailer spewing smoke.

About an hour out of town appear the first pastures dotted with cattle—the driving force behind the history and wealth of Buenos Aires. In addition to grazing land, wealthy city dwellers own luxurious weekend and vacation homes at elite clubs which offer facilities such as golf courses, swimming pools and tennis courts.

Still the road continues another hour before it reaches the classic scenery of the pampas: endless pastures of rough grass, broken only by the cattle, clumps of trees, and the occasional *estancia* house. A rancher's home is typically a broad, low building painted either white or pink, and preceded by a long, tree-lined drive.

The easiest way to get a closer look at an *estancia* is to take a tour from downtown Buenos Aires. This excursion, often called a *fiesta gaucha,* is a whole day outing at a real *estancia,* set up to handle tourists. Though the tour may head to any one of several *estancias,* the basic itinerary is the same: plenty of food and wine, a show of regional singing and dancing, horse-riding, demonstrations of gaucho sports, relaxation, and fresh air.

The tour begins with the trip of two or more hours west or northwest, making the gradual transition from one of the largest cities in the world to the wide open pampas. Upon arrival, the eating begins with *empanadas,* the traditional Argentine meat pies. After an opportunity to stroll around the grounds of the *estancia,* ride one of the horses, and settle into the slower pace of life, the word arrives that lunch is ready in the semi-open shelter.

The main event: As with any true meal in the pampas, the main event is meat. *Asado de tira* arrives first. These beef ribs are roasted outdoors on stakes next to a wood fire, just as the gauchos prepared them 200 years ago. They are followed by steaks, sausages, kidneys,

and other organs, all grilled over wood coals. Anyone who still has room for more is welcome to second helpings. Bread, salad and a dessert of *pastelito,* a traditional crispy pastry filled with jam, add variety to the meaty meal. And of course, the long tables come with enough bottles of wine and soft drinks to keep everyone happy.

During and after lunch, a pair of dancers flirt and stomp the *gato, zamba,* and *escondido,* accompanied by guitar and accordian. Both singing and dancing are in the gaucho style, especially the *malambo de boleadora,* a rhythmical feat of coordination performed by whirling a *bola,* a gaucho lasso with weighted balls on the ends. As the music speeds up, the *boleador* keeps rhythm with the tapping of the *bola* against the floor until the *malambo* ends in a frenzy.

The gauchos are most skillful in the outdoors, so after lunch has settled a little, the entertainment moves onto a field for *sortija, pato* and calf-riding. *Sortija* requires a smooth horseman with a steady hand. Riding at full speed, the competitor tries to aim a needle-like stick through a ring *(sortija)* hanging from a pole. *Pato* is a team sport played on horseback with what looks like a soccer ball with handles—a humane substitute for the duck *(pato)* originally used by gauchos.

Pampas horsemen: Though the men at the *estancia* maintain some of the dress and customs of the gauchos, these horsemen of the pampas disappeared in the 19th century. They made their living by hunting the plentiful wild cattle and the ostrich-like *ñandu,* selling the hides and feathers, and eating as much meat as they wanted, leaving the rest to rot. As the pampas were divided into huge *estancias,* the mixed-blooded, fiercely independent gauchos were seen as good-for-nothing thieves by the "civilized" men of rural Argentina. Barbed-wire fences dealt the final death blow to the gauchos. Deprived of the open plains and wild cattle, they had no choice but to work for wages on the

estancias. Since their demise, the gauchos have been symbols of Argentine freedom and independence.

The citizens and streets of **San Antonio de Areco** have preserved a bit of the image of the gaucho and his times. Though Areco is less than two and a half hours from Buenos Aires by bus, in 1725 and the following decades, its fort marked the frontier between land settled by Europeans and the land of the Indians. As well as a stage-coach stop on the **camino real** from Buenos Aires to Peru, Areco was a common meeting place for gauchos.

One of the *pulperías,* where the gauchos met to drink and buy supplies, has been preserved as part of the gaucho museum in Areco. The museum also features a replica of an *estancia* house, containing paintings and artifacts from gaucho and *estancia* life. The museum is named for Ricardo Guiraldes, the novelist who made Areco famous with his *Don Segundo Sombra,* a *gauchesco* novel about a man from the area.

The memory of Don Segundo Sombra and reverence for the gaucho lives on in one of Areco's better known citizens, artist Osvaldo Gasparini. He sketches gaucho scenes with pen and ink and sells them for a song to the school children and tourists who visit his studio and gallery. The attraction, as much as the drawings, is Gasparini himself. He dresses as a gaucho, and loves to tell stories about his life, especially the few years in the 1930s when Don Segundo Sombra looked after him.

San Antonio de Areco has many craftsmen like Gasparini. In fact, just a block down the street, Homero Tapia fashions stirrups from ram horns, a traditional craft of the pampas. Another couple of blocks down, Juan Jose Draghi works in silver, using original designs from the region for knives, belts, and horse tack.

City of pilgrimage: Luján was also a frontier town in colonial Argentina, but today it is better known as the holy city of Argentina. The images of the Virgin Mary that can be seen in any subway station in Buenos Aires and in shrines across the country are replicas of the Virgin of Luján, housed in the basilica there. Though the city has a lovely river and a large museum complex, Luján rates as one of Argentina's most visited cities, primarily because of the basilica and the Virgin.

The story goes that in 1630, a man was carrying two small statues of the Virgin from Brazil to Peru. When crossing a river not far from Luján, his cart got stuck in the mud. The cart finally moved when one of the statues was taken off, so the man determined it wanted to stay. A shrine grew up around the Virgin of Luján, and was later moved to its present site.

Today, the original statue stands high above the altar of a grand gothic **basilica**, finished in 1935. In the interior of the basilica hang many signs made entirely of silver medallions given in thanks to the Virgin of Luján for illnesses cured and petitions granted. The medallions are in the shapes of arms, legs, bodies, and internal organs, depending on the part of the body healed.

Twice each year, hundreds of thousands of pilgrims walk the 40 miles (60 km) between the city of Buenos Aires and Luján. The pilgrimage ends with an open-air mass in the plaza facing the basilica. Less hardy visitors can cut the trip down to about two hours by taking the bus or train from Once Station, in the center of Buenos Aires.

After the basilica, the **Historical Museum** deserves a visit. One of the most complete museums in Argentina, it covers not only the local history of the Virgin, Indians, gauchos and *estancias*, but also the history of the entire country from the colonial period to recent years. The building itself is a museum piece, which served as the *cabildo*, or town hall, of Luján two centuries ago.

After visiting the museum, it is time for a relaxing, scenic boat ride on the river, and time to breathe in the pure air and to enjoy a meal at one of the outdoor restaurants along the banks.

visit to
a estancia
volves an
utdoor
sado
arbeque)
ad a ride
cross the
ampas.

TIGRE

For more than 100 years, the streams and canals of the **Tigre Delta** have been a favorite weekend refuge for *porteños* of all ages.

Every Sunday afternoon, thousands make the hour-long journey to the delta to relax among the elegant monuments commemorating the faded glories of Argentina.

Trains leave regularly from the Victorian cast-iron **Retiro** station, moving through the northern suburbs to stop at Tigre. Dozens of small wooden ferries leave the wharves across the road to service the waterways which are the veins of the region.

A tree-lined promenade follows the main river which is its usual murky brown. Weeping willows reach down the water in between the open-air restaurants and cafés, while assorted food vendors, soapbox politicians and charlatans crowd the footpaths. Across the river are the various English-style rowing clubs, with their magnificent grounds and ostentatiously impractical clubhouses. Every March and November, the waterways are taken over by the rowers for regattas.

Boating on the delta : Meanwhile, every other type of sailing craft seems to ply the Tigre delta. The boats may be more modern, but the atmosphere has changed little since the homesick English traveler John Hammerton recorded in his 1920s travel guide that Tigre "awakens memories of the Upper Thames on summer days :

"Crews practising in outriggers; lonely canoeists; launches scurrying along, well-laden with passengers and delightfully oblivious of the 'rules of the road;' and the gilded youth showing the paces of his new motorboat and translating his Florida swagger into terms of the river."

Numerous tourist boats and local

Boating on the river delta in Tigre.

ferries head farther out into the delta to quieter zones for lunch. Homes along the way range from turn-of-the-century stone mansions, English cottages and Italian villas to little wooden shacks painted bright blue and green. Ferries stop at many of the broken-down piers to drop off newspapers and pick up mail.

Restaurants range from the up-market **El Gato Blanco** to the sleazy tourist trap **El Toro** which boasts a huge white statue of a bull as well as a reindeer's head, both of which are set above a plastic fireplace.

Faded elegance: By far the most unique excursion is that to the **Hotel El Tropezón** in the farthest reaches of the delta, where visitors come for lunch or a cheap overnight stay, and to get a taste of 1920s elegance.

An old lady waits on the pier for the morning ferry to travel the hour-and-a-half upriver. The hotel is at the intersection of the major boat routes to Paraguay and Uruguay, in what is jokingly referred to as "the jungle of Buenos Aires."

Built in the late 1920s at the peak of Argentina's wealth, the hotel has tried to maintain its style and standards despite the country's declining fortunes. El Tropezón (the blunder) was named by its original owner, but the hotel was in fact a raging success, luring the most fashionable *porteños* away from the city. Today, it is run by the founder's five spinster daughters, all of whom are in their fifties.

The wooden hotel is painted beige. On the wrought-iron fence around its patio, are sculpted tiny red flowers. The garden is crowded with real flowers from all over the world. The grass is so lush it seems to glow green. The center-piece is a twisted cactus flanked by *art-nouveau* lamp-posts which no longer work.

A set lunch is eaten on the patio among dozens of tables which will never be filled. Drinks can be ordered in a dark wooden bar next to which is an ancient looking icebox and a framed picture of Jesus of the Sacred Heart.

Outside, the ocean-going cargo ships are slowly squeezing their way through the river.

The clean spartan rooms have beds with what feel like original 1920s mattresses. The bathrooms have glistening tiles and polished brass fittings, but the metal pipes which burst years ago have not been repaired so that now there is no hot water.

An indoor games room still has its wooden piano and faded photographs of fishermen displaying their hauls alongside grinning chubby girls clad in shorts. At the back of the room is a print of national heroes San Martin and Belgrano with the heroic figure of Freedom carrying the Argentina flag. The emblem reads: "There Arose Upon the Face Of the Earth a Great and Glorious Nation."

At dusk, the ferries start making their way back to the Tigre terminal where trains rattle back to the present, towards the bright light of Buenos Aires.

ON THE BEACH

When the summer heat smothers Buenos Aires, Buenos Aires migrates to **Mar del Plata**. By the millions, *porteños* flock to this Atlantic City of Argentina, fleeing the heat and the hustle of the city—but not the crowds.

On a typical Friday in January or February, six trains, 14 planes, hundreds of buses, and a traffic jam full of cars leave Buenos Aires for Mar del Plata 250 miles (400 km) away. The city of 500,000 residents swells with three million tourists in those two months. Mar del Plata has enough beaches to absorb such numbers, but as one visitor commented, "you just can't see the sand."

Mar del Plata was an exclusive resort graced with vacation mansions belonging to the Argentine elite at the turn of the century. Today, though the wealthy and their mansions remain, middle-class Argentines, and workers who pay special rates in union-owned hotels make up the tourist majority.

Most visitors rent an apartment or house for two weeks or a month in Mar del Plata. Many also rent one of the beach tents lined up in colorful rows, where they spend their days chatting, eating and relaxing. If a cold spell strikes, the bathers can take long walks on the ramblas along the beach or go downtown to shop for local sweaters and *alfajores* (sweet cakes). Nightlife is supplied by casinos, discotheques, and theatrical productions, which all follow the migration from Buenos Aires to Mar del Plata.

Those left back home are constantly reminded by broadcasts from Mar del Plata and photographs of scantily-clad beachgoers in magazines and newspapers, of the beach they are missing. Even sports and political news have Mar del Plata datelines, since the games and politicians migrate too. The only

Marble lion outside Argentino Hotel in resort village of Piriapolis, just outside Monte-video.

204

consolation in Buenos Aires is the lack of crowds. They're at the beach.

Punta del Este: For most of the year, Punta del Este is a quiet Uruguayan town. The top crust of Montevideo may drive out for a weekend at their ocean home, but usually the long beaches are stirred only by the surf. Then, suddenly, cars with Argentine license plates are jamming the streets. Buenos Aires newspapers are outselling Uruguayan dailies three to one. Neighbors on the sidewalk are gabbing in *porteño*. When Argentines are released for summer vacation, Punta del Este becomes a second Argentina.

Only a select group of Argentines can afford Punta del Este, and most of them prefer it that way. They already complain that their resort "isn't what it used to be,"—20-story condominiums, which offer more affordable rates, are replacing the summer estates that dominated the point for most of the century. But one of the taxi companies which operates in Punta del Este still uses exclusively Mercedes-Benzes.

In the previous century, the village lived off the plentiful fish, whales, sea lions and salt found at the point where the Rio de la Plata blends into the Atlantic Ocean. The endless sand created such a nuisance that camels had to pull the salt carts, and forests were planted to halt the advancing dunes.

Now it is the Argentines who are advancing on Punta del Este, to enjoy the sand rather than fight it. Off the sand, vacationers enjoy Uruguay's most exclusive little shopping district. Several sweater stores sell the country's famous hand-knits, some so intricate they resemble tapestries.

When the cool breezes that blow across the point become winter's colder winds, the shutters close on most of the town. A few small hotels, shops, and restaurants stay open, however. It is time for long walks on empty beaches and afternoons at a quiet café. It is time to enjoy the other Punta del Este—the Uruguayan one.

enos
res
oves to
e beach
Mar del
ata in
cember.

COLONIA DEL SACRAMENTO

An easy day trip from Buenos Aires can be made to the old Portuguese settlement of **Colonia del Sacramento**, across the muddy Rio de la Plata in neighboring Uruguay.

Not only does Colonia provide an escape from the pace and crowds of Buenos Aires, it is one of the few surviving colonial relics in the southern zone of South America.

The Portuguese presence in this otherwise Hispanic country is the result of Spanish greed. The explorer Juan Diaz de Solis landed near Colonia in 1516 thinking he was on the way to the riches of the Orient. Unfortunately, he only took six men ashore with him. Instead of finding gold, they were ambushed by wild Indians and, according to contemporary reports, eaten.

History: Later explorers refused to bother with Uruguay, being much more interested in the stories told by shipwrecked sailors of a "white king" who ruled a fabulously wealthy land to the north.

While the Spaniards were chasing their dreams of gold, the Portuguese slipped down from Brazil in 1680 to found Colonia for the far more profitable purpose of smuggling.

Although Colonia was founded by the Portuguese as a rival to Buenos Aires, it is difficult to imagine two more different results.

A short hydrofoil ride or a more leisurely trip by ferry crosses the river to a completely different world.

Dreamlike: Arriving in Colonia at lunch-time from the Argentine capital can be an unnerving and dreamlike experience. There are only 10,000 people in the town and few of them are in the streets. The only signs of activity are dogs wandering aimlessly and old men sitting in the shade of sycamores, sucking *mate* through silver straws.

The steamer arriving in Colonia.

The colonial part of the town is largely intact or restored, jutting into the Rio de la Plata so that water is at the end of every street.

With the scattered palm trees, it would be an idyllic semitropical setting except for the odd color of the river. The Rio de la Plata looks like silver in the morning, copper in the afternoon and gold at dusk.

While the buildings of Buenos Aires are often extravagant and indulgent, the lines of the Portuguese architecture are clean and symmetrical. An old parochial church has twin plain towers and a simple clock. There is a plaza with neat gardens and ancient trees, usually with more gardeners than visitors. Crooked streets with crumbling white-washed houses lead down to the water where a lighthouse warns of Uruguay's treacherous coastline.

The streets may be deserted but the restaurants are packed and noisy. Unlike dining in much of central Buenos Aires, which is formal, lunch in Colonia is long and relaxed. The tables have plastic cloths, the walls are decorated with religious paintings, and a television blares a soccer match.

Vegetarians should beware: even more than in Argentina, meat is difficult to avoid at any meal. Even the Hotel Italiano in this Portuguese enclave of an ex-Spanish colony serves steaks which dwarf the plate on which they're served, slightly overdone and unsullied by sauce or mustard.

An extended walk should follow lunch along the riverside to the remains of colonial fortifications and groups of weeping willows. There is a 200-foot (30 meter) stretch of beach around which the local soccer club seems to be endlessly jogging. The sun bounces from the white buildings on the road from the town and there are no sounds but the cicadas and the wind.

Some 2.5 miles (four km) farther out stands a colossal and lavish bullring which was built at the turn of the century with no expense spared, but which has not been used for decades.

Museums and antique cars: There are also three small museums to visit. The restored building containing the **Spanish Museum** is more impressive than its exhibits; the **Municipal Museum** has two suspicious policemen guarding decaying stuffed birds; but the **Portuguese Museum** has a fine collection of 18th-century furniture, carved from mahogany and with cordovan upholstery.

Towards evening, a few bicyclists and horse-drawn carts appear in the streets. Many of the town's cars are antique Fords and Chevrolets, including crank-starters in working condition. There used to be many more until the late 1970s, when foreign automobile museums snapped them all up.

Colonia has a number of small hotels. Since the Uruguayan coast is a playground for rich Argentines in summer, these range from the luxury class (one even with a small casino) to cheap and comfortable *pensiones* looking out over trees to the water.

Colonial lighthouse in Colonia.

MONTEVIDEO

In his affectionate ode, *Montevideo*, the great Argentine writer Jorge Luis Borges wrote of the Uruguayan capital: *You are the Buenos Aires we once had, that slipped away quitely over the years you are ours and all revelers, like the star mirrored in the waters. False door in time, your streets contemplate a lighter past.*

Borges' nostalgic recollection of **Montevideo** is shared by many who've been there: a city that looks like Buenos Aires might have several decades ago, when life moved more slowly and locals never strayed far from home without a thermos jug of hot water and a *yerba mate* gourd in hand.

Night ferry: A side trip to Montevideo is easily made from Buenos Aires, and the best way to go is by an overnight ferryboat called the **Vapor de la Car-** **rera**. During warm months boats leave every night for Montevideo; every other night during the off-season. You can check availability at the company's main office at Florida and Lavalle.

The river crossing costs between US$20 and US$30, and includes a sleeping berth in a cabin for two or three. For a little more you can have a room with private bath in the lower, less wave-rocked quarters. But the trip usually goes quite smoothly even when the waters are agitated. In any case, the ferryboat is highly preferable to the hydrofoils that also ply the river, whose passengers frequently emerge looking like they've been on a lengthy carnival ride.

You can catch the Vapor de la Carrera at **Darsena Sud**, near the barrio of La Boca. It leaves at 9 p.m. and normally arrives in Montevideo about 8 the next morning, just long enough for a good night's sleep.

But sleeping is probably the least interesting thing to do during this night

Approaching Montevideo after a nighttime river crossing.

crossing. If weather permits, the upper deck is a fine place to do some star gazing—and to watch sparkling Buenos Aires fade into the horizon. As the boat steams down the estuary, you can have dinner in the large dining hall. The menu options are usually limited to steak or chicken—this is not the Queen Elizabeth II.

After dinner, there's usually disco dancing at one end of the boat. There are also a couple of bars and one-armed bandits for diversion.

In the morning the boat chugs toward the sunrise, close to the Uruguayan shore. As it approaches Montevideo, you can see the large rise which inspired a Galician navigator's exclamation, *Monte vi eu!* (I saw a hill!), a remark that reportedly inspired the city's name.

South American Switzerland: Landing in the Montevideo harbor may give you the sensation of having traveled not only down the river but also back in time. On sycamore-shaded streets, old British Leyland buses maneuver around spark-showering trolley buses, scooters, motorcycles, bicyclists and masses of pedestrians. Ancient automobiles, spared the corrosion of harsher climates, mix with recent models on the city's streets.

Uruguayans themselves are an older population than their Argentine neighbors, a consequence of generally small families and an exodus of younger Uruguayans during a period of military rule that lasted from 1973 until 1985. One and a half million Uruguayans—half the country's population-live in or around Montevideo.

Generally, they're regarded by visitors as less pretentious and more friendly than Argentina's *porteños.* Perhaps because this is such a small country—the smallest Spanish speaking nation on the continent—Uruguayans tend to be passionately interested in their country's affairs.

Uruguay was this hemisphere's first welfare state early in this century,

aving
enos
es on the
ry for
ntevideo.

earning the somewhat misleading title of "the Switzerland of South America." The argricultural wealth that financed the wide array of social services provided by the state has been spread increasingly thinner over the decades, and today Montevideo looks a little shabby. Its charm lies in the Old World dignity and graciousness of the people who live there. Montevideans still find time for the afternoon siesta, and, like Argentines, they like lingering lunches and dinners.

Argentina, in fact, has always been Uruguayans' cultural point of reference—they call Uruguay the Eastern Republic of Uruguay, and themselves Easterners (*Orientales*), in reference to the colossus to the wèst. Some liken the relationship to that of Canada with the United States. Yet you'll quickly notice some significant differences between Montevideo and Buenos Aires.

Perhaps the most striking change from Buenos Aires is the racial mixture in Montevideo. While its inhabitants are predominantly of European descent, there are also many with African origins. Montevideo's blacks have kept alive the rhythms of *candombe* music, first developed in the southern barrios of Buenos Aires before that city's black population disappeared. You can often hear the drumming of candombe at Montevideo's plazas and street markets, as well as during the annual New Year's and pre-Lenten carnival street celebrations.

A more subtle difference from Buenos Aires is Uruguay's fiercely laic tradition. The Catholic Church plays no role in the state, and religious holidays have all been given secular names: Christmas is the Feast of the Family, Holy Week is Tourism Week.

Montevideo is the kind of city that can be seen in a day or two. You may want to make the rounds in a day and catch the 9 o'clock ferry back to Buenos Aires, or else take a bus (two hours) to Colonia, the picturesque port opposite Buenos Aires, and from there take a

Plaza de la Constitucion in Montevideo's colonial quarter.

pleasant ferry ride back to town.

A stroll through town: A good place to start seeing Montevideo is by going to **Plaza Cagancha** (also called Plaza Libertad) on the city's main thoroughfare, **Avenida 18 de Julio**. There you'll find the main tourism office with plenty of brochures and free maps of the city and surroundings (Montevideo is, after all, a resort town and promotes tourism skillfully).

From Plaza Cagancha it's an easy walk down the 18 de Julio to the city's main square, **Plaza Independencia**. Along the way you'll pass several shopping arcades filled with boutiques, as well as a series of bustling coffeehouses in the avenue.

Strolling along the 18 de Julio and window-shopping is a popular pastime for the gregarious Montevideans. Economic difficulties in recent years have made window shopping a necessity as well as a form of entertainment.

Plaza Independencia is at the beginning of the 18 de Julio. The antennae-peaked scalloped tower to the left as you approach the square is the famous **Palacio Salvo**, for some a monumental eyesore and for others an endearing symbol of the city on a par with the Obelisk in Buenos Aires.

In the middle of the square is the subterranean tomb of General Jose Artigas, leader of Uruguay's fight for independence from both the Portuguese and the Spanish. The cream-colored palatial building o the south side of the square is Government House, the strictly ceremonial presidential office.

Further down the south side, just off the square, stands the city's cultural palace, the stately **Teatro Solis**. Even if you don't attend one of its plays or concerts, it's still worth a look inside.

The arch at the west end of Plaza Independencia marks the entrance to the **Ciudad Vieja** (Old Town). This port-flanked peninsula has the city's oldest and most picturesque buildings. **Plaza Constitución** (Ituzaingro and Sarandi) is a pleasant place to stop. Facing the plaza on one side is the

Cathedral (circa 1800); on another side is the ancient **Town Hall.** The **stock exchange building** (**La Bolsa**), the **Banco de la Republica**, and the imposing **Customs House** (**Aduana**) are all north of the plaza and worth seeing.

Look for the **Mercado del Puerto** on **Calle Piedras**, near the Aduana. This is a congenial place for a leisurely lunch or dinner, with restaurants inside and on the fringes of the market. Succulent seafood is available at several places; grilled beef, almost everywhere.

Buying wool and leather: Shopping in Montevideo is best in terms of woollen or leather goods. A knitting cooperative called **Manos del Uruguay** has several shops with beautifully knitted and loomed woollens made for export. (As the country's major export, Uruguayan wool is generally high quality—usually better than what can be had in Argentina.)

Leather prices are generally lower than they are in Buenos Aires. Details such as zippers and buttons on clothing articles also tend to be sturdier than those used for Argentine leather goods.

If the weather is warm, save time to visit Montevideo's beaches. They're clean, broad expenses of sand that are popular sunning spots on weekends. Also worth a visit are several large parks: the rambling **Parque Rodo**, with a small lake, an amusement park, and the **National Fine Arts Museum**; **Parque El Prado**, featuring a large rose garden and the municipal fine art and history museums; and **Parque Batlle y Ordóñez** (named after the great social reformer president who pioneered the concept of the welfare states). And don't miss the beautiful **Legislative Palace**, constructed almost entirely from domestic pink marble.

If you're running low on currency and have a major credit card, you have one more reason to visit this off-shore banking capital. Uruguay is the only South American nation where you can obtain US dollars by simply charging them to your credit card.

arble lion
tside
gentino
otel in
sort
lage of
riapolis,
st outside
ontev-
eo.

TRAVEL TIPS

GETTING THERE

Buenos Aires is the first stop on the route of any seasoned visitor to Argentina. Yearly visitors such as skiers from Europe and the United States and Canada booking every available flight to the Argentine ski resorts of Bariloche (in the province of Rio Negro) and Las Lenãs (Mendoza) will stop in Buenos Aires for a quick rich shot of big city life before plunging in the white wilderness of the South.

BY AIR

From New York, fly Aerolineas Argentinas, Pan American, Eastern, LAn-Chile, Varig. From Miami: same. From Toronto, Montreal and Vancouver: Canadian Pacific airlines. From Europe: KLM, Swissair, Alitalia, Lufthansa, Iberia, Aerolineas Argentinas, Varig, etc. Charter flights, tours prove a good buy, since services are greatly improved. Argentine travel agents are making a major effort to deliver the goods on schedule in a bid to reach a long-sought-after international standing.

BY SEA

Major world carriers visit Buenos Aires periodically. For those with time and money, Prudential Lines, to name one, sails its luxury liners from Vancouver to Buenos Aires with stops in Tacoma, San Francisco, Los Angeles, Buenaventura, Guayaquil, Callao and Valparaiso, passing through the Straits of Magellan. The liners accommodate about 120 passengers. The return route goes through Santos, Rio de Janeiro, La Guaira (Venezuela) and the Panama Canal.

OVERLAND

Several all-comfort luxury buses feature daily and (in many cases) hourly trips joining BA to major cities in the neighboring countries of Uruguay, Paraguay, Brazil, Bolivia and Chile.

Argentine railways are run by the government, sometimes not to the tighest of schedules or to the greatest physical comfort of the traveler. But they get there, and they are very inexpensive. A good way to travel the great expanses of Argentina. Main train terminals in BA are Retiro (northern lines), Once (western line) and Constitución (southern line).

Remember, whether you get in to Buenos Aires by train, bus or plane, your best friend is the Tourism Secretariat, and do steer away from the "friendly" limousine, or taxicab driver or that smiling promoter of downtown hotels and restaurants.

TRAVEL ESSENTIALS

TRAVEL PAPERS

You will need a passport and a tourist visa to enter Argentina. For customs regulations, contact your travel agent. Proper clearance for special equipment such as cameras, videos, typewriters, computers and tape recorders may be arranged through your travel agent.

MONEY

The Argentine Austral was born to bear its own weight against the US dollar. It was worth US$1.20 upon creation in mid-1985, but has lost considerable ground since then. At press time the Austral stood two-to-one against the dollar, but miniscule devaluations eat at the Austral almost weekly.

With respect to the dollar, The Austral is valued officially at one rate and unofficially, at the "parallel" rate. The parallel rate is illegal but recognized by everyone from small shop owners to television economic forecasters.

As for credit cards, all major names are honored almost everywhere you go, including most hotels, restaurants, tea houses, gas stations and clothing and shoe stores throughout town. The same applies to travelers's checks, although not on such a wide scope.

GETTING ACQUAINTED

CLIMATE

Buenos Aires' climate is a slave of the Rio de la Plata (River plate). It is a city of an average humidity of 45 to 60 percent in the summer months (December to March) and as high as 70 to 95 in the winter (June to September). Humidity is to such an extent the star of the show in BA that a coin expression goes, *Lo que mata es la humedad* (the killer is the humidity), as opposed to temperature which in the mild climate zone of Buenos Aires is an average of 50 F to 65 F in winter and around 90 F in the summer. The river is big enough to moderate the climate of the city and sprawling suburbs.

Spring will find BA in the tender bloom of its jacaranda blues and "palo borrocho" pinks and soft yellows. Throngs of bustling short-sleeves, coat-around-arm, tie-loosened hopefuls fill the downtown pedestrian strips in the renewed restlessness of the season. You will have to pick your way carefully in promenades, in city parks and around main historical monuments. Hundreds of sun worshippers will have taken their places, shirts off, skirts up a bit, coats and cardigans rolled tight behind their heads. No hurry then for the office boy on his lunch break, or the harried businessman between bank errands.

The crowds thin out miraculously come mid-December, though. At Christmastime, only half of Buenos Aires is at home.

The other half is self-exiled along the Atlantic coast, this time doing that for which they rehearsed every lunch break throughout spring, sun-tanning to their heart's content.

Summer is not Buenos Aires' favorite season. Too hot and humid. But there is an attraction to the city then: it's empty. No lines at restaurants, banks, or bus stops. That, for a city dweller, is a brief blessing. In fall, the crowds are back, tanned and ready to resume the fight. Fall is the best season in Buenos Aires. A good time to feast one's eye on the splendor of city colors and lights, and on the pretty *porteñas* in their autumn finery.

Capricious and mercifully short, winter in Buenos Aires is a furtive attacker that takes good straight jabs at disconcerted city dwellers, letting them enjoy periods of mild balmy weather in between. You can go from coat to a short-sleeve T-shirt and back again inside a 12-hour-span. Warning: No matter what time of the year you decide to hold your romantic affair with "La Perla del Plata" (The Pearl of the River Plate), bring a medium-weight coat and one summer outfit.

COMMUNICATIONS

POSTAL SERVICES

Varyingly unreliable. You will have to wise up to wildcat strikes and slowdowns and to learn to make provisions for your mail. Regular mail lies literally at the bottom of the barrel. (friendly postman's advice: Invest a couple more cents in letters going out of the country and send it registered:) Never enclose valuables. Even checks have been repeatedly known to stray from their due destination.

TELEPHONE SERVICES

If your call is long-distance and abroad, walk the short distance from your hotel to the telephone exchange and place the call there personally. Trying to get a long-distance operator during business hours, or on weekends, or late at night is a job that will demand saintly patience. However, ENTel's (state telephone company) public relations department is amazingly helpful and effectively bilingual.

RADIO

There are two radio stations which offer music non-stop, allowing only for a couple of minutes interruption per hour for newscasts and commercials. Pop on Radio Laser 102, classical on Radio Clásica. Distinct but equal in their top-level musical selection.

TELEVISION

There are four metropolitan TV stations, three private (Channels 9, 11 and 13) and one state-run, ATC or Channel 7. Channel 2, broadcast in the capital of the province of Buenos Aires, La Plata, is also viewed in the city of Buenos Aires, although reception is not always good.

NEWSPAPERS

There are two major dailies, *Clarfn*, the most widely read, which follows a popular line, is run as big business, stressing business and middle-of-the-road political and social views, reducing editiorial involvement to a minimum, with juicy police stories, tales of misery and deprivation, etc.

On the other end of the rainbow stands *La Nación*, geared for middle to upper-middle class readers with a refined taste for news and editorials. No controversial issues published here either.

Another traditional Buenos Aires daily is *La Prensa*.

Businessmen feed avidly on *Ambito Financiero*, a weekday business paper known for its scoops and controversial shop gossip. *Financiero* is also a booming business organization.

The *Buenos Aires Herald* is the only English-language newspaper in BA, and in Argentina, for that matter. Founded in 1876 originally as a maritime paper, it is an uncompromising daily whose loud and clear message has transcended the country's boundaries on such thorny issues as human rights, the evils of dictatorship, oppression, the Malvinas war and the "disappeared" Argentines.

MAGAZINES

A foreign observer once said newsstands on Buenos Aires streets were the best-stocked in the world. He was possibly very close to the truth. You can bet you will find your favorite magazine on any display of the downtown Florida newsstands. But if you do not, just ask the newsvendor for it. He will surely be able to give you the address of the local distributor. You may also wish to go to one of the major bookstores on the same street or to one just around the corner.

BOOKS

Foreign books are quite difficult to obtain in Argentina as import duties are high and there is much redtape involved in bringing in foreign publications. There is only a precious trickle of them coming in each month. The bookstores may nevertheless prove quite helpful in putting you on the right track to your sought-after volume. Give them a call. **Ateno**, on Florida (block between Corrientes and sarmiento) is a three-story-high haven of the written word. Fiction and otherwise. In the basement you will find a moderate-size selection of English and American books (plus French and Italian). A run-of-the mill sprinkle of classics and current best-sellers.

The **ABC**, on Córdoba and Maipú is better stocked, and it adds to its displays luxury editions, as well as records and an array of art book. The bookstore is German-owned and run. Tops.

Another German-oriented bookstore is **Goethe**, on Corrientes 200, right across the avenue from the Goethe German Institute, of learning and culture promotion. Periodic sales and discounts make the Goethe bookstore an interesting place to visit while in BA.

Specializing in textbooks, dictionaries and business books is the **Rodrigues** bookstore, on Florida, in front of Ateneo. It is run like a college bookstore, not a very romantic place for a book lover since there is not enough room to browse around and attendants are over-zeolous.

Other bookstores are:

Casa pardol Marcelo T. de Alvear 894 (antique books).

Hachette. Córdoba 936. Tel: 392-6497.

Rivadavia 739, phone 34-8481 (French books and magazines).

Kier. Av. Santa Fe 1260. Phone 41-0507. (Art and philosophy books)..

Libraries are few and far between in BA. But for the avid English/American reader, there is a golden corner of silence with records, tapes, magazines and newspapers from the United States, at the Lincoln Center, on Florida 935, a few steps from the San Martin park, the Plaza and the Sheraton. It is open from 9.30am to 6.30pm. Don't forget to take along your passport, which will be checked (and you frisked) at the downstairs entrance.

EMERGENCIES

City Medical Attention: 34-4001
Intoxications: 87-6666
Police: 101, 37-1111
Fire Department: 23-2222
Burns: 923-3022
Coronary Care: 107
Suicide Prevention: 826-1551

HOSPITALS

British hospital: Perdriel 74-23-1081
French hospital: Rioja 951-97-1031
German hospital: Pueyrredón 1657-821-4083
Dental hospital: Pueyrredón 1940-941-5555
Eye hospital: San juan 2021-821-2721

GETTING AROUND

· ADDITIONAL INFORMATION

For information on further detailed lists of services available in BA, your key source is the Tourism Bureau, greatly refurbished and considerably humanized under the current Secretary of Tourism, Francisco Manrique, a man who to the best of his knowledge and possibilities (government funding, etc) is making a major effort to place Argentina back on the world tourist map. Offices on Sarmiento 1551, 5th floor. The Secretariat publishes a handy monthly magazine called *Where*. An unassuming practical guide to things to do and places to go in the city. (Available in English.)

TRANSPORT

CAR RENTAL SERVICES

You may do your hiring from the airport as you arrive. There are booths of the major car rental companies in the main lobby both at the Ezeiza International and at the Metropolitan airport. If you have decided to wait, or just to shop around, these are the downtown addresses:

Avis: Suipacha 268, 7th floor, Tel: 45-1943.

Hertz: Esmeralda 985, Tel: 312-0787.

Rent-A-Car: Marcelo T. de Alvear 6789, Tel: 311-0247.

Serra Lima: Córdoba 3100, Tel:s 821-6611/84.

If you are intimidated by the mad traffic and suicidal drivers on the streets of BA, a chauffer is a reasonably-priced alternative.

Alas: Callao 756, Tel: 42-4192.

Agencia Ecuador: Ecuardo 1022, Tel: 824-3187.

Agencia Paraguay: Paraguay 238, Tel: 824-4211.

Autos Delfino: Laprida 1128, Tel: 843154.

Continental: Esmeralda 1077, Tel: 312-4352.

Del Plata: Carabelas 295, Tel: 35-0749.

Turismo Plaza Mayo: Azopardo 523, Tel: 33-4705.

SUBWAYS

Buenos Aires' subway system serves most of the city, with five main lines cutting across all directions. The state-owned subway allows free transfers from one line to another at certain stops.

TRAINS

Most trains arrive at the Retiro, the station closest to downtown Buenos Aires. At peak times, there is a train every ten to fifteen minutes.

TAXIS

The BA taxicab is easily spotted: Black body, yellow on top, with light-on yellow sign over the roof when it is free. There is also a "flag" which also should be up and lit reading "*libre*" (free).

If you are not sure how far away your destination is, ask the desk clerk at your hotel how much the fare should be. Every cab must carry a price list, which usually hangs on the back of the driver's seat, for the perusal of the passenger. Check on that list against the number on the meter. Next to that number you'll find the price. This rather complicated system is a way of helping the drivers keep pace with inflation, but unfortunately some drivers take advantage of it by suggesting that foreigners pay the number on the meter, rather than the price on the chart. Tipping in taxis is not customary, unless it's to round out a number. Try to have some small bills handy: drivers often don't seem to have change.

RADIO TAXIS

Pidalo SA (translates: Ask for it) at 9993-4991/9

WHERE TO STAY

Hotels
*** Deluxe
** First class
* Moderate

Buenos Aires Sheraton (***)
High-rise commanding magnificent view of the River Plate, port area, in front of the historical Torre de los Ingleses and the Retiro train terminal. Uncrowded, it stands atop a tiny rise in one of the very few "hilly" areas of the city. 24 stories, 800 rooms, heated pool, tennis courts, sauna, roof-top bar, a sprinkling of top-notch international restaurants, High-level entertainment. A favourite of traveling business people. San Martin 1225/75.

Plaza (***)
A favorite of visiting royalty and heads of state. Very French, very formal, host to high-fashion shows etc. Superb service. Known for its well-stocked wine cellar. Jewelers, furriers, banks and travel agencies have shops on the ground floor. Florida 1005.

Bauen (***)
250 rooms, 32 suites and two penthouses. Callao and Corrientes. View from 19th-floor restaurant is breath-taking.

Hotel Libertador (***)
Modern, glass-plated. Maipú and Córdoba. Convention halls. Two excellent restaurants, El Portal and the Pérgola.

Hotel Presidente (**)
9 de Julio avenue and Córdoba. A favourite with the business community. 300 rooms.

Claridge (**)
180 rooms. Known for its excellent restaurant. Tucumaan 555, a few steps from the glittering Florida shopping strip

Gran King (**)
Right on Florida, corner of Lavalle. Advice: Look both ways before stepping out into the mainstream of Florida shoppers and office commuters on their break.

República (**)

250 rooms. Fairly new. On 9 de Julio avenue.

Continental (**)

A few streets away from the main maddening crowd, on an avenue adorned twice a year by blooming jacaranda trees. Steer away from it if you are allergic, it could send you into sneezing fits by mere approach. Otherwise very stately hotel. Good eating. Diagonal Roque Saenz Peña 725.

Salles(*)

On Cerrito and residente perón. Modern and efficient. Pleasant setting, with a view of the 9 de Julio greenery and in fall, and spring, the "palo borracho" pink, yellow and cream flowers on the trees and carpeting the minuscule park areas separating the main central avenue from two lateral streets, Cerrito to the West and Carlos Pellegrini to the East. A few blocks' walk from the banking and shopping area.

Dos Chinos (*)

Close to the constitución train station. 14 floors, 120 rooms. "E" subway line takes less than 10 minutes to downtown BA.

Nogaró(*)

Reasonable. Famous Bob's Bar Avenida Julio A. Roca (Diagonal Sur) 562. Good cooking at the Chez Louis restaurant.

Tres Sargentos (*)

Reconquista 730. A favorite with smart shoppers.

If your stay in BA promises to be lengthy or if you are searching for a bit of privacy, there is a wide range of service hotels or apartments. Among them, the Embassy Building, Córdoba 860, Edificio Esmeralda, at Marcelo t. de Alvear 842, or "Πosadas 1325", or Edificio Arenales, Arenales 855.

FOOD DIGEST

Dining out is a favorite pastime with *porteños*, but the menu is by no means the main attraction. Restaurants are places to socialize, to observe and be observed, to show off a new outfit and share a bottle of tinto until the small hours of the morning. The restaurants listed below were chosen for their long-standing popularity and reliability, but as in any big city, fashions and phone numbers change quickly. However, don't be afraid to try any clean, well-lighted place that strikes your fancy. It's hard to make a bad decision on a restaurant in Buenos Aires: prices are low for visitors with dollars, and the food is almost universally fresh and well-prepared in a simple Southern European style.

DOWNTOWN RESTAURANTS

La Veda. Florida 1. 331-6442. Basement floor, lunch only.

Camara de Sociedades anónimas. Florida 1. 3rd floor.

Deck Grill. Florida, corner of Sarmiento, 1st floor.

Blab. Florida 325. Tel: 394-2873. Closed weekends. Excellent bar.

Au Bon Air. Tres Sargentos 496. Tel: 313-2135. Ferydoun Kia's combination of Oriental, classic and personal touches is a challenge to the palate.

Catalinas. Reconquista 875. Tel: 313-0182.

Restaurante de la Vieja Panadería. 25 de Mayo 597. Tel: 3117544.

Down Town Matías. San Martín 979. Tel: 35-3627.

El Figón de Bonilla. Leandro Alem 655.

Las Nazarenas. Reconquista 1132. Tel: 312-5559.

Cardinale. Buenos Aires Sheraton Hotel

La Cabaña. Entre Ríos 436. Tel: 37-2639. Argentina's beef emporioum.

Plaza Grill. Plaza Hotel. Santa Fe corner of Florida.

Pizza Hut. Lavalle 876. Tel: 392-5041.

Cabildo 1978. Tel: 782-3787. Open every day, noon to midnight. Pizza and salad bar.

RESTAURANTS IN RECOLETA

El Gato Dumas. R. M. Ortiz 1813. Tel: 804-5828. Trendy, imaginative menu.

Au Bec fin. Vicente Lopez 1825. Tel: 801-6894. One of Buenos Aires' most popular restaurants. Dinner only 8pm-2am. Reservations advised.

Lola. Roberto Ortiz 1811. One of the newest additions to Recoleta, and one of the best.

Harper's . Junin 1763. Tel: 801-7155/7140. Open every day for brunch and dinner.

Clark's II. Junin 1777. 801-9502. Even more impressive than the original Clark's. Old-fashioned bar.

Estilo Munich. Roberto M. Ortiz 1878. Tel: 44-3981. Open daily.

Norte. Junin 1767. Tel: 801-9648. Good continental fare, reasonably priced.

Brasserie Lipp. Ayacucho and Alvear. (Alvear Hotel).

POPULAR EATERIES

Pippo's Parana 356. Montevideo 345 and 356.

Chiquilín. Montevideo and Perón.

La Payanca. Suipacha 1015. Suipacha and Santa Fe.

Los Chilenos. Suipacha. (Across street from La Payanea)

Guerrin. Pizza on Corrientes and Uruguay.

La Americana. Callao 77.

La Lecherísima. Santa Fe 1726, Corrientes 839, Reconquista 1235.

CAFÉS AND CONFITERIAS

Tortoni. Av. de Mayo and Maipu

Confitería Ideal. Suipacha 384. Tel: 35-0521

Richmond. Florida 468. Tel: 392-1341

El Molino. Rivadavia 1801. Tel: 45-5848

Las Violetas. Rivadavia 3899. Tel: 981-0170

La Biela. Av. Quintana 600. Tel: 42-4135

El Rosedal Caseros 2822. Tel: 91-1301

Steinhauser Cafe. Av. Cabildo 1924. Tel: 781-0861

Florida Garden. Florida and Paraguay

St. James. Cordoba and Maipu

Café de los Angelitos Mitre 926. Tel: 201-9497

THINGS TO DO

AMUSEMENT PARKS

Ital Park. Libertador and Callao, only a few blocks from Retiro station. Open every day, weekdays from 2pm, weekends from 10am, Rides, games, shows for the youngest. Refreshments. Tel: 41-6405

Parque de la Ciuded. Cruz and Escalada. Open on weekends (Saturdays as from 1pm, Sundays as from 11am). Tel: 601-3332.

RIDES

Treat yourself to a Bing Crosby-Grace Kelly style coach ride through the shady greenery and wide promenades of the Palermo parks. You can hire coach services at the entrance of the Zoological Gardens, Plaza Italia. Take your camera along. Another 19th-century treasure is pedal boat rides on the Palermo lakes. Very romantic in the spring and autumn, a bit breezy and wet in winter, but still a challenge for those jet-lagged legs of the long-distance traveler.

ZOOS

Buildings in an elaborate turn-of-the-century style. The variety of animals is considerable, but their living conditions are appalling, by 20th century standards.

ANIMAL WORLD

Animal World is an altogether different story. Mr Jorge Cuttini, a former elementary teacher gone wild beast-lover and keeper, has done a marvellous job bringing up a wide array of very happy big wild animals. His elephants, Bengalese tigers, pumas and lions, live free and undisturbed in his home-made haven outside the town of General Rodriguez, on highway 22. You don't want to miss this exemplary drive-through animal retreat, or chatting a bit with controversial owner Cuttini.

CULTURE PLUS

MUSEUMS

Natural Science: Av. Angel Gallardo 470, Tel: 982-0306.

Spanish Art "Enrique Larreta": Juramento 2291, Tel: 783-2640

"Isaac Fernández Blanco": Museum of Spanish-American Art. Suipacha 1422. Tel: 393-6318/9394.

San Martin Cultural Center: Sarmiento 1551. 46-1251.

Cultural Center of the City of Buenos Aires: Junin 1940 803-1041.

Modern Art: Corrientes 1530. Tel: 49-4796.

"Eduardo Sivori": Museum of Plastic Arts. Corrienties 1530, Tel: 46-9680

City Museum: Alsina 412. Tel: 331-9855.

José Hernández Folk Art Museum: Libertador 2373. Tel: 802-7294

Historical Museum of the City of Buenos Aires: Republiquetas 6309. Tel: 572-0746.

Buenos Aires Planetarium: Sarmiento and Roldán (Palermo parks). Tel: 771-6629.

Cabildo Historical Museum: Bolivar 65 (across the street from Plaza de Mayo and Government House). Tel: 301-0593.

National History Museum: Defensa 160. Tel: 27-4767.

National Museum of Decorative Art: Libertador 1902. Tel: 802-0914.

National Museum of Oriental Art: Libertador 1902. Tel: 801-5988.

National Fine Arts Museum: Libertador 1473, Tel: 803-8814.

Botanical Gardens: Across the street from the Zoo. Worth an unhurried visit. A haven of peace and quiet, featuring hundreds of rare species of plants and trees.

ART GALLERIES

Alberto Elia, Azcuenaga 1739, Tel: 803-0496

Angelus, Suipacha 834, Tel: 311-8213

Arte Nuevo, Balcarce 1016, Tel: 362-5393

Atica, Libertad 1240, P. Baja "9," Tel: 42-3544

Christel k, Arenales 1239, p. Baja "C," Tel: 44-3917

Del Retiro, Marcelo T. de Alvear 636, Tel: 311-2527

El Mensaje, Arenales 867, Tel: 393-0109

Federico Ursomarzo, M.t. de Alvear 1418, Tel: 41-9636

Feldman, Junin 1142, Tel: 83-7257

Jacques Martinez, Florida 948, 1p., Tel: 311-4028

Miro, M.T. de Alvear 865, Tel: 311-2265

Praxis, Arenales 1311, Tel: 44-6254

Rubbers, Suipacha 1175, Tel: 393-6010

Ruth Benzacar, Florida 1000, Tel: 313-0408

Soudan, Arenales 868, Tel: 393-1500

Van Riel, TAlcahuano 1257, Tel: 41-8359

Velazquez, Maipu 932, Tel: 311-0583

Vermeer, Suipacha 1168, Tel: 393-0502

Wildenstein, Cordoba 618, Tel: 392-0628

SHOPPING

ANTIQUES

San Telmo has rows of little dusty shops as well as palace-like emporiums of works of art and atiques from all over the world, by the best artists and artisans living and dead. On Sundays a stupendous antique fair assembles at the San telmo plaza. You will not want to miss it, even if you don't do any actual buying. Take your camera and comfortable shoes. You will probably hear a number of street musicians, including a peppy Brazilian *ecola da samba* (they'll have the entire market swing in a few minutes). You'll also see artisans at work, poets reading their works, young groups doing theater, pantomine, and impromptu tango. A few names and addresses to remember in the antique market are:

Antique Casa Pardo: Defensa 1170. Tel: 361-0583.

Bontempo: Callao 1711. Tel: 41-8265.

Galleria Studio: Libertad 1271. Tel: 41-1616.

Gallery Space: Carlos Pellegrini 985, Tel: 312-1342. Marcelo Torcuato de Alvear 628. Tel: 4236.

Naón y Cia: Guido 1785. Tel: 41-1685.

Roldán y Cia: Rodriquez Peña 1673, Tel: 22-4714. Defensa 1084, Tel: 361-4399. Florida 141, Tel: 30-3733 (auctions) Santarelli. Florida 688, Tel: 393-8152

Saudades: Libertad 1278, Tel: 42-1374

Vetmas: Libertad 1286, ∏hone 44-2348

Zurbarán: Cerrito 1522. Tel: 22-7703 (also art gallery).

FURRIERS

Carles Calfun: Florida 918, Tel: 311-1147.

Maximilian: Marcelo T. de Alvear 684 Tel: 312-0623.

Pieles Libero: Guido 1890. Tel: 44-5501

Berthe: Santa Fe 1227. Tel: 41-2284
Ana-Ra: Cerrito 1020. Tel: 393-6441

JEWELLERS

Santarelli: Florida 688. Tel: 393-8152

Ricciardi: Florida 1001 (Plaza Hotel). Tel: 312-3082.

H. Stern: At the Plaza Hotel, Sheraton and Ezeiza Airport.

Belgiorno: Santa Fe 1349. Tel: 41-1117. Best silver designer jewelry.

Antoniazzi-Chiappe: Av. Alvear 1895. Tel: 41-6137. Santa fe 896. Tel: 311-4697.

Guthman: Viamonte 597. Tel: 312-2471

Jean Pierre: Alvear 1892. Tel: 42-8303.

Ricardo Saúl: Quintana 450. Tel: 41-1876.

LEATHER CLOTHES

Chiche Farrace: Florida 940. Ciudad del **Cuero Shopping Mall, stand number 43:** Tel: 311-4721.

Echeverria 2252 "23": Belgrano. Tel: 781-2885. Libertador 16465. San Isidro. Tel: 747-8881.

López: Marcelo T. de Alvear 640. Tel: 311-3044.

Sagazola: Libertador 7112. Tel: 70-3988 (Nuñez). Guido 1686, Tel: 42-5428.

Jota U Cueros: Tres Sargentos (behind Harrod's) 439.

Lederland: Talcahuano 862. Tel: 41-6693.

LEATHER GOODS

Rossi y Carusso: Santa Fe 1601. Tel: 41-1538.

López: Marcelo T. de Alvear 640. Tel: 311-3044.

Pullman: Esmeralda 321. Tel: 45-5959. Florida 985, ∏hone 311-0799.

Sagazola: Libertador 7112, Nuñz. Tel: 70-3988. (see under Leather Clothes) Agué. Cerrito 1128. Tel: 393-3066.

Hersé: Florida 961. Tel: 311-1842.

RIDING GEAR

López Taibo: Corrientes 350. Tel: 311-2132.

Rossi y Carusso: Santa Fe 16011. Tel: 41-1538.

H. Merlo S. y Cáa: Juncal 743. Tel: 22-6116.

H. **Melos y Cia**: Julio A Roca 1217, Hurlingham. Tel: 665-4859.

LADIES SHOES

Norberto: Florida 817. Tel: 311-1488.
Peruggia: Alvear 1866. Tel: 42-6340.
Avella: Quintana 309. Tel: 41-5198.
Boniface: Florida 891. parera 145. Santa Fe 1781.
Botticelli: Florida 891. Quintana 488 Tel: 44-3906.
Lonté: Rodriguez Peña 1221.
McShoes: Florida 849. Tel: 312-4781.
Raffi-Lu: Alvear 1824. Tel: 44-2398. Libertad 1157. Tel: 44-5695.

MEN'S SHOES

Boniface: Florida 598. Parera 145. Santa Fe 1781.
Delgado: Corrientes 161. Tel: 331-0173.
Grimoldi: Florida 251. Tel: 394-2405.
Guante: Florida 271. Tel: 394-7127.
Guido: Quintana 333. Tel: 41-4567, Rodriguez.
Peña 1290: Tel: 42-9095. Florida 704. Tel: 392-7548.
López Taibo: Corrientes 350. Tel: 311-2132.
Los Angelitos: Florida 529. Tel: 393-4477.
McShoes: Florida 849. Tel: 312-4781.
Callao 1714: Tel: 44-6535.

PRET-A-PORTER

Christian Dior: Quinta 545. Florida Corner of Viamonte.
Elsa Serrano: Mansilla 3045. Tel: 824-9571.
Graciela Montefiore: Alvear 1889.
L'Interdit: Uruguay 1196. Tel: 42-5602.

DESIGNERS

Gino Bogani: Rodriguez Peña 1044. Tel: 44-0862.
Best Seller: Alvear 1883.
Nina Ricci: Alvear 1539. Tel: 22-8283.

ARGENTINE REGIONAL GIFTS

Martin Fierro: Santa Fe 904. Tel: 392-6440.
Artesanian Argentinas: Montevideo 1386. Tel: 44-2650. Non-profit organization which promotes the work or Indian artisans living in the north and northwest of Argentina.
El Altillo de Susana: Marcelo T. de Alvear 515. Tel: 311-1138.
Rancho Grande: Leandro N. Alem 564, Tel: 311-7603.
Matra: Defensa 372. A state-run cooperative for local craftsmen.
Kelly's: Paraguay 3431 Sweaters, ponchos and scarves of Ilama wool.

SPORTS

PARTICIPANT

BOATING AND SAILING

There is boating in the **Tigre** (River Plate delta) some 45 minutes north of the city. From Retiro station, the train ride to Tigre is both fast and interesting. The train crosses through old stately suburbs as well as populous neighborhoods such as Belgrano. Tours of Tigre are also available through T-bar SA, on Libertador 14434. Tel: 798-9969/9043. There you will find sail ships, sail boats, motors, kayaks and windsurf boards. There you can also contract cruises to Uruguay's main tourist and nautical resort, Punta del Este, as well as to Brazil.

GOLF

Municipal Golf Course. Tornquist and olleros, palermo woods. Tel: 772-7576.
Argentine Golf Association: Corrientes 538. Tel: 394-3743/29972.
Jockey Club and Blue Course, Links Golf Club, Club Náutico San Isidro, are other possibilities, although not so readily available, since they are strictly private clubs. Another possibility is afforded by a stretch of good golfing grounds on the Costanera. It is on Costanera Norte and

Salguero. It is run by the local golf association and you can rent your clubs there.

SQUASH

Posadas Squash Club. Posadas 1265, 7th floor, Tel: 22-0548. Two courts, plus sauna, whirlpool, closed-circuit TV, bar and restaurant.

Olimpia Cancilleria. Esmeralda 1042, Tel:s 311-8687. Five courts. One racquetball court. Plus gym, sauna, bar.

TENNIS

Almost everywhere in the city and suburbs are municipal courts, well lighted and with round-the-clock security. With instructors, if desired. Your best bet is inquiring about the nearest one at the hotel where you are staying. Some private courts that may be worth your looking into are:

Baakerloo: Pampa 1235, Belgrano neighborhood. Three clay courts.

Break Point: Yatay 943, Caballito neighborhood. Two courts.

Bustamante Tennis Bar: Sanchez de Bustamante 1256. Tel: 88-6277.

Caballito Tennis Club: José María Moreno 953, Cabollito. Three clay courts.

Daria Kopsic: Hernandarias 2050, La Boca neighborhood. Eight clay courts (two indoors). Tel: 28-3276

Parque Norte: Cantilo and Guiraldes (Costanera Norete) Tel: 784-9653.

Solís Tennis Courts: Solís 1252. Seven clay courts.

Tatum Tennis Club: Yerbal 845. Caballito. Five clay courts

Tennis Colonial: Donato Alvarez 224. Two courts.

Municiapal Courts: Parque Sarmiento. Av. del Tejar 4300, Saavedra. Fourteen hard courts. Tel: 541-3511 Parque José Hernández. Hernández 1302. Parque de Palermo. Hard and clay courts. Tel: 782-2619.

WATER SKIING

There is a water skiing school in Tigre at the jorge Renosto establishment. Tel:s 875-0128-783-5181. Renosto is a former South American Ski Champion. Equipment provided.

WIND SURFING

Parque Norte, Cantilo and Guiraldes, (Constanera Norte).

El Molino. Elcano and Perú, Acassuso. Hoopika. Italia and river, Vicente López.

SPECTATOR

BOXING AND WRESTLING

At the downtown **Luna Park**, **Corrientes** and **Madero**, right on the waterfront. The Luna Park also brings to Buenos Aires top shows from around the world, such as top-level circuses, ballets, singers and other performers.

PATO

It is a combination of polo and basketball on horseback. Very exclusive clubs.

POLO

Clubs in the neighborhood of Palermo, and in the suburbs of Hurlingham, San Isidro and Tortugas.

LANGUAGE

The Spanish spoken in Argentina is to the Castilian Spanish of Spain what American English is to BBC English: it stands on its own; proudly, enriched and developed by local custom and refreshingly unperturbed by "how it should be said." The most vivid grammatical contrast is between the Spanish *tu* form (second person singular, informal), and the Argentine *vos* form. Example: Instead of the Spanish *Tu vienes*? (Are you coming?) the Argentine will ask, *Vos venis*? The concept of vos has ancient roots in the Castilian vosotros (second person plural). Speakers of Castilian will observe that the verbs corresponding to vos are conjugated similarly to the Castilian vosotros verbs, with some variations. The subject is thorny even for advanced students of Argentine Spanish, but fortunately Argentines are all familiar with the standard *tu* form. As in the rest of Latin America, "you" plural is expressed by third person plural with the pronoun *ustedes*. To use the same example, *Ustedes vienen*? (Are you all coming?)

Slang: Slang is an equivocal business, as most visitors know from using it in their own languages. It's an undercurrent of language with precise meanings, and unless it's used impeccably, can make the speaker sound foolish or even rude. Thus the following is a descriptive, rather than proscriptive, list of some commonly used *porteño* slang words. Note: Spanish translation in bold and *porteño* translation in italics).

Woman
Mujer
Mina

Man
Hombre
Tipo, Flaco

Child
Niño
Pibe, Purrete, Pebete

To look
Mirar
Junar

To eat
Comer
Mangiar

To sleep
Dormir
Apolillar, Torrar

To chat
Charlar
Chamullar

The best expression of slang is in the heartfelt tango. When a foreigner gets to the point of understanding the lyrics of old-time tango, he will have gained a certain insight into the world of slang, and will be better able to understand the thoughts, actions and emotions of a *porteño*.

USEFUL ADDRESSES

CREDIT COMPANIES IN BUENOS AIRES

American Express: 312-0900
Choice International: 362-0235
Diners Club: 22-4545
London Card: 34-2170
Antique Casa Pardo: Defensa 1170. Phone 361-0583.
Bontempo: Callao 1711. Phone 41-8265.
Galleria Studio: Libertad 1271. Phone 41-1616.
Gallery Space: Carlos Pellegrini 985, Phone 312-1342. Marcelo Torcuato de Alvear 628. Phone 4236.
Naón y ciaa: Guido 1785. Phone 41-1685.
Roldán y Cia: Rodriquez peña 1673, phone 22-4714. Defensa 1084, phone 361-4399. Florida 141, phone 30-3733 (auctions) Santarelli. Florida 688, Phone 393-8152
Saudades: Libertad 1278, Phone 42-1374
Vetmas: Libertad 1286, Πhone 44-2348
Zurbarán: Cerrito 1522. Phone 22-7703 (also art gallery).

CONSULATES

Austria: 802-7195
Belgium: 33-0066
Canada: 312-9081
Denmark: 312-6901
Ireland: 44-9987
Norway: 312-1904
South Africa: 311-8991
Sweden: 311-3080
Switzerland: (also in charge of British affairs in Argentina ever since the 1982 South Atlantic conflict) 311-6491
United States: 774-7611
West Germany: 771-5054

AIRLINES

Aerolineas Argentinas: 393-5122
Aero Mexico: 392-4821
Aeroperú: 311-6431
Air France: 312-7331/5
Alitalia: 3112-84211/5
Austral: 313-3777
Avianca: 312-3621
British Airways: 392-6037
British Caledonian: 392-3489
Canadian Pacific: 392-3732
Cruzeiro0Varig: 35-5431
Eastern: 312-3641
Ecuatoriana: 311-1117
Iberia: 35-2050/9
Japan Air Lines: 392-7198
KLM: 311-8925/6
LADE: 361-7071
Lan Chile: 311-5334/8
LAPA: 394-5829
Lufthansa: 312-8171
Pan Am: 45-0111
South African: 311-8181/6
Swissair: 311-8933/88

ART/PHOTO CREDITS

Artes, Museo de Bellas	163
Bemporad, Fiora	19, 22, 23, 24, 26, 28, 29L, 30, 31R, 32, 33, 35, 36, 37L, 37R, 41, 51, 55R, 75, 79, 81, 82, 84, 86, 88, 118, 119R, 120, 130, 132, 136, 144, 145, 147R, 151, 152, 158, 159, 174
Bemporad, Fiora/National Archives	42, 43, 45, 46, 47, 48
Bemporad, Fiora/Witcomb Collection	38/39, 40
Museo Fernandez Blanco	175R
Boroughs, Don	3, 18, 20L, 56, 58, 59, 69, 97, 104, 105, 106L, 106R, 111, 131R, 133L, 135R, 137R, 154, 155, 164, 165, 167R, 176, 177, 178, 179, 181R, 182, 183, 184, 187, 189, 190, 191, 192, 193R, 194, 195, 196, 197, 198, 199R, 201, 212
Courtesy of Ed de la Flor	83
Doura, Miguel	65, 68L, 109R, 128, 129, 143, 209
Encinas, A.	205
Gil, Eduardo	Cover, 5, 6, 7, 10, 11, 12, 13 21, 54, 63, 64, 90, 91, 98, 99, 100, 101, 103R, 107, 108, 110, 112, 117, 122R, 124, 127R, 138, 139R, 156, 166, 171
Gowar, Rex	161
Hooper, Joseph	20R, 168, 169, 170
Joly, Marcos	8/9
Schulte, Jorge Juan	14, 15, 102
Ocampo, Alex	16, 17R, 149, 172/173
Perrottet, Anthony	53, 70, 72, 114, 123, 126, 133R, 202, 203R, 206
Welna, David	60, 61, 66L, 67, 76, 113, 115, 125, 134, 137L, 140, 141, 148, 185R, 204, 207L, 208, 210

INDEX

D

Y